The Impossible Bourbons

The Impossible Bourbons

Europe's Most Ambitious Dynasty

OLIVER THOMSON

'The great nobles in general, the Bourbons in particular, were not
noted for their tender-heartedness.'
Philippe Erlanger, Louis XIV

AMBERLEY

'The Bourbons had a strange beauty of their own.'
Harold Acton, *The Last Bourbons of Naples*.

First published 2009
Amberley Publishing
Cirencester Road, Chalford,
Stroud, Gloucestershire, GL6 8PE

www.amberley-books.com

© Oliver Thomson 2009

The right of Oliver Thomson to be identified as the Author
of this work has been asserted in accordance with the
Copyrights, Designs and Patents Act 1988.

British Library Cataloguing in Publication Data.
A catalogue record for this book is available from the British Library.

ISBN 978 1 84868 356 3

Typesetting and origination by Amberley Publishing
Printed in Great Britain

CONTENTS

PREFACE

There have been numerous excellent biographies of the individual Bourbon kings of France and there are many fine histories of France, but there is no recent account of the French Bourbons as a dynastic family, let alone one that includes the two other great branches of the family that took over Spain and half of Italy, not to mention some of the lesser but still fascinating branches like the princes of Condé and Conti. This book aims to analyse the rises and falls of this extraordinary triplex dynasty which at one point ruled huge areas across five continents, had incredible wealth and for much of the time had absolute power. For good and ill it had a substantial effect on the lives of many millions of people.

For the sake of convenience most of the chapters contain short biographies of individual kings and queens and their more significant relations, so they can be read as self-contained excerpts or as part of a connected narrative.

The book is divided into four main parts. The first considers the rise of the Bourbons before they won their first major throne. The second looks at the three main royal branches in the period before all three were deposed during the French Revolution and its aftermath. The third looks at the same three branches during their restoration after the fall of Napoleon, the demise of the French and Italian Bourbons and the extraordinary double come-back of their Spanish cousins. Finally part four takes in a world-wide tour of the dynasty's most impressive monuments from Bourbon itself to Versailles, then via Madrid and Naples to Montréal, New Orléans, San Francisco and beyond.

NOTE ON NAMES

For the French Bourbons I have used the French spelling of their names, for the Spanish Bourbons the Spanish form and for the Italian Bourbons the Italian. Many of the Bourbons changed names or titles mid-stream, like the Duc d'Enghien became Prince de Condé, the Duc de Chartres became the Duc d'Orléans, Dauphins and Spanish Infantes became kings, Mme Scarron becomes Maintenon etc., so to avoid confusion I have tended to use the best known of the names sometimes even before they were actually applied. We also have tiresome changes of name and number like Carlo IV of Naples turning into Carlos III of Spain, or Ferdinando IV of Naples turning himself into Ferdinando I of the Two Sicilies. Another potentially confusing feature is the similarity of Christian names, especially in the early part of this saga where there is a profusion of Louis and Philippes. In the later parts the problem is more the use of double-barrelled Christian names like Marie Louise or Marie Antoinette. More recently still the family, by incessant intermarrying acquired double-barrelled surnames like Borbon y Battenberg, some even triple-barrelled and these I have kept to a minimum. I have also tended to use the local version of each Christian name, for example Charles in France becomes Carlo in Italy or Carlos in Spain. I apologise for any short cuts that offend anyone, but I have tried my best to make sure that names do not get in the way of the fascinating people who bore them.

LIST OF ILLUSTRATIONS

FAMILY TREES

PLATE SECTION, BETWEEN PAGES 96 AND 97

1.   The fortress at Bourbon l'Archambault
2.   Château Lavardin
3.   Moulins Cathedral
4.   Charles III, Duke of Bourbon
5.   Henri IV enters Paris
6.   Louis XIII
7.   Louis XIV
8.   Louis de Bourbon, the Great Condé
9.   The execution of Louis XVI
10. Felipe V of Spain
11. Carlo IV of Naples/Carlos III of Spain
12. Fernando IV of Spain
13. Alfonso XIII of Spain
14. Queen Isabella II
15. Ferdinando I of the Two Sicilies
16. Louis Philippe at the barricades
17. Château Pau
18. Versailles
19. Palacio Real, Aranjuez
20. Caserta

ACKNOWLEDGEMENTS

My usual huge thanks to my wife Jean for sharing the trip of exploration and to my DACE class at the University of Glasgow for their constant stimulation. A special thanks to the staff at Amberley for their patience and expertise.

'A hero is a thief who does at the head of an army what robbers do on their own.'

Father Mascaron

INTRODUCTION

Of all the dynastic families in European history the Bourbons were in many respects the most remarkable. Only they managed to hold the crowns of three kingdoms simultaneously. Not only in the mid-eighteenth century did they rule France, Spain, half of Italy and the southern Netherlands but at the same time virtually the whole of the South American continent apart from Brazil, most of Central America, most of the West Indies apart from Jamaica, a huge swathe of North America including Florida, California, Louisiana and much of eastern Canada plus the Philippines, half of Morocco and trading stations in India and West Africa. Thus a huge proportion of the world's wealth was under their control and this was reflected in their extraordinary levels of ostentation and extravagance. They also showed remarkable resilience for though they lost all three of their kingdoms and empires during the revolutionary period they won most of all three back. They lost all three again in the nineteenth century but regained one of them, Spain, only to lose it and win it back a third time in the twentieth.

It took nearly 700 years for the family to claw its way up to its first throne but just over a century after that to win the next two and very nearly a fourth, Poland. They produced a few men of genius but on the whole were of average ability, ambitious, greedy, arrogant and determined. Some of them were sound administrators, but many of them made horrendous errors of judgement which caused themselves and their subjects great suffering. Several of the less famous were quixotically brave; several were traitors. Their daughters were often handed over to loveless marriages for the sake of political advantage and their wives were often ignored for the sake of more pliable mistresses or for what Winston Churchill describes as other 'disgusting habits'. Due to the application of Salic law except for Spain there was only one ruling queen produced between the three branches, the notorious Isabella II, but there were several effective female regents. With a total of 23 kings and one queen the Bourbons between them ruled for 610 years averaging a remarkable 27 years each.

The Bourbons caused large numbers of unnecessary wars leading directly and indirectly to massive suffering. They were hugely self-indulgent, yet that self-indulgence has left behind a superb architectural and cultural heritage spread over five continents. They were nearly all obsessed with hunting and killed vast numbers of animals. They also nearly all married their own cousins, often first cousins, usually other Bourbons, sometimes Habsburgs, so their degree of inbreeding was very considerable, resulting in numerous cases of mental and physical abnormality, not surprising given that all the royals from Louis XIII onwards were descended from Juana the Mad of Castile. For example, of the twelve children of the last official Duke of Parma six were declared mentally defective whilst the current King of Spain had two haemophiliac uncles and a deaf mute. The two brothers Louis XVI and Louis XVIII both suffered from a 'sexual impediment'. Similarly of the senior Bourbons three Spanish kings were clinically depressed, one thought he was a frog whereas of the Condé Bourbons one thought he was a wolf and another expected to be reincarnated as a horse.

This book might appear to be about rather unattractive, self-opinionated elitists who enjoyed undeserved power and wealth: that is partially true, but they were at the same time ordinary human beings in the grip of vast long-term forces who in different ways also changed the course of events, sometimes for better sometimes for worse. Frequently an understanding of their personal lives helps to explain key events in European history for in many cases a deep sense of personal insecurity was veiled by a compulsory veneer of superficial arrogance. So this is an unashamed multiple biography of both the famous (or notorious) and less famous members of an extraordinary family traced for over a thousand years.

'France was no less affected by the biology and personality of the Bourbon, Bonaparte and Orléans dynasties than by mass movements of nationalism, revolutionary liberalism...'

Philip Mansel, *Paris between the Empires*

FROM SMALL BEGINNINGS 910-954

Like so many great dynasties the Bourbons had a long gestation period. Between the first known appearance of the family in 910 and the acquisition of their first proper crown in 1589 there was a period of over six centuries during the first three of which their progress was slow and uninspiring.

A few centuries, however, seem only a short period compared with the millions of years the hot springs have been bubbling up from the deep volcanic rocks of the Massif Central. The ancient Gauls had such a reverence for springs that they had a god called Borbo whom they worshipped, and the Romans who loved hot water harnessed one of them and called the place after its god – *Aquae Borvonis*. Many years later the little town was conquered by the Franks and turned into a frontier outpost called Bourbo (now Bourbon l'Archambault), and the massive rock above the town made an excellent site for a new castle close to the vast oak forest of Le Tronçais which was rich in game.

The ancestor of the Bourbon family was a young *viguier* or castle-keeper called Adhemar or Aymar (*c.* 870-920) who held an estate and small castle at what is now called Châtel de Neuvre (then Deneuvre), on a promontory that dominates the valley of the River Allier. This lies some fifteen miles from Bourbon near where the Allier widens as it meanders and begins to deepen on its long journey to join the Loire. A few miles to the north is the more recent town of Moulins where the Allier was deep enough to be used by sea-going ships.

Adhemar was a soldier (*miles clarissimus* in the documents) owing allegiance to the Count of Auvergne and was part of a frontier force intended to keep order in the independently-minded province of Aquitaine that lay to the south-west. According to a probably fabricated legend he was descended from Charles Martel, the leader of the French Army that won a famous victory against the Saracens at Poitiers in 732. It was this success that gained Charles his nickname of Martel (Hammer) and was the foundation upon which his grandson Charles the Great (Charlemagne, 747-814) became first the king of France and then Holy Roman Emperor. Yet whatever relationship Adhemar's grandparents had to the new Carolingian dynasty does not seem to have brought them any immediate benefit so we can guess that it was either illegitimate, on the female side or perhaps both. It was to be nearly a hundred years after Charlemagne's death before this branch of the family won any serious promotion.

Thus it was one of Charlemagne's feebler successors, Charles III the Simple (879-929, King of France from 884 till deposed in 922) who in the end perhaps acknowledged Adhemar's existence and set the family on the road to fame and fortune. The life-changing moment that brought him to the king's attention took place some fifty miles to the east in 910 at Cluny. There he attended the hand-over by his overlord William the Pious Count of Auvergne of the site for what became the most influential new monastic order in Europe. Adhemar was so impressed by this new order of spiritually dedicated monks that he himself a mere five years later decided to provide a site for a second abbey in one of his own estates at Souvigny, just a few miles to the west of his castle. Whether motivated just by piety or more mundane considerations Adhemar's generosity was to prove a major benefit for his family, for it brought into the area a whole new range of skills associated with a fast-expanding, highly respected monastic order. The prestige of hosting what was one of the first daughter houses in what became a network of over a thousand monasteries was considerable but it also gave Adhemar and his successors access to literacy and legal skills which were to help lift them to a higher level than the numerous other minor vassals of the area. In addition the family may well have had an early connection with another monastery founded in 936 at Chantelle a few miles to the south and dedicated to St Vincent – it still survives, as does the delightful priory church at Souvigny.

While many of the later Bourbons were far from saintly it is likely that this early association with an influential group of monks was very helpful to the rise of the family. What is more two of the earliest abbots of Cluny, Mayeul and Odilon had a soft spot for Souvigny and chose it for their retirement. They both died and were buried there and were men of such impressive sanctity that they soon won canonisation. St Mayeul (*c.* 906-94) had survived being buried alive by Saracens whilst on his way over the Alps to see the Pope and Odilon (962-1048) too was believed to have performed miracles, so their tombs attracted pilgrims to the new abbey, which added to the flow of pilgrims that already passed through the Allier valley on their way south to Santiago de Campostella.

Meanwhile King Charles the Simple was undergoing a period of crisis, which nine years later was to cost him his throne. This crisis had been brought on by the invasion of France by the Vikings under their ambitious leader Rollo who by the year 911 had pushed inland as far as Chartres and was within a day's march of Paris. Though in the end Rollo's siege of Chartres was a failure Charles the Simple could not drive him out of France and bought peace by ceding him huge tracts of western France which soon became the independent duchy of Normandy.

What Adhemar's role had been in fighting against the Viking mercenaries we do not know but Aimon (*c.* 900-60), the eldest of his three sons by his wife

Ermengarde, married Aldesinde, the daughter and heiress of Guy the royal representative holding the castle of Bourbon. Promotion by means of a good marriage was to be a hallmark of the rise of the Bourbons. So when Guy died Aimon took over both Bourbon and the royal authority that went with it, with the blessing of Louis IV (r. 936-954), thus becoming the first Sire de Bourbon at a time of great disturbance. Also on his father's death round about 920 he had taken over the estates of de Neuvre.

It was to be a feature of the Sires de Bourbon, like many land-holding families, that when they were old men and afraid of death they gave generously to the church, but their sons resented this and tried to claw back the donations till they too grew old. Thus Aimon initially grabbed back some of the benefices handed over to the abbots of Souvigny, but eventually around 953 confessed himself a miserable sinner and not only gave them back but added another estate at Bressoles for good measure.

THE NINE ARCHIBALDS

Aimon and his wife Aldesinde had seven children, the eldest son being Archambaud or Archibald. In fact, he was to be followed as Sire de Bourbon by nine generations of Archibalds interrupted only by a couple of girl heiresses who were therefore Dames de Bourbon and passed the title on to their sons, for this family ignored Salic law when it suited them.

The first Archibald or Archambaud I (c. 940-959 *Archibaldus Burbunensis Comes* or *Princeps*) was known as Le Franc and presided during the period when the Carolingian dynasty finally fell from power and was replaced by the Capets with whose fortunes the Bourbon family's were later to be inextricably linked. Indeed Archambaud I claimed some kind of relationship with Hugh Capet who became the new king of France shortly after his death. Amongst the few other facts known about Archambaud was that he married a Rothilde de Limoges or Rotgardis or Rohaud de Brosse which suggests that the family had acquired some properties to the west in the Limousin. Certainly he added Bessay in the south-east but failed in his attempts to take over Saint Pourçain and Ebreuil. Overall the objective now was to dominate the fertile and well-wooded area between the rivers Cher and Allier. He and his wife had only one child that lived to adulthood.

Archambaud II (c. 960-1032) known as Le Vert or Le Vieux had an unexplained three-year gap in the middle of his period of holding the lordship during the troubled reign of King Robert II (966-1031) but in general was an aggressive man who steadily increased the wealth and power of the family. He attacked his neighbour the Count of Nevers, extracting new territory from him towards the north and won the archbishopric of Bourges for one of his own younger sons, Aimon whilst the other married the heiress of Montluçon.

Archambaud, referred to in some documents as a count (*comes*), married Ermengarde de Sully and had four children. He began the construction of a large new castle at Hérisson, the Hedgehog, which guarded the crossing of the River Aumance and became an important new fortified base for the family facing the frontier of Aquitaine.

It was allegedly this Archambaud II who lost his way whilst hunting in one of the many forests of the area and was rescued by a pretty miller's daughter, for whom he subsequently built a lodge at Moulins. Moulins as its name suggests was then very much a milling town as the River Allier there is both wide and quite fast. In fact it was also a port for sea-going ships despite the long distance to the Atlantic via the Loire. Archambaud's creation of an extra home for the family presages the growth of Moulins as later their capital and main residence. In addition Archambaud founded the impressive new Benedictine monastery at Le Montet as if Souvigny was not enough. Nevertheless on his death as often happened he split his inheritance between two of his sons, the next Archambaud getting most of it but the younger son Gerard inheriting Montluçon.

Archambaud III (fl. 1032-78) had three or four nicknames, one Le Blanc, so a different colour from his father (though white was to be the iconic colour of the later family), the second Le Jeune, so a different age group and the third du Montet, some fifteen miles south-east of Moulins where he built a massive church as part of his father's new monastery. His fourth soubriquet of Sire de Montluçon suggests that this increasingly important town thirty miles south-west of Moulins which had been acquired by his brother Gerard had now passed to him. Meanwhile by intimidation or other means he took over other properties such as Neris, Murat, Ainay-le-Vieil, Jenzat, the fortress of Gannat known as the 'gateway to Occitania' and Cusset near Vichy, so the area controlled by the Bourbons was expanding quite rapidly.

Archambaud III was perhaps rewarded for services rendered to Henri I of France (r. 1031-60), the tireless but rather unlucky Capet who had to juggle with the fickle friendships of his rebellious brother Robert and William the ruthless new Duke of Normandy. In 1054 Archambaud served in the campaign against the Normans and one of his daughters Ermengarde actually married Fulk Count of Anjou, the ancestor of the Plantagenet kings of England.

With his wife Deaurate, or Edernud, Archambaud had four children and donated the chapel of La Faye to the family abbey at Souvigny, for like his predecessors in his youth he had seized properties back from the Church but in old age repented and gave them back, particularly to the monastery of St Michael at Montet where he and his wife were buried and the new priory of St Bernard at La Chapelaude. In addition around 1050 he built the important new castle at Murat, between Montluçon and Le Montet which in due course became the third largest in the Bourbon portfolio.

Archambaud IV (fl. 1078-95) was known as Le Fort, a euphemism for a man who was violent and aggressive. As part of his ruthless trail of acquisition he imprisoned his neighbour Hugh Count of Nevers and attacked the Archbishop of Lyon. As a result he added Mazirat, Neuville, and Ygrande in the west to his possession plus to the north Le Moutier, Le Veurdre and La Chapelle-aux-Chasses. However, all this aggression plus the usual youthful meanness towards the monks of Souvigny led to the threat of excommunication and even Pope Urban II was involved. The Pope was on his way to Clermont to make his famous call for the First Crusade and saw the merit in baronial quarrels being made up as a prelude to knights signing up for the Holy Land.

In the midst of the negotiations, however, the old warrior died, thus avoiding a dangerous trip to the Middle East.

Archambaud IV had married twice, the first time to Philippe d'Auvergne, the second to Beliarde and had six children. Like his predecessors in old age he sought a place in heaven by being a donor of property to the church, this time the church at Neuville near Montaigu and to the Chapter of St Ursin of Bourges just before he died. But he was also still acquiring property for he took over the castle at Chantelle on its promontory above the river Bouble south of Moulins which became a favourite with succeeding Bourbons. It was also he and his son William who built the new castle at Montluçon.

Archambaud V (*fl.*1078-96) had the nickname Le Pieux, which inevitably suggests a contrast with his father, indicating a tendency towards spiritual rather than military prowess and perhaps a lesser degree of physical health. This is perhaps corroborated by the fact that his death, apparently in his mid-forties followed very quickly after his father's.

His son Archambaud VI (1090-1116) in theory took over the patrimony at the age of only six, hence his nickname Le Pupille but in fact authority was quickly usurped by his uncle Aimon, known as Vaire Vache or Spotted Cow. However, the boy's mother Luce had remarried and her new husband Alard de la Roche helped her to come to the rescue. They appealed for justice to King Louis VI the Fat (*r.* 1108-37) who was remarkably energetic despite his chronic obesity and accused Aimon not just of usurping the title but also of exploitation, brigandage, robbery of pilgrims and kidnapping merchants passing through the territory. In addition he was casting covetous eyes on the royal town of Saint Pourçain, a place where the French King kept arms and treasure. Louis who was making substantial efforts to bring the feudal vassals of France into some form of discipline, to encourage towns and create prosperity responded to the call. He summoned Aimon to appear at court and when Aimon failed to obey he besieged him in his most northerly castle at Germigny l'Exempt.

Aimon's previous attitude of cocky defiance now vanished immediately and he threw himself at the king's feet, begging for mercy. Unfortunately the wretched Archambaud VI seems to have benefited little from this victory, probably because he died very soon afterwards and left no children. Aimon managed to persuade the king that he was a reformed character and probably also a useful one to the government, for the frontier in the south was still fragile. Not only did he shortly resume his role as Sire de Bourbon but was appointed royal protector of the very town which he had himself in his previous career been trying to capture: Saint Pourçain. As an even greater reward Aimon's son was allowed to succeed him. He had married Aldesinde and they had four children including the next Archambaud.

Archambaud VII (1100-71) took over in 1120 at the age of twenty and held the lordship for half a century. Most of his first two decades in control coincided with the reign of Louis the Fat and the rest with Louis VII the Young (r. 1137-80) perhaps most famous as the cuckolded husband of Eleanor the heiress of Aquitaine. As the late king's second son he had been brought up to take a high position in the Church but on his elder brother's death had to change roles. His resultant piety and perhaps also his reluctance to spend time with his wife resulted in his somewhat naive departure in 1147 to join the Second Crusade, which had been preached the previous year by St Bernard.

Amongst many distinguished French knights who accompanied King Louis was Archambaud VII who had quite recently in his late thirties married Agnes of Savoy or Maurienne, the younger sister of the king's mother the pious but unattractive Queen Adelaide, so he was the king's uncle by marriage. They shared the horrendous crossing of Anatolia from Constantinople to Antioch, during which many died from thirst and exhaustion. Thereafter the crusade became hopelessly bogged down in local politics as rival factions wanted to use the French Army for their own ends. One of the leading personalities, Raymond of Toulouse disagreed with the king's priorities and deliberately undermined the king's already volatile marriage so that Eleanor, who had joined them in the Holy Land, would leave him and take back her dowry, the huge province of Aquitaine. In the end Louis was persuaded after a month in Jerusalem to attempt the capture of Damascus. This ended in humiliating failure and one of the few to come away with any credit was Archambaud who safeguarded the dangerous retreat and saved numerous lives. For the king it was a major disaster not just because of his abject military incompetence but also the irretrievable breakdown of his marriage. Its annulment in 1152 resulted in the feisty Eleanor replacing him very rapidly with Henry II of England and transferring her valuable inheritance of Aquitaine from France to England, a damaging loss of territory for the French crown.

Archambaud VII meanwhile returned to Bourbon after a three-year absence, his image greatly enhanced. He brought with him numerous trophies including many fragments of what he chose to believe was the true cross and these he presented to the monks of St Vincent at Chantelle, his favourite abbey.

The turning of Aquitaine into a huge English enclave had important repercussions for the Bourbons because Auvergne of which Archambaud VII was now made Lieutenant General became a frontier outpost. His château at Hérisson was close to the new frontier and was captured at one point by the English or simply settled by English-paid mercenaries or freebooters with the agreement of Archambaud. At some point he tried to recoup his losses by snatching the château of Jaligny. Meanwhile he made some headway in the Auvergne and added Bellesnaves, Charroux and Montaigu to the list of Bourbon possessions, but though like his father he tried to seize Saint Pourçain, which was a key town for holding the frontier, he was not allowed to keep it. He retained Hérisson, Huriel, Epineuil and Saint Desire as a theoretical vassal of the count of Champagne. His only recorded good work was to found a leper sanctuary at Souvigny in 1140 but out of enlightened self-interest he did grant freedoms to many of the towns in the Bourbonnais such as Montluçon and Moulins as a means of ensuring their future loyalty.

Despite their late marriage he and Agnes had two children but their only son, another Archambaud, who had married Alix de Bourgogne died before his father and it was thus a granddaughter who succeeded to the patrimony when he died in 1171 just about the time when the English captured Montluçon.

The new head of the house of Bourbon was now for the first but not last time to be a woman: Mahaut or Mathilde Dame de Bourbon (1165-1227) was only six when she took over and was clearly a very eligible match. She luckily still had her grandmother Agnes of Savoy to act as her guardian. Her first marriage to Gaucher de Vienne took place when she was eighteen and lasted ten childless years during most of which he was away fighting, either the routiers in Châteaumeillant or the Saracens in the Holy Land, for he joined King Philip II Augustus (r. 1180-1223) on the Third Crusade in 1189. When he returned after three years away in the east he suspected, perhaps with justification, that his wife had been unfaithful (this was one of the hazards of crusading) for he beat her, flung her in one of their dungeons and arranged for the Church to excommunicate her. She had too many important allies however – one of them the king – so the churchmen were persuaded to change their attitude. She was released and allowed to divorce him in 1195 on grounds of consanguinity – he was related to her mother's family. Gaucher took this reverse very badly and proceeded to burn and pillage the Bourbonnais in revenge. The solution was to find her a husband strong enough to defend her and thus King Philip Augustus recommended one of his trusted knights, Guy II de Dampierre (1155-1216) who was ten years her senior, and had good properties of his own. He became the new Seigneur de Bourbon as well as Seigneur de Dampierre, which was south-west of Paris. So not only were the Bourbon estates substantially increased overall but some of them were closer to the capital and to the notice of King Philip II Augustus.

Philip Augustus had shared the leadership of the Third Crusade with the more impetuous Richard Coeur de Lion and did much to consolidate the French monarchy during his forty-four year reign. In particular he increased the power of France by defeating Richard's brother King John at Bouvines in 1214, so consolidating Normandy back into the French fold together with Maine, Anjou, Touraine and the overlordship of Brittany. The Sire de Bourbon played his part in these campaigns, particularly in 1211 with a three-year stint as constable in charge of in the suppression of the Auvergne, to the south of his own estates. This included his capture of over a hundred castles including Châteldon, Mauzur and the supposedly impregnable Tournoel. In addition he helped consolidate the defences of the Bourbonnais with two new forts guarding the approaches to Montluçon, the donjon at Ronnet and Château de l'Ours.

Meanwhile Philip Augustus also turned Paris into a more effective capital by building new city walls, paving the streets, developing Nôtre Dame Cathedral and starting a new royal castle at the Louvre. At some point, however, Philip Augustus used his power to the detriment of the Bourbons for he confiscated some of their estates in 1209 for an unspecified misdemeanour or perhaps simply to satisfy his own drive to centralise power. This was not before he had helped Guy de Bourbon recapture Château Hérisson and Montluçon while the English king was still shut up in a castle on the Danube.

Philip Augustus was succeeded for the last few years of Mathilde's life by his son Louis VIII (*r.* 1223-6) who was in his mid-thirties. He continued the rapid expansion of the French kingdom undertaken by his father with his main efforts concentrated well south of Moulins in the Languedoc. He conquered the county of Toulouse aided by the excuse that he could call his war there a crusade because of the number of Albigensian heretics in the area. He died in suspicious circumstances before he was forty, either from deliberate or accidental food poisoning or possibly some sexual aberration.

Just before her second wedding Mahaut had dedicated the completed Benedictine priory at Le Montet and soon afterwards she produced the first of seven children, a son Archambaud VIII Le Grand (1197-1242) who was twenty when he took over the lordship of both Bourbon and Dampierre in 1216 and seven years later was appointed Constable of Auvergne like his father. Soon afterwards came the accession of the new boy king Louis IX (1215-70, king from 1226) later known because of his crusading zeal as St Louis but who at this point was only eleven years old.

Archambaud VIII had shared in the brutalities of the so-called Albigensian Crusades, where the wretched Cathars of Provence were systematically persecuted and he now thrived under the new king. As the Bourbons continued to add relentlessly to their portfolio of castles and estates he acquired Nizerolle, Vartenne, Billy, Jenzat, La Palisse and Châteldon to the south and built the new Château de la Bruyere-l'Aubepin. It was his closeness to Louis IX which was to earn a royal marriage for the Bourbon family in the next generation and thus totally change its fortunes. In the meantime, however, like some of his predecessors, he had a serious disagreement with the Archbishop of Bourges and it was ten years before he at last submitted to the Church in 1239. Archambaud was still only in his mid-forties when he was killed in 1242 at the Bridge of Taillebourg near Saintes leading a royal force against some kind of counter-attack launched by the dispossessed of Languedoc. His and his wife's elegant tomb at Abbaye de Bellaigue in Virlet survives.

Archambaud VIII's first marriage to Guigone de Forez produced three children and his second was to his neighbour and close relative Beatrice de Montluçon, daughter of another Archambaud, so Montluçon which had been given earlier to one of his uncles now returned to the main family, and the king endorsed this as part of Archambaud's reward for help against the

English. One of his daughters, Marguerite (1211-56) became the third wife of Teobaldo, the King of Navarre and thus the first queen from the Bourbon family with a foretaste also of the important link with Navarre three centuries later. On her husband's death she acted as regent for their young son.

The constable's son Archambaud IX (c. 1215-49) took over in his late twenties and in 1228 had married Yolande de Châtillon, the heiress of Nevers of which he thus became the count, another step forward for the family. Like his father, he was made Constable of Auvergne by Louis IX; however, seven years later he followed the saintly king on the calamitous Sixth Crusade and was killed in Cyprus before he even had a chance to fight the infidel. He and his wife who had accompanied him to the east were both buried in Nicosia. The king made it to Palestine only to suffer defeat and capture, so that it cost a million marks to ransom him. Yet when he returned at last to France he must have had a soft spot for his dead companion for later he was to plan the momentous match which set the Bourbons on the road to their first crown.

Meanwhile Archambaud IX had left only two daughters so the elder of them, Mahuat or Mathilde (1234-62) took over the patrimony as Dame de Bourbon, Comtesse de Nevers et Tonnere. At the age of fourteen she married Eudes de Bourgogne but when she died in her late twenties after producing three daughters he took himself off to the Crusades and never returned. He died and was buried in Acre.

So in 1262 most of the Bourbonnais (three small areas were taken out as dowries for Mahaut's three daughters) passed to Archambaud IX's younger daughter Agnes (1237-87) who was in her mid-twenties. She had already made a good first marriage to Jean de Bourgogne, Seigneur de Charolais and the younger brother of her sister's husband, who like him was a junior member of the Capet royal family, yet another sign of the increasing prestige of the Bourbons. With her second husband she was less lucky for Robert II Comte d'Artois, a nephew of King Louis, spent much of his time away in Naples where he was acting as regent and where she seems to have died before him. He later tried to snatch some of his stepdaughter's inheritance.

As it turned out the only surviving child from these two marriages was a girl from the first of them, Beatrice (1257-1310). Meanwhile King Louis IX was by this time in his mid-fifties and had devoted the previous eighteen years to sensible government and reform. But now in for what was in those days a late-life crisis he decided to embark on another crusade and died of the plague in Tunis before he could do any damage to the infidel. The eldest of his seven surviving sons Philip III Le Hardi (r. 1270-85) had been with him in Tunis and took over as the new king, adopting a less pious approach to warfare which took him mainly to Spain and an early grave. Hasty, ill-planned and too prone to pleasing his favourites his only real achievement was the near annihilation of the remaining Albigensian heretics which resulted in most of

Provence coming under royal control. Nevertheless shortly after his accession he organised the marriage of his fifth brother Robert to the granddaughter of their father's dead fellow-crusader the Sire de Bourbon, a union believed to have been planned by St Louis before his departure to Africa. Thus in 1272 took place the momentous match between young Beatrice and Robert de France (1256-1318) who had just been made Comte de Clermont. It was due to this marriage that three centuries later the Bourbons were to inherit the crown of France.

With a bride of fifteen and a royal bridegroom one year older it might have been a fairy-tale marriage, but this was far from the case. When they were both twenty-one he was involved in a near-fatal head injury while taking part in a tournament to celebrate a visit by one of his other brothers Charles of Anjou who had become Prince of Tarento and claimed the crown of Sicily. For the next forty years Robert survived in virtually a brain-dead condition, spending most of his time in Paris. He outlived his wife Beatrice who made her château at Murat into a comfortable home, by seven years and his brother King Philip by fifteen. Anyway, before his accident Robert had fathered a son, Louis (1280-1342), who would carry on the Bourbon line after Beatrice died in 1310.

Meanwhile King Philip had been succeeded by his son, Robert's nephew, Philip IV le Bel (the Fair r.1285-1314) who added Champagne, Brie and Navarre to the French kingdom by marrying Queen Joanna of Navarre. Philip is perhaps best remembered for his ruthless pursuit of church money, both the huge funds normally extracted by the papacy and the massive treasure collected by the Templars. The first resulted in his quarrel with Rome and the setting up of the Avignon Papacy, the second in the cruel torture and execution of the Templar leaders.

Louis the new head of the Bourbon family was thirty when he took over during the final years of Philip le Bel. He was known initially as Louis de Clermont or Louis Monsieur and nicknamed Le Boiteaux because of some limp or deformity or possibly because of a war wound. At the age of seventeen in 1297 he had fought with distinction at the battle of Furnes and was knighted by the king at Compiègne. However, his conduct received varying reviews in Philip's disastrous Flemish campaign of 1302 when he led what was described as either a commendable rearguard action or an infamous retreat during the Battle of the Golden Spurs (so-named because of the many knights' spurs were captured by the Flemings) at Courtrai, which proved that Flemish infantry could take on French knights. He then contributed to the improvement in French fortunes in 1304 at the battle of Mons-en-Pevelle. In 1308 he had the dubious honour of escorting the king's daughter Isabelle to London for her marriage to Edward II, but was so extravagant in his personal display of grandeur that he had to ask his mother Beatrice to mortgage four of her properties to help him repay his creditors.

Some accounts suggest that Louis was prone to nervous disorders if not total breakdowns and this perhaps inherited tendency was also noted in his granddaughter Jeanne who became queen of France and passed the strain on to her paranoid son Charles VI the Simple whose daughter in turn passed it on to Henry VI the neurotic king of England.

Meanwhile Louis was rewarded with the post of Great Chamberlain whilst still in his early twenties and married Marie de Hainaut with whom he had six children.

With the king's death, however, in 1314 France was heading into an unexpected period of disaster. For all three of Philip IV's sons died within fourteen years of each other, as if doomed by the curses of Pope Boniface and the dying Master of the Templars. Not only did all three die but they left not one surviving son between them, so that ironically Philip's only living grandson and legitimate heir was the utterly unacceptable Edward III King of England. This was to mean a century of war in which the Bourbons were to play an often brave part but sadly often on the losing side.

In the meantime Philip's eldest son King Louis X le Hutin lasted only two years (1314-16) during which he was compelled to withdraw most of the governmental reforms brought in by his father. He killed himself at the age of twenty-seven by over-indulgence in wine after a hot game of ball.

Louis of Bourbon was confirmed as Comte de Clermont by the next brother, the pliable Philip V le Long (Tall r.1316-22), whose reign saw the horrific victimisation of Jews, lepers, monks, beggars and all others on whom the woes of society could be blamed. He died before he was thirty leaving only two daughters. This left the third brother Charles IV Le Bel (the Fair r. 1322-8) who promoted Louis to Comte de la Marche (including Montferrand, d'Issoudun and Saint-Pierre-le-Mont) in 1322 in return for him surrendering Clermont and for undertaking the delicate mission to see the Pope in Avignon and arrange for the king's divorce on grounds of adultery. In 1324 Louis took part in the military campaign against the English and Gascons during which he captured l'Agenais. Charles meanwhile concocted a plot with his sister Isabelle, the Queen of England to dethrone and murder her wretched husband Edward II in 1327. That same year Louis was made the first Duc de Bourbon – there were only three other dukedoms in France at this time – along with the return to him of Clermont. This promotion was followed less than a year later by Charles IV's death in his early thirties, childless despite three marriages. The extinction of the main Capet dynasty marked a new turning point in the fortunes of the Bourbons.

3

THE BOURBONS DURING THE HUNDRED YEARS WAR

'It laid the foundations of France's national consciousness even while
destroying the prosperity and political pre-eminence which France had once
enjoyed.' Jonathan Sumption, *Trial by Battle*

Thus the promotion of the Bourbons to a dukedom and the death of the last
male in the mainstream Capet dynasty took place within the single year 1227-8.
Though the new Duc Louis was a grandson of King Louis IX he was only
the son of a sixth son and not himself a serious contender for the throne.
Much closer were another grandson and a great grandson. Obviously the least
acceptable to the French was young Edward III king of England: he was the
son of Philip the Fair's daughter Isabelle who had married Edward II, and thus
great grandson of the Saint King. His accession would mean the absorption of
France by England, which at this time still claimed Normandy and Aquitaine,
but it could be argued by Salic law that his inheritance through a woman was
invalid. The alternative was Philip of Valois, a first cousin of Duc Louis de
Bourbon and the son of his father's elder brother Charles of Valois.

So Philip of Valois as the man on the spot took over as King Philip VI
(r. 1328-50) backed by Louis Duc de Bourbon and immediately laid on a show
of strength by subduing a rebellion in Flanders. Louis himself fought at the
battle of Mont Cassel in 1328. The new king gave up his claims to Navarre
but held on to Brie. Edward III, however, was waiting to reassert his claim and
Philip proved himself more of a showman than a detailed administrator. He
was constantly short of money. Yet after six years on the throne he had grown
so over-confident that he deliberately provoked Edward III into starting a war
by supporting the Scots King David II, invading Gascony and interfering in
Artois. As Mackinnon put it 'Two mad kings could make the world dance to
their music', or Sumption 'This succession of destructive wars separated by
tense intervals of truce and by dishonest and impermanent treaties of peace
is one of the central events in the history of England and France as well as
of their neighbours who were successively drawn into it: Scotland, Germany,
Italy and Spain.'

By the time the Hundred Years War began in 1337 Duc Louis, in his late
fifties, was too old to join in the fighting but strengthened the defences of
his two main castles at Bourbon l'Archambault and Moulins ready for the

onslaught. Three years later the French fleet was destroyed by the English at Sluys after King Philip had rashly dismissed too many of his experienced officers and two years after that Duc Louis de Bourbon died at the age of sixty-two.

The fate of the next three generations of the Bourbons was inevitably linked to the long war against the English. The fortunes of Duc Louis's own six children (plus one bastard) were to be varied and dramatic: two sons were killed in battle and three made royal marriages.

His eldest daughter, Beatrice (1320-83) who was given Creil as her dowry when she married the German-born Jean de Luxembourg (r. 1310-46), King of Bohemia, the blind hero who died as a volunteer fighting for France at the Battle of Crécy in 1346, a battle where the superiority of the English longbow negated the prowess of France's famed cavalry.

His younger daughter Marie de Clermont (d. 1387) also became at least a theoretical queen if not an empress, for after a first marriage in 1325 to Guy of Cyprus, Prince of Galilee she was widowed in Nicosia in 1346. In Naples in 1347 she married the ambitious Robert of Tarento (1326-64) who claimed the imperial crown in Constantinople through his Valois mother. Robert had also claimed to be Despot of Romania, and King of Albania. He seized power in Naples and fought to hold on to Greece, but spent the first four years of their marriage imprisoned in Hungary for murder. At his death in Naples in 1364 Marie still held Corfu and sixteen mainland Greek castles, but sold her rights in Achaia for 6,000 gold pieces. She survived another two decades as a widow in Naples where she was buried in Santa Chiara.

So far as his sons were concerned Louis had made the radical decision to split his massive inheritance in two, perhaps he thought quite rightly that it was now so large as to attract jealous eyes from the throne or perhaps he thought it too much for one man to handle. Anyway he left the dukedom of Bourbon to his eldest son Pierre but the county of Marche to his second son Jacques and, as we shall see, it was to be this junior branch which in the end triumphed while the senior was doomed to disappear.

Louis's eldest son Pierre, second Duc de Bourbon (1311-56, duke from 1342) married the new king's sister Isabelle de Valois and it was perhaps this connection that led him to adopt a conspicuously extravagant lifestyle, one that even with his now vast estates he could not afford in a period when France had lost around a third of its population due to the Black Death. The cost of further extending his already huge fortresses must have been considerable. He had taken part in the 1339 attack on Bordeaux and was made joint commander of the army in the north in 1342, the royal lieutenant on the south-west frontier in 1345. He tried hard to hold together the French forces against Henry of Lancaster, spending a very difficult winter besieged at his headquarters of Agen. He was made governor general of Languedoc. He was wounded the next year fighting in the main French Army against

Edward III at Crécy where King Philip mismanaged his larger army and suffered 15,000 casualties.

Pierre continued a prominent career as soldier and diplomat, including the painful negotiations that led to the surrender of Calais in 1347. Over the next few years the country suffered from plague and 50,000 died in Paris alone. Edward III's son the Black Prince was able to campaign with impunity deep into French territory – he reached Bourges and some of his freelance Gascons penetrated into the Bourbonnais itself. When King Philip was succeeded by his son Jean, (John II the Good *r.* 1350-64), things barely improved. Pierre was in such a weak position by 1356 that he bribed the Gascons to surrender Felletin since he could not capture it by force of arms. He was killed in his early forties at the battle of Poitiers, where as at Crécy the French had a larger force and should have won. He died in the act of saving the life of his new king Jean, a useless sacrifice as the king was captured and held for a huge ransom. At this point Duc Pierre had been recently excommunicated by the Church because his extravagance had brought on bankruptcy and in this unholy state he was refused a Christian burial. His body was rather unkindly kept in the church at Poitiers as security for the payment of his debts to the Church. Only when his son offered all his property to the Pope was the burial allowed to take place. He left one son and six daughters. His wife Isabelle retired to a nunnery after his death.

At this same battle at Poitiers his younger brother Jacques, Comte de la Marche (1319-62) who had saved the life of Philip VI in an earlier skirmish shared some of the blame for the disastrous defeat by the Black Prince as he along with several other prominent French nobles allowed themselves and the king to be taken alive by the English and held in London for ransom. Jacques had theoretically been given Ponthieu for his earlier gallantry, and married Jeanne de Châtillon, the heiress of Condé marking the first association of the Bourbons with that town, probably the one in Brie with which they were later to be famously associated. (The alternative is Condé l'Escaut in the north, which came in 1487 by the marriage with Marie of Luxembourg and is close to Enghien, which also became a Bourbon title). In 1350 he had been put in charge of all French forces in Languedoc, then a year before Crécy on his own merits was given the prestigious post of Constable of France. He was based at Caen in 1355 when all seemed set for a major defeat of Edward III by superior French forces. Nevertheless he was against the risk of a pitched battle and adopted the usual delaying tactics of proposing single combat between the two kings, an offer he knew would be refused but which always helped with the propaganda. Like his colleagues, however, he was guilty of over-confidence in the French cavalry and underestimated the potency of the English longbow. He had been badly wounded at Crécy, was renowned as 'the Flower of Chivalry' so he found the criticism hurtful and resigned as constable.

On his recovery Jacques was once more in charge of the army in Languedoc but morale was poor, the troops rebellious and he failed totally to prevent the devastation wreaked by the lightning attacks of the Black Prince. Thereafter came his disastrous role in the battle of Poitiers and his period as a prisoner.

In the end, after his release by the English, Jacques was fatally wounded along with his son Pierre in a battle at Brignais in 1362 whilst attempting to purge the countryside of stray mercenaries and brigands – *tardvenus* or routiers. He had an army of 5,000 men under his command but rashly regarded his opponents as amateurs, failed to keep a good look-out and was caught totally unprepared. The defeat was an additional and unexpected shock for the unfortunate King Jean II and the end of a career in which he had been one of France's most competent generals yet been defeated by smaller enemy forces due to over-confidence and a failure to appreciate that men of lower class like longbow men or mercenaries could in this period outfight traditional French cavalry. His surviving sons were to have equally adventurous careers in the next period.

Meanwhile we turn to the children of Duke Pierre. As in the previous generation, several of his six daughters were would-be queens. The elder, Jeanne (1338-78) married the Dauphin (he was the first to bear this title) Charles of Valois, the physically weak but mentally astute heir to the throne, who acted as regent during the long captivity of his father after Poitiers and eventually in 1364 was crowned with awe-inspiring ceremonial at Reims as Charles V the Wise (r. 1364-80). He had with great skill recovered many of the territories lost to the English and ruthlessly suppressed all opposition. Sadly Jeanne died at the age of forty giving birth to a daughter, Katherine and Charles himself died soon afterwards, leaving the throne of France to their twelve-year-old son Charles VI the Foolish (r. 1380-1422) whose mental health problems have been blamed on his mother's Bourbon antecedents. His courtiers tried successfully to debilitate his immature mind with a surfeit of debaucheries so that he was to spend much of his life in a strait-jacket. He was the first half-Bourbon king but turned out a paranoid schizophrenic who nearly murdered his own bodyguards after succumbing to the heat during a campaign in 1392. He suffered regular bouts of insanity for the rest of his life especially after the accidental fire during a fancy dress party in 1393.

Duke Pierre's second daughter Blanche (1339-61) suffered an even more tragic fate for in 1353 she was sent as a bride to King Pedro the Cruel (r. 1350-69) of Castile who was so infatuated with his current mistress, Maria Padilla, that he put his new wife in prison the day after their wedding at Valladolid. His annoyance with her was exacerbated by the fact that Duke Pierre was so close to bankruptcy that neither he nor his son could afford to pay her dowry. She spent some months in the fortress of Siguenza and then died suddenly, probably poisoned, at Medina Sidonia at the age of twenty-three. The Bourbons gathered a small army to seek revenge and it was led by Jean

Comte de la Marche (1342-97) Blanche's first cousin and the son of Jacques the Constable. Like his cousin he had been captured at Poitiers. He invaded Castile in 1366-7 and Pedro was removed from his throne, an action which was politically useful since for a while he was an ally of the English.

Another of Pierre's daughters, Bonne, also had a reasonably colourful career for she was the ancestress of the house of Savoy. Charlotte married King Jean I of Cyprus, but Marie, having eloped with an unsuitable mate, was locked up by her family for the next thirty years.

The outnumbered brother of the six girls, Louis le Bon II (the Good) of Bourbon (1337-1410) took over the dukedom as a teenager after his father's death at Poitiers in 1356. It seems that perhaps like his sister and father he suffered some level of mental instability. During the captivity of King Jean II he visited him in London as he tried to organise the collection of the huge ransom of bullion and land which had been demanded and allegedly played cards with the Queen. Born at the Château Montluçon he gained a reputation as a chivalrous knight, allegedly saving the life of the dauphin, his brother-in-law, in 1350. He founded his own order of knighthood *De l'Ecu d'Or*, and was kind to widows and orphans. Obsessed with the fashionable craze for chivalrous love he begged the king to found a Court of Love in Paris as an antidote to the Black Death which was sweeping the city. He would have disapproved of the king's younger son who stood as hostage for his father's release, then broke his parole, but equally he would have approved of King Jean who for the sake of his honour but with great political naivety voluntarily returned to London and died a prisoner three years later.

Meanwhile Louis had to spend a further four years in London where he had acted as a hostage for the payment of King Jean's ransom which never materialised. On his return in 1360 Louis found his duchy in a terrible state due to the ravages of the English and the disloyalty of his local barons. His great castle at Bourbon l'Archambault had twice been captured by the English or their allies (1356 and 1359). He summoned his vassals for a Christmas celebration where he forgave them and announced his new motto of 'Hope'. Then he drove the English out of the Bourbonnais in a short but effective winter campaign followed by the recapture from the English of the castle La Buyere-l'Aubepin. Five castles he actually bought back from the Gascon mercenaries, the Albrets, who were holding them. But his troubles were far from over for in 1363 his other great castle at Hérisson was captured and it was not till 1368 that he was able to capture the notorious routier Le Bourc Camus from Navarre and lock him in the dungeons of Moulins. Then in 1369 Belle-Perche was raided by Gascon routiers who kidnapped his mother Isabelle de Valois and kept her hostage for three years.

One of the lessons learned was that his castles were far from impregnable and at Bourbon he raised all of its fifteen already massive towers an extra twenty meters and strengthened them to hold cannons, also adding the additional tower named *Qui qu'en grogne*, allegedly to intimidate his own people. He also completed new castles at Montluçon where he built town walls and Verneuil and repaired those at Hérisson, Murat, Billy and Belle-Perche. The towns of Vichy, Villefranche and Varenne were also treated to new walls and Moulins given the first part of its future great cathedral.

He did also conduct a memorable siege, one of the first using artillery, of the castle at La Roche Aigueperse near Montpensier which had been occupied by English mercenaries and which soon afterwards became the seat of a major new branch of the Bourbon family.

Louis had married Anne de l'Auvergne when she was only fourteen and she brought him Forez as her dowry but at this stage the Bourbons despite large land-holdings rarely had enough income to pay the huge expenses of defending their dukedom. Even though he added to his holdings with Vichy, La Combraille, Beaujolais and the principality of Dombes, which was over the border in the German empire, his castle-building expenses outweighed his income. Certainly he devoted more energy than his predecessors to creating an administrative and financial infrastructure for the government of the region but it was still too little to support his massive building programme.

At the age of forty-three in 1380 after a deathbed request from his brother-in-law King Charles V the Wise he acted as one of the guardians for the king's son the wayward young Charles VI Le Bien-Aimé or Well-Beloved, later the Foolish who was having one of his periods of mental breakdown. The king's mother Jeanne who was Louis's sister had died earlier, but their mother the indomitable Isabelle (and the young king's grandmother), a widow, was still alive and she backed Louis in his difficult task of trying to control the country under a schizophrenic king, hampered by the fact that his fellow regents, the king's uncles all had different agendas and that the crowds of Paris exploited their divisions to riot.

Louis seems to have applied the same kind of fairness on a larger scale that he had already shown in the Bourbonnais and was popular except among the rapacious senior nobles who simply wanted to increase their own patrimonies. He joined in some of the successful campaigns led by Bertrand de Guesclin, and played an important part in the battle at Rosebeque in 1382 against the Flemings, gaining the reputation of an ideal royal servant. Yet the plans to invade England in 1386-7 were wrecked by disagreements at the top so the Hundred Years War was set to continue.

Then in his mid-fifties in 1394 during an interval in the war with England Louis, like his ancestor and namesake Saint Louis, responded to the call for a crusade. He was put in charge of the French contingent along with a Genoese naval force that would attack the Barbary pirates in Tunisia, who were not only Muslims but a menace to peaceful shipping. He besieged the pirate base at Mahdia and although he failed to capture it extracted a treaty from the Saracens that the activities of the pirates would be curtailed.

Louis remained a keen château builder, rebuilding La Roche Othon near Hérisson, extending Murat and Montluçon, which he turned into his favourite residence and where he also built some fine churches. In his early seventies Louis was still fighting and contemplated dying in the Holy Land or becoming a monk. But after writing an affectionate farewell to his wife Anne he had to defend his duchy, particularly its eastern estates in Beaujolais against an invasion from Burgundy. He memorably repelled the Burgundians just before he died at the advanced age of seventy-two in 1410 and was buried in the family priory at Souvigny.

Meanwhile his cousin Jean de Bourbon (1342-97) who had survived both capture at Poitiers and the deaths of his father and brother at Brignais as well as the adventure in Castile in 1366 was now Comte de la Marche and became also Comte de Vendôme in 1374 marrying its heiress Catherine in 1364 thus founding a major new branch of the family which later produced the first Bourbon king of France. He rose to be lieutenant general in Limousin, helping to drive out the English. He began the rebuilding of the two massive rock-top castles of Vendôme itself and nearby Lavardin.

Jean's eldest son Jacques de Bourbon (1370-1438) had a colourful career as Comte de la Marche and de Castres. In 1396 he led an army of 10,000 men to help defend Hungary from the Turkish invasion begun by the aggressive Sultan Bajazet. He took part in the siege of Bandins and was appointed chamberlain. He married the Infanta Beatrice of Navarre and took money from various sources to help fund an extravagant lifestyle, even setting out in 1407 to burn Plymouth and stir up a Welsh rebellion against the English but been driven back by storms. Then in 1415 he headed off to Naples to marry its Queen Joanna, a lady in her early forties described as 'no beauty or wit but profligate'. He promptly imprisoned his new wife, styled himself King of Naples and executed her lover Alopo before resuming his aggressive and extravagant habits which soon made him very unpopular with his subjects. They rebelled and restored Queen Joanna who took a new lover Caraccioli and flung Jacques in prison for two years. He returned to France in 1422 and was made governor of Languedoc, then ostentatiously retired to a monastery in 1438, claiming that he had received the call from Saint Colette. Never one to do anything by halves he dressed in rags and had himself wheeled into the cloisters in a manure barrow. He repeated this form of entry when he went on tour and died as a monk four years later. One son also became a monk while another Louis was killed at Agincourt and a third, Pierre, was murdered at La Rochelle in 1422 after being captured by the English.

Jacque's brother Louis de Bourbon (1378-1446), who became Comte de Vendôme held not just Vendôme but later also Castres in the Aligeois and La Marche to the south-west of Bourbonnais. He had campaigned in Brittany, Flanders and Castile, then became grand master of the king's household and an ambassador to England but had been involved with the Armagnac faction

and some fairly unsavoury pillaging in 1413. He led the left wing at Agincourt
with 600 picked men and sustained huge losses. He was captured and even
managed to father a bastard by a Sybil Boston while he was a prisoner in
London. He was not ransomed for eight years after which he resumed fighting
the English in 1423 when unfortunately he led the French to defeat at Cravant.
However, the greatest service he rendered was to be the man responsible for
bringing Jeanne d'Arc (Joan of Arc) to meet King Charles VII (*r.* 1422-61) at
the Château Chinon. Up to this point none of the authorities had taken her
seriously. As chamberlain it was Vendôme who supervised the famous scene
where the king hid amongst his courtiers in the hall, but Jeanne managed to
pick him out from the crowd. She insisted on calling him the dauphin because
he had not yet been crowned due to Reims being in enemy hands. Vendôme
then organised a more private meeting between the Maid and the king, which
resulted in her being given the chance to save Orléans where he fought beside
her, as he also did at Jargeau.

Meanwhile there had been a change of leadership in the senior branch of
the Bourbon family. Louis Duc de Bourbon's son Jean (1380-1434) born at
the Château Moulins became the fourth Duc de Bourbon on his father's death
in 1410. He was known as Jean le Bon in imitation of his distant cousin King
Jean le Bon of France who had died a prisoner in London in 1364 and his own
destiny was to be similar. Thus though he was a near contemporary of his
Vendôme cousin he was not to share his later successes.

Charles VI the Foolish was king throughout most of Duc Jean's life and
latterly so imbecilic that he was confined in a strait-jacket, whilst his relations
fought each other for power. In this chaotic situation Jean became a supporter
of the Orléans/Armagnac faction and joined in the attempted coup against
the Duke of Burgundy at Gien so that he was outlawed in 1411. Nevertheless
he himself had acquired the additional dukedom of Auvergne by marrying its
twice-widowed heiress Marie de Berry in 1400. In 1414 he was again involved
with the Armagnac faction against the Duke of Burgundy and led the brutal
siege of Soissons after which he ungallantly executed his defeated opposite
number de Bournonville, partly, according to rumour, because his bastard
half-brother had been killed by a crossbow during the attack.

Like his father Jean was obsessed with ideals of chivalry and in 1415 made
a vow along with sixteen of his knights that they would wear leg irons every
Sunday for two years until they met sixteen opponents willing to fight them to
the death: the order of the *Fer du Prisonier*.

At about this time the new king of England Henry V noted the continual
chaos in Paris and decided to take advantage of it by bringing an invasion
force across to Harfleurs. In the chivalrous spirit Duke Jean offered to take
on King Henry in single combat but there was little risk of his accepting. His
vow to fight to the death was never fulfilled for he signally failed to do so on
the field of Agincourt where he led the front division but instead surrendered

to an English man-of-arms, Ralph Fowne and was lucky not to be killed like many of the other prisoners of lesser rank. He thus spent the last twenty years of his life as a prisoner of the English, though in extreme comfort – he was able to send for his four falconers from Bourbon. He was allowed home on parole to try to raise a huge ransom in gold but failed because his living expenses kept eroding the sum that had been collected so he died in London aged fifty-four. An alternative French version of the story has him three times successfully collect the required ransom and three times have it rejected because of his reputation as 'the scourge of the English'. He was therefore out of action during those remarkable years from 1429-31 when the presence of Joan of Arc seemed to transform the fortunes of the French Army and created a mood in which at long last the English invaders could be driven back across the Channel.

Remarkably the year 1422 saw the deaths of two key players whose very different royal careers had dominated the penultimate period of the Hundred Years War. The death of the imbecillic Charles VI of France who by this time thought he was made of glass and would not even answer to his own name was followed by that of the much younger and hyperactive Henry V of England who had been mad in a totally different way and worn out by his lust for conquest and glory plus perhaps a consumptive chest.

With Duke Jean stranded in London it was to be his son Charles (1401-56) known as the Count of Clermont who was to be the other main Bourbon supporter of Joan of Arc. He had to stand in for his imprisoned father from the age of fourteen and then to wait nearly twenty years to inherit the title Duc de Bourbon. As a young man under the title Count of Clermont he took charge of the French Army at the famous Battle of the Herrings where he might well have beaten the English with his early bombardment but for the impetuosity of his Scots mercenaries under John Stuart of Darnley who disobeyed orders and dashed into battle too early so that he had to stop firing. So he lost the battle, the English managed to get through to Orléans with their herrings and other supplies and the morale of France reached its lowest ebb.

Like his cousin Louis of Vendôme, Charles of Bourbon at this point seems to have played a key role in the advancement of Jeanne d'Arc, for in the record of her trial she attested that he was one of the men who had witnessed her hearing voices, so clearly she regarded him as a key early supporter of her claims though perhaps later he thought she had overreached herself. He was a key ally of King Charles VII (r. 1422-61) who at this time was nicknamed by the English 'The Little King of Bourges' because that city was his main base and most of France was in English hands. Even Joan of Arc refused to call him anything but Dauphin, since although he had been king for over five years she did not regard his coronation as valid. Later Charles of Bourbon was one of two nobles chosen to serve the meal after Charles VII's coronation at Reims which Jeanne had made possible, yet she was not invited to the supper.

Similarly Charles had a minor breach with the Maid when the king sent him to summon her for a meeting at Saint Denis when she was busy fighting on the outskirts of Paris and did not want to be distracted. However, the fact that she called for him as a witness during her trial indicates a strong element of trust.

Less in doubt was the continued support for Jeanne from Louis de Bourbon, Count of Vendôme – the man who had led her to meet the king/dauphin at Chinon. In his early fifties he still fought alongside *La Pucelle* at the assault of the fortified town of Jargeau east of Orléans when she went seriously on the offensive and was herself first up the scaling ladders despite a crack on the head from a missile. It was all part of her plan to make possible what she regarded as a proper coronation of the king at Reims. Alongside both Louis and Jeanne was the subsequently infamous Giles de Retz, later known for his alleged child abuse as the Blue Beard, and associated with Jeanne in the English propaganda designed to blacken their names as witches. Louis continued to fight at Jeanne's side during the Aisne campaign when she tried to outflank the Burgundians at Soissons but was impeded by a governor appointed by Charles Bourbon of Clermont. Soon afterwards she was cut off and captured by the Burgundians at Compiègne, but essentially she had achieved all that she had intended.

The third member of the Bourbon family to back Joan of Arc was Charles of Clermont's younger brother Louis of Montpensier (1405-86) who was on her Loire campaign. This enterprising young Bourbon founded an important new branch of the family at the hilltop fortress of Montpensier at Aigueperse, south of Gannat. He was helped by two excellent marriages to heiresses in the Auvergne and his progeny were to play a major part in the Italian wars.

When Charles of Clermont did eventually become Duke of Bourbon after his father's death in 1434 his career was something of an anti-climax. For a variety of reasons once the war was nearly over he seems to have fallen out with Charles VII, now called the Victorious, who had his own special favourites, leaving men like Charles of Bourbon without the promotions they thought their rank deserved. To make the atmosphere even worse in 1437 France was smitten by poor harvests and plague but the king seemed to lead an ever more hedonistic lifestyle with his exotic mistress Agnes de Sorel.

The discontent climaxed when Bourbon joined with the king's impatient seventeen-year-old son, the Dauphin Louis (later Louis XI) in a rebellion given the name Praguerie in imitation of a similar recent event in Prague. This was provoked by an announcement by the king to the Estates General that he was forming a new professional army to tackle the problem of wandering ex-mercenaries or *Ecorcheurs* (literally flayers), survivors from the Hundred Years War who were still devastating the countryside.

For Bourbon and his cousin the Count of Vendôme this royal move presented a threat to their traditional role as leaders of a feudal army. Bourbon himself seems to have made an unsavoury alliance with some of the ex-mercenaries under their leader the Spaniard Rodrigo de Villandandro, known as *L'Empereur des Brigands* and the known instigator of a massacre near the Bourbon castle at Hérisson. Charles had let Villandandro marry his bastard sister and loaned him castles at Ussel, Montgilbert and Châteldon. Bourbon himself had provocatively imprisoned the bishop of Clermont and demanded a ransom, so he was perhaps closer to the brigands than he was to the king.

The Praguerie rebellion was, however, ill thought-out and Bourbon found himself pushed back into his home territories by the royal army. There even his own tenants would not support him, the cities of Auvergne shut their gates and the Dauphin changed sides when the king offered him what he wanted. The king attacked Hérisson and Bourbon thus lost one of his greatest fortresses. So he was in an impossible position and was persuaded to submit without further fighting. The infamous Villandandro was banished in 1443 to pursue his mercenary career back in Spain.

Charles de Bourbon's poor relationship with King Charles continued, particularly when Agnes Sorel died of poisoning in 1450 and the increasingly paranoid king suspected his recalcitrant nobles of plotting her demise.

When Charles himself died six years later in 1456 he was succeeded by his son Jean II (1426-88) who had played a more active role in the last stages of the Hundred Years War than his predecessor. Still in his early twenties he acted as a senior officer in two key battles which finally saw the expulsion of the English from all France except Calais. The battles of Formigny (1450) and Castillon (1453) were not just significant in bringing the ridiculously long war to a close but also for the first serious use of artillery in world history. The reward for Jean was to be given the king's daughter, Jeanne de Valois, as his bride.

Five years after the death of Charles Bourbon came the death of his namesake King Charles the Victorious, the man for whose throne Joan of Arc had paid such a dreadful price. His last two decades had seen him become increasingly eccentric and more interested in a succession of new mistresses than affairs of state. In the end beset by a mixture of real and imagined ailments he seems to have starved himself to death.

Duke Jean was made chamberlain for the new king, his brother-in-law Louis XI (*r.* 1461-83) but despite his record as a soldier he was dissatisfied and was prone to fits of pique. Described perhaps with slight exaggeration by Bridge as 'the richest nobleman in Christendom' he emerged from the Hundred Years War with vast estates which now included Beajeau, Forez, Clermont en Beauvais, Château Chinon in Nievres and Dombes. This was perhaps why he was so angry when as the price for his younger brother Pierre being allowed to marry Louis XI's daughter Anne in 1463, he was made to hand over to the young couple Clermont, Beaujeau in Beaujolais and Dombes.

Despite his marriage to Jeanne de Valois, two subsequent marriages and a significant number of bastards Duke Jean produced no surviving legitimate heir. So the dukedom went very briefly to his next brother who was a cardinal and did not need it, then a day or so later to his younger brother Pierre who had married the daughter of King Louis XI, Anne de France.

Until the final decades of the Hundred Years War (1337-1453) very few Frenchmen had distinguished themselves in battle and the Bourbons, though great proponents of knightly honour and magnificent armour were no exception, but at least a number of them had paid for their over-confidence with death or imprisonment.

In the end the tide had been turned by a young peasant woman with none of their advantages and whose cruel death, despite all their ideals, they and their king did nothing to stop. Yet it is possible that but for the early support of two key Bourbons she might never have come to the king's attention and never helped change the course of history.

Unlike many noble French families who were wiped out during the long war the Bourbons as a family not only survived but had added to their estates, had regained most of their huge wealth and were poised to play a prominent role in the next period of French history. There were now also three significant branches of the family; the Dukes of Bourbon, the Counts of Vendôme and Montpensier: all three were poised for dramatic action over the next century. The first of the three was so rich and powerful that it excited the envy and hatred of the Crown yet few could have predicted just how dramatic was to be its fall.

THE BOURBONS – FROM AYMAR DE NEUVRE TO BEATRICE

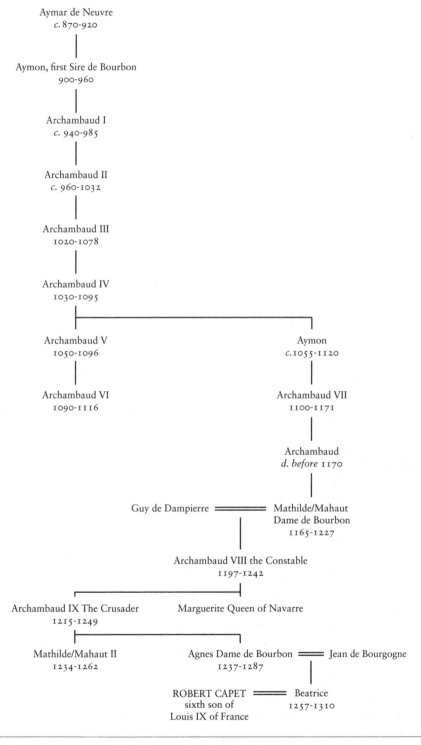

Aymar de Neuvre
c. 870-920

Aymon, first Sire de Bourbon
900-960

Archambaud I
c. 940-985

Archambaud II
c. 960-1032

Archambaud III
1020-1078

Archambaud IV
1030-1095

Archambaud V
1050-1096

Aymon
c.1055-1120

Archambaud VI
1090-1116

Archambaud VII
1100-1171

Archambaud
d. before 1170

Guy de Dampierre ════ Mathilde/Mahaut
Dame de Bourbon
1165-1227

Archambaud VIII the Constable
1197-1242

Archambaud IX The Crusader
1215-1249

Marguerite Queen of Navarre

Mathilde/Mahaut II
1234-1262

Agnes Dame de Bourbon ════ Jean de Bourgogne
1237-1287

ROBERT CAPET ════ Beatrice
sixth son of   1257-1310
Louis IX of France

Family tree continued on page 47

4

THE BOURBONS AND THE
ITALIAN WARS

'A la cour du roi chacun pour soi.' Traditional saying

Despite the obvious failings and mental instability of three of the last four Valois kings there were still at this time plenty of relatives closer to the throne than the Bourbons when the deviously ambitious Louis XI became king in 1461. Yet the Bourbons had proliferated considerably and with their various branches now held a dukedom and owned very substantial territories: the Bourbonnais itself, Clermont, Auvergne, Montpensier and Vendôme. So given their huge wealth and an occasional streak of truculence it was not surprising that clashes with the ruling dynasty became more frequent. As we have seen there was the Praguerie in 1440 when the Bourbons had backed the attempted coup by Louis when he was still the Dauphin and impatient to replace his father.

Duc Jean II de Bourbon despite his close marital connections with the Valois and his distinguished war record fell out with Louis XI who irritatingly deprived him of the governorship of Guienne and soon afterwards supported the rebels of Liège against their master Louis Bourbon (1438-82), the prince bishop of the city who was later murdered there. Then when Jean's younger brother Pierre married the king's daughter Anne, Louis made a very reluctant Jean hand over large tracts of land including Clermont, Beaujolais and Dombes to the bridal couple. It was a classic case of divide and rule.

For this reason Jean and his namesake Jean VIII de Bourbon, Count of Vendôme, (1428-75) who like him had played a prominent part in the wars against the English now played a similar role in the opposition to the centralising policies of Louis XI. In 1465 the two Bourbons joined with several other great lords at Nantes in the so-called League of Public Good in which they hypocritically claimed to stand up for the rights of ordinary people. This led to their dramatic confrontation with the king and an indecisive battle at Montlhery. King Louis was forced to make concessions to the rebels but had no intention of honouring them and soon regained the initiative by attacking Bourbon on his home ground, capturing both Hérisson and Montluçon castles and destroying Murat to teach him a lesson.

Duke Jean now focussed on accumulating great wealth at the expense of his neighbours in the Auvergne, just as his brother the pluralistic cardinal Charles de Bourbon, Archbishop of Lyon and Bishop of Clermont had exploited the citizens of Clermont. He spent huge sums on modernising his castles and hiring numerous artists and poets such as the talented but violent François Villon to celebrate his successes.

However, when in 1475 there was a new plot to depose Louis XI and Jean was asked to be regent he had learned his lesson and refused. Instead together with his brother Pierre he helped to put down the revolt and in 1477 their former ally Charles the Bold of Burgundy was defeated and killed. Jean was made constable of France as his reward.

King Louis XI died in 1483 aged sixty leaving as his heir the thirteen-year-old Charles VIII the Affable (1470-98). Jean, who was only three years younger than his old master, found that he now had to play second fiddle to his own younger brother Pierre (1437-1503) who had married the old king's daughter, Anne of France. They had been chosen to share the regency for his nephew Charles VIII. Anne was twenty-two, eight years older than her brother, the somewhat immature and unprepossessing king. She was a tall, determined woman who could dominate him with ease and, if nothing more, was certainly a gifted partner for her husband Pierre de Bourbon. Their joint portraits on the famous Moulins triptych show a woman of steely determination who had endured a loveless childhood in the court of her ruthless father. She was also extremely rich – it is recorded that she once spent 14,000 livres on three ruby and diamond ornaments. She thus took charge of France along with her husband Pierre but they had to mollify his elder brother the Duc de Bourbon by letting him continue as constable. They also had to stand by when the vindictive Jean took his revenge on the former king's administrator in the Auvergne, Jean de Doyat, and insisted on the poor man being condemned to mutilation.

However, the grumpy old Duke Jean was still not satisfied and though he was also briefly governor of Languedoc he joined the rebellion of 1488 against his brother and sister-in-law's régime, and instead supported Louis of Orléans, who was at this point the heir apparent. Then soon afterwards Jean died, and since none of his three marriages had produced any children – though he did have several bastards – the dukedom passed to his brother.

After a very short interval during which the oldest surviving bother, Charles the cardinal, held the dukedom for a few hours it was passed to the joint regent, Pierre. Duke Pierre II had already been governor of Languedoc in 1466, and when he married his princess had been given Châtellerault as well as large swathes of his brother's estates. During his brother's final years he was governor of France and heavily involved in the 'Mad War' (*Guerre Folle* 1485-8) against the recalcitrant nobles angered by the attempt to take over Brittany and by the power being wielded by the Bourbon couple whilst they managed the teenage king. Some five thousand were killed at the Battle of Saint Aubin du Cormier between the rival factions.

By 1489 Charles the Affable had come of age and the duties of Pierre and Anne as regents were over, so the couple at last returned to Moulins. By this time Pierre's only son Charles had died and as he was in his fifties it was likely that for the first time in two centuries the dukedom of Bourbon would have no male heir. Neither obviously could his other brother Charles Cardinal Bourbon, archbishop of Lyons, provide a male heir despite the fact that Louis XI had once referred to him as 'a good fellow who would absolve almost anyone from sin'. He makes a cameo appearance in Hugo's *Hunchback of Nôtre Dame* and Hugo comments 'he would rather give alms to a pretty girl than an old woman... and was never averse to a thorough good dinner.'

Thus the couple resumed life in the castle at Moulins which had been made into a luxurious palace by Jean the previous duke, with the forty-five meter high tower the *Mal Coiffée*, but Anne now added her own superb annexe known as the Pavilion of Anne of Beaujeau. Anne spent more time at Chantelle, which she also modernised and from which she still sent written notes of advice to her brother the king. Surprisingly after fifteen years of marriage in 1491 she gave birth to a daughter Suzanne so at least there was a female heiress, but if she left no children the dukedom would be threatened with extinction, many of its properties would revert to the Crown and the mighty power of the Bourbons would come to an end.

By 1494 when he embarked on his war to capture Naples Charles VIII the Affable was still in his early twenties, extremely ambitious and styling himself the new Charlemagne. By this time Pierre and Anne of Beaujeau had been sidelined, partly because Charles no longer wanted the dominance of his bossy sister and partly because the Bourbon couple were opposed to the war policy, for they had a good relationship with the Sforzas of Milan. Nevertheless Pierre was left in charge of the country during the king's absence and for the next year Moulins was the effective capital of France.

One of the king's most favoured officers in the campaign was Pierre's cousin Gilbert de Bourbon, (1448-96) Count of Montpensier, an experienced soldier who had been a lieutenant general for Louis XI in Poitou and the same in Paris in 1493. Having crossed the Alps in 1494 the French captured first Florence and then Rome where Louis was crowned king of Naples and Jerusalem as well as receiving the vacant imperial throne of Constantinople. But the success was superficial.

One of the first Bourbon casualties of the Italian war was François Count of Vendôme (1470-95) who died at Vercelli at the age of only twenty-five, but before doing so he had made a good marriage to Marie of Luxembourg who brought with her as part of her dowry the estates of Condé (*sur* l'Escaut) and Enghien which were later to become famous branches of the Bourbon family. Charles Bourbon (1489-1537) the son of François and Marie took over Vendôme and later was to be made its first duke in 1514.

In 1495 the French lost the disastrous the Battle of Fornovo where Matthew, the Bastard of Bourbon, one of the grumpy Duke Jean's extra-marital products, became the king's favourite warrior and later a marshal. The war had gone deceptively well to start with, for initially many Italians imagined it was a war of liberation but they were soon disillusioned by the brutality of the troops, so factions which had backed the French changed sides. Gilbert Bourbon of Montpensier himself was involved in some of the ruthless looting and massacres in Tuscany. Moreover inflation, famine and disease followed the army's path. Gilbert appeared to be hugely successful, for he was made Duke of Sessa and governor of Naples and he took a beautiful Italian wife Chiara Gonzaga. But the French victories had been against badly organised troops and the Aragon kings of Naples were not going to tolerate such a humiliation for long. Having lost all his booty at the disaster of Fornovo Charles VII returned to France leaving his subordinates to cope as they might and taking with him amongst his troops the first germs of syphilis. Duke Pierre had to be summoned from Moulins with reinforcements to rescue the king's rebellious cousin Louis of Orléans who was trapped in Novara. Louis was still deeply distrusted by King Charles, but as all the royal couple's children had died young he was still the next in line to the throne.

Gilbert Bourbon of Montpensier was left stranded in Italy with only a few troops. He was defeated at the battle of Pozzuoli and the French sent no further reinforcements or ships to rescue his beleaguered army. He died along with most of his men in the malaria-ridden swamps near Naples. His beautiful widow Chiara Gonzaga survived and continued to create uproar in court circles with her series of love affairs. In fact she was believed to be the model for the heroine of the *Heptameron* who kept six lovers locked up for her delectation.

The French invasion of Italy had achieved nothing and the king himself died soon afterwards in 1498 at the age of twenty-eight after knocking his head on a low lintel, leaving his throne to a very surprised Louis of Orléans (Louis XII 1462-1515), who had attempted unsuccessfully to overturn his predecessor ten years earlier. Louis was then even more surprised and pleased that his former enemies Duke Pierre and Duchess Anne chose not to make his accession difficult, but both King Louis and Duke Pierre had a problem and they needed each other's help. Pierre's main preoccupation was with the survival of his great dukedom intact after his death and with his son dead and only a sickly seven-year-old daughter, Suzanne, to take over he needed the new king's help to bypass the legal difficulties of a handover. Louis in his turn wanted their support in his own tricky negotiations to get rid of his wife, the disabled Jeanne who just happened to be Duchess Anne's sister, so that he could marry his predecessor's widow, Anne of Brittany, the only way to keep Brittany under French rule. So for a time it suited the king and Pierre to sink their differences and work together.

Despite Gilbert of Bourbon's defeat it was the Montpensier branch of the Bourbons which remained prominent in the next generation. Gilbert's eldest son Pierre was meant to marry Suzanne, the heiress of Duc Pierre, and thus reunite two major portions of the Bourbon inheritance, but for some reason seems to have made a mess of things and been replaced by Charles d'Alençon. To offset his failure he decided to win glory in the next Italian war and took part under Berault Stuart in a near-suicidal attack on Capua in 1501 when he was eighteen. One version of what followed is that he found his father's tomb at Pozzuoli, opened the lid and died of shock. Certainly he died at Pozzuoli but the alternative version is that he was killed in a skirmish or, like his father, died of malaria.

There was now a change of circumstances for the main Bourbon line. Five years after the accession of Louis XII, Duke Pierre II died and his redoubtable wife Anne of Beajeau or France decided that d'Alençon was not a strong enough character to marry her daughter Suzanne. So she had the engagement cancelled and switched her attention to the able second son of Gilbert, Charles of Montpensier (1489-1527) who had the advantage of being himself a Bourbon and of having already inherited the Montpensier part of the Bourbon estates so that he would reunite them with the Bourbon dukedom. With the king's help the legal difficulties were circumvented and Charles, at the age of fifteen, married the fourteen-year-old Suzanne in 1505 at the ducal palace in Moulins, becoming the most powerful and wealthiest duke in France. He held not only the Bourbonnais but also Auvergne, Forez, La Marche, Beaujolais, La Combaille, Clermont, Gien and Dombes. If required he could have mustered some 40,000 troops. He had a personal guard of two dozen archers and a hundred men-at-arms.

An accomplished soldier, the new young Duke of Bourbon, now known as Charles III, soon enjoyed a meteoric career under Louis XII. After a successful junior command against Genoa in 1507 he played a major part in the victory of Agnadello two years later and the Spanish campaign of 1512, after which he was made governor of Languedoc. Then during the combined Tudor and Habsburg attack of 1514 he was appointed Lieutenant General of Burgundy and took Soissons. He was made constable of France the next year at the age of only twenty-five.

King Louis XII had with the backing of the Bourbons and of the Borgia pope, Alexander VI, dispensed with his first wife Jeanne (the hunchback later made a saint for her charitable works) so that he could marry the late kings's widow Anne of Brittany and keep her inheritance in the family. After her death he had married Mary, the sister of Henry VIII but he had produced no sons, only a daughter Claude. She had married his nephew and, for the time being, closest male heir, François of Angoulême, so yet again there was likely to be a minor change of dynasty within the Capet/Valois fold.

Known as the 'Father of his People' at home because of his relatively benign policies Louis pursued a disastrous foreign policy. He had given up Naples as a target and was concentrating on Milan of which Charles de Bourbon was made briefly governor just as his father had been governor of Naples. But overall the campaign met with no more success than that of Charles VIII.

Disastrously Louis XII lost the Battle of the Spurs to his future brother-in-law Henry VIII of England despite an ill-judged diversionary campaign by the Scots at Flodden. He died two years later at fifty-two and just a few weeks after his marriage to the teenage Mary of England, leaving no male heir despite his three wives. So the crown went to his nephew and son-in-law, the ambitious and extravagant François of Angoulême (François I, r.1515-47) who was only twenty-one.

Like his predecessor François had had to live for some years in the expectation that he would never wear the crown, for all it had required was for King Louis to produce a son and his hopes would be dashed. He had received plenty of psychological support during this period from his bitter and intensely ambitious mother Louise of Savoy who as it happened was more of a mainstream Bourbon than Charles the new Duke of Bourbon himself. She had been forced at an early age into a loveless marriage with the middle-aged and thoroughly debauched Charles of Angoulême who had largely ignored her, as had her Bourbon relations. She thus had a grudge against the Bourbons, in particular their new duke Charles who was a mere Montpensier but whose charismatic persona and fighting abilities had a tendency to put her son the new king in the shade. It was just a matter of time therefore before this vindictive woman would use her new power to the disadvantage of Duke Charles.

For the first six years of the new king's reign the career of Charles Duc de Bourbon continued to flourish. François I confirmed his appointment as constable and immediately renewed the Italian War, crossed the Alps like Hannibal and won a major victory at Marignano where Bourbon's tactics played a major part in the victory. Sadly the duke's younger brother François Duc de Châtellerault was killed as were three thousand other Frenchmen, but so were four times that number of the Swiss mercenaries fighting for the emperor. Two other prominent Bourbons fought here, Charles (1489-1537) the new Duke of Vendôme and his brother Louis who had married Charles III's sister and been made Prince of La Roche sur Yon.

At this point Charles Duke of Bourbon was not only the most successful military commander in France but having reunited by his marriage the two main branches of the Bourbons he held three duchies in France plus three more large estates in the Holy Roman Empire, so he was probably also the wealthiest landowner. However, everything started to go wrong for Charles with the death of his wife Suzanne at Châtellerault in 1521. She had borne three children who died in infancy, so since Charles was only Duc de Bourbon by right of marriage and he had no son there was now the possibility that other claimants might challenge him for the title and many of his estates could revert to the crown.

That possibility soon became a reality. King François, perhaps jealous of Bourbon's huge wealth and goaded by his vengeful mother Louise of Savoy who as a Bourbon believed she had a claim to the duchy, inaugurated a series of minor humiliations to irritate the constable. There had already been rows between them over the expenses of campaigns. Louise, the king's mother, offered an easy solution: despite the fact that she was in her mid-forties while Charles de Bourbon was just past thirty she suggested that they should marry. To her disgust he rejected her so she was determined to ruin him. So came the next humiliation inflicted on him by her pliant son. The duke was removed from his usual position in charge of the advance guard in battle, then deprived of his post as constable and threatened with the loss of the dukedom he had gained through his late wife.

Duke Charles's mother-in-law Anne of France took his side in this crisis even though her daughter was now dead, for what mattered to her was the preservation of the duchy. Charles had been a faithful husband to Suzanne and only one mistress, Madeleine de Bouce, and one illegitimate child were ever attributed to him apart from the legend of his later affair with a Mogul princess. Anne advised Charles forcibly to switch alliances to the Emperor Charles V, who was already his overlord for the principality of Dombes. But she died soon afterwards and did not live to see the outcome. The Emperor Charles V now dangled the possibility of a Habsburg bride, his sister Eleanora, and the crown of Provence as bait for Charles to change to the imperial side. Along with Henry VIII he emphasised the advantages to Bourbon of deserting a French king who was trying to deprive him of his inheritance. In 1523 King François having heard of the intended treason called on the duke at Moulins but nothing was resolved. Yet it seems that Bourbon saw no possibility of reconciliation and made his decision to head for the border.

King François immediately set about confiscating all the Bourbon estates including the huge Forêt de Tronçais and destroyed several of the duke's castles such as Chantelle. Charles was almost as rapidly made a lieutenant general of the imperial army of Charles V in Italy. In 1524 he won his first battle against his own countrymen near Gattinara. He then he led the emperor's troops in an invasion of Provence and after capturing several cities such as Aix and Frejus he laid siege to Marseilles which proved too tough a nut to crack. King François retaliated by besieging Pavia in Italy but Bourbon gathered together a new imperial army and counterattacked. The French got in the way of their own guns and, with between 5,000 and 8,000 killed, were disastrously defeated by Bourbon and his allies. François I was made a prisoner by some of Bourbon's men, and was not to be released from Spain until he had promised to surrender Artois, Flanders, Burgundy and all his Italian territories – promises which he had no intention of keeping.

Charles of Bourbon had proved one of the emperor's most successful generals just as he had been for King François, but in the prolonged negotiations for peace Charles V chose to renege on the kingdom and the royal bride that he had promised to him. Equally François I reneged on all his promises to restore Bourbon's estates, claiming oaths were invalid if made under duress. Instead the Bourbon inheritance passed to his mother Louise of Savoy. It seemed Charles had just switched allegiance from one untrustworthy monarch to another. Ironically his distant cousin Charles IV of Bourbon, the first Duke of Vendôme, acted as co-regent of France while King François was a prisoner and was later made governor of Paris, so as one Bourbon star fell another rose.

In 1527 Charles was once more in charge of an imperial army in Italy but his situation had still not been clarified. Neither had his troops been paid, so he was in an awkward position, but he now had the opportunity to let his army win its own pay-off by capturing the richest city in Europe, Rome, where Charles V was planning to be crowned by the Pope. As the army had no artillery the only way to capture the city was by storming the walls. Charles de Bourbon insisted on being the first man up the scaling ladders, made himself conspicuous by wearing a white tabard and was hit by a musket shot. Thus he died in the moment of victory. Benvenuto Cellini the Florentine jeweller and sculptor later boasted unconvincingly that he was the sniper who killed both the former constable and later William the Silent. At least Charles could not be blamed personally for the atrocities committed by his troops after his death, but in the eyes of the Church he had committed sacrilege so he was excommunicated. In 1562 his body was exhumed so that it could suffer posthumous humiliation, standing upright in armour till 1660 when at last the Church consented for him to be reburied. The vindictive Louise had only lived to enjoy her new estates for a further four years and some of them were restored to Charles's sister Louise of Monpensier who married a Vendôme Bourbon, Prince of La Roche sur Yon.

While Charles de Bourbon left no legitimate children he did, according to some sources, have an extraordinary affair with a Mogul princess from Delhi. This resulted, according to one version, in the birth of a boy, Jean Philippe, (1525-60) who after numerous adventures became a courtier of the Emperor Akbar (r. 1556-1605) in Delhi, was made captain of the royal guard, chief of the harem, promoted to the rank of Nawab, married Akbar's sister-in law and founded a new branch of the Bourbons who later settled in Bhopal. The alternative account of Jean Philippe's parentage suggests that he was the son of one of Duke Jean II's bastards who had married a Busset heiress and begun a new branch of the family. Whatever the truth of this the family in India survived into the modern era as the Fratcis or Bourbons in Bhopal.

A huge effort had been made with the marriage of Charles and Suzanne to reunite two of the main branches of the Bourbon family so that the vast estates of the Bourbonnais, Montpensier and Châtellerault had come together under a single owner. Charles's younger brother François had even been given an extra dukedom in 1514 only to be killed a year later at Marignano so that the title passed to Charles who thus at the height of his career had three dukedoms and the office of constable, only for it all to be snatched away. Then just when he might have been reconciled with King François he sacrificed his life in a foolhardy act of bravery leaving no direct heir. Most of the estates remained confiscated and the old dukedom of Bourbon was gone forever. It could have been a mortal blow to the family, yet the surviving junior branch of Vendôme and Condé was growing rapidly in power and wealth. It still had one asset that was more valuable than all the estates which had been forfeited, a few drops of royal Capet blood which within seventy years of the disaster were to give the Bourbons far more wealth and power than had looked likely in the 1520s. No one in 1527 could have foreseen that the extended royal family of the Valois/Capets would self-destruct and suffer such a succession of reproductive failures.

THE BOURBONS – FROM BEATRICE TO HENRI IV

Family tree continued from page 36

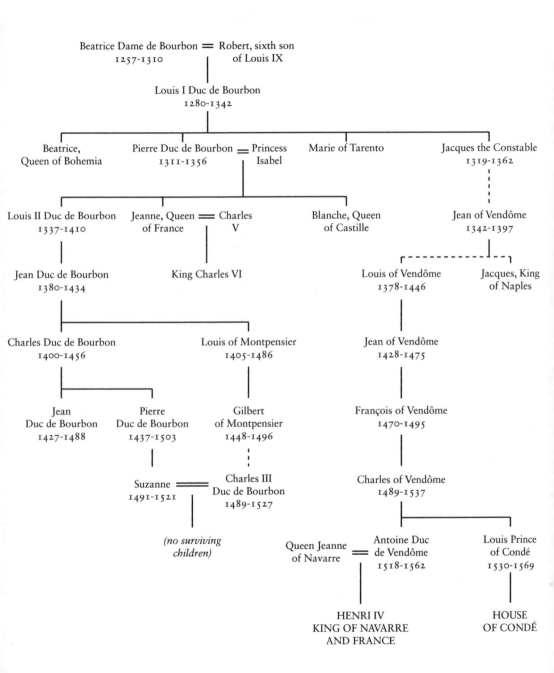

5

THE RELIGIOUS WARS AND THE END OF THE VALOIS

'Nobody who likes to relax inside his armour should take the trouble to make war.' Henri of Navarre

The deaths of both François I and Henry VIII in 1547, followed eight years later by the retiral of the Emperor Charles V led to a period of great turbulence. It was thirty years since Luther had nailed up his ninety-five theses in Wittenberg and a decade since John Calvin, son of a Picardy lawyer, had written the inflammatory preface to his *Institutes* dedicated to François I. In the aftermath France had been swept by an almost millennial religious frenzy. The new French Protestants were particularly fanatical so persecution only served to make them more so. Similarly the die-hard Catholics adopted an equally combative stance and perceived themselves the victims of a satanic plot.

The division between the two sides grew deeper the more they became embroiled in conflict and violence. Though there were obvious geographical preponderances for both parties many of the Huguenot enclaves were isolated from each other, many towns and districts had their own religious fault-lines. Thus even families could be divided by religion and the Bourbons were no exception, yet religion was to play a major role in their final rise to supreme power and by a coincidence the two ablest Bourbons of this generation were both Protestants.

François I had not been an avid persecutor of heretics, perhaps because his sister Marguerite the Queen of Navarre had shown Protestant tendencies. She had been influenced by the Calvinist missionaries who from their base in Geneva had focussed their efforts on southern France. Another who held him back was his mistress the Duchesse d'Etapes. He made an effort at suppression after the saturation of Paris with Huguenot placards in 1534 but only kept it up for another year so that most of the Vaudois moved over to Calvinism and the new sect gathered adherents in the south and west.

François's son, the new king Henri II (born 1519, r. 1547-59), who took over at the age of twenty-eight was a much more enthusiastic persecutor, partly because of the influence of his mistress Diane de Poitiers. He attended the burnings of Huguenots in Paris 1548-50 which resulted in around ten thousand others fleeing to Geneva and even more deeply entrenched fanaticism.

Henri II and his wife Catherine de Medici produced nine children, seven of whom survived to adulthood, so no one would have predicted that just over four decades after his accession he and all his sons would be dead and that thus the Valois/Capet dynasty would be extinct. As it happened the main line of Bourbon had also become extinct with the childless death of Duke Charles the Constable who by the time he was killed on the ramparts of Rome had already been deprived of his three dukedoms. So it was the junior branch of the Bourbons who came to the fore at this time as the senior surviving relatives of the royal family. Charles IV de Bourbon (1489-1537) had been promoted to Duc de Vendôme in 1515, acting as regent when King François was captured and held prisoner after the defeat at Pavia. He was made governor of Paris in 1527 shortly after his cousin the ex-constable's death had left him the senior surviving member of the Bourbon family.

Charles Duc de Vendôme had a remarkably large family considering the plague that ravaged France in 1516-17 when he was in his late twenties. It was to be one of the remarkable features of this generation that two of the sons became leaders of the Protestants in France, a third, Louis, became a cardinal archbishop, one of his daughters the wife of the leader of the Catholic side, the Duc de Guise, and another an abbess. To what extent this sectarian diversity was based on genuine belief and how much on political expediency it is hard to judge, but as the number of Valois males continued to diminish, the Bourbons' political prospects were bound to rise and in such a climate their religious affiliations became particularly significant.

When Charles died in 1537 the new Duc de Vendôme was his eldest son Antoine (1518-62) a man regarded as vain and unstable who nevertheless became the ancestor of all the Bourbon kings. He was born at the family's château at La Fère in Picardy near Reims but also held the Château Lavardin near Vendôme and substantial other estates. At the age of thirty he married Jeanne d'Albret the heiress of Navarre, the small Pyrenean kingdom which had lost its southern half to Aragon a few decades earlier but was still notionally independent of France. Antoine thus found himself in a Huguenot enclave so that he became not only head of the house of Bourbon but a potential leader of the Huguenots. His wife was not just the daughter of the King of Navarre, Henri II, but of the royal Valois princess Marguerite, sister of François I and a talented writer, author of the popular *Heptameron*. She was a dedicated Calvinist and herself also a poet. Sadly Antoine, who had no strong religious views, could never make up his mind which was the better side to support and was to earn the nickname *Le Grand Tergiversateur* ('Turncoat') and was described as '*ondoyant* (undulating)'. He had a reputation for being calm and brave in battle, but impetuous, hyperactive and chronically unfaithful to his wife.

In 1553 Antoine and his wife at last produced their first son, the future Henri IV of France, but only after she had made a dangerous last minute dash from La Fère to one of her father's castles at Pau so that the baby could be blessed by his grandfather with a traditional dash of wine and a smear of garlic. Maybe this move away from Picardy was prompted by the fact that Antoine had begun an affair with a catholic mistress, La Belle Rouet, Louise de la Berauderie, who the very next year produced another son for him, the bastard Charles who later became a bishop. With his affections split between a strict Calvinist wife and a more relaxed Catholic mistress, Antoine took Navarre for granted and concentrated his ambitions in Paris. Yet when his father-in-law Henri of Navarre died in 1555 – perhaps of a venereal infection – and his wife inherited the kingdom he was happy enough, for a while, to play the Calvinist, accepted the title of King of Navarre and enjoyed the additional new estates of Albret, Béarn and Foix. He was present at the major Huguenot rally in Paris in 1558 but then changed sides to fight for the king against the Austrians. He brought his wife and now four-year-old heir Henri to attend the wedding of the Dauphin to Mary Queen of Scots and then left the little boy motherless to be trained in the decadent atmosphere of St Germain-en-Laye. In 1559 he was in Guienne when Henri II was accidentally killed in a tournament and was himself too slow getting back to Paris to grab any portion of the subsequent regency organised by the pro-Catholic Guises. The new king François II (1559-60) was an unhealthy teenager married to Mary Queen of Scots who had a Guise mother, so the strength of the Guise hold on power increased.

In 1560 Antoine's youngest brother Louis Prince of Condé (1530-69) led an attempted coup at Amboise, to sieze the young invalid King François from the clutches of the Guise family and turn France in the direction of Protestantism. The plot failed and the bodies of many of the conspirators were hung from the castle walls. Antoine had not supported the conspiracy and was party to his brother's arrest afterwards, but supposedly secured his freedom by resigning his own right to be part of the regency team. However, his ambition was still not satisfied so he reconverted to Catholicism and was given the title of general. He escorted the dowager Queen Catherine de Medici back to Paris from Fontainebleau yet at the same time was plotting against her to try to win a role in the regency. This remarkable woman, daughter of the Medici Duke of Urbino, was a widow at forty and spent the next thirty years of her life trying to preserve the Valois dynasty in the shape of her four sons, three of whom became kings but one after the other let her down by dying without leaving any male heirs. Described by her third son Henri as '*Madame la Serpente*' she was a woman of remarkable ability and determination.

Meanwhile King Antoine of Navarre drove his own queenly wife out of her home for letting her Huguenot friends vandalise his chapels in Vendôme. Philip II of Spain was trying to bribe him to change sides with an offer of the crown of Sardinia. In the end he was fatally wounded while leading a royal army at the siege of Protestant Rouen in 1562.

Two of Antoine's brothers had already been killed in battle, François soon after winning the field at Cerisoles in Italy in 1544 when he was still in his early twenties and Jean at the Battle of St Quentin in 1557. Thus it was their hunchback youngest sibling Louis Prince of Condé who was left available as the preferred leader of the Huguenots. He had been brought up amongst converts and married one, Eleonore de Royza, who brought him the additional lands of Conti (sur Seller near Amiens) which was to provide a new title for their younger son. He had served as a youngster in the army of Henri II from 1551-7 when his daring raid helped save Metz from the Spaniards and again did well as a cavalry commander at St Quentin but failed to win further promotion, so after a spell in Geneva listening to sermons he took over as the Huguenot leader, despite the fact that his personal morals were far from Calvinistic. Condé was involved in two conspiracies, the first at Amboise to kidnap the king from his minders, the second after which his brother induced him to surrender. He was condemned to death but reprieved when the new king died, as the regent Catherine de Medici needed allies to offset the huge power of the Guise family. His brother Antoine as we have seen helped secure his release by surrendering his own claims to a role in the regency.

In 1562 the Guises were responsible for a massacre of Huguenots at Wassy. Condé left Paris and joined Admiral Coligny at Meaux where they became joint leaders of the Huguenots and effectively started a civil war. They seized Orléans and it was around this time that Condé's eldest brother Antoine King of Navarre and Duke of Vendôme was killed with the royal army at Rouen, leaving his young son Henri (1553-1610) who thus succeeded him as the senior Bourbon at the age of nine. A year earlier his father had taken him to the court at St Germain en Laye, away from his mother's influence, so that he could be tutored as a good Catholic with a smattering of Latin and Greek. There he became friends with the two other Henris who were to play a big part in his early career; Henri d'Anjou the future king and Henri de Guise the future head of the most powerful Catholic family.

Louis of Condé was captured again after an indecisive battle at Dreux, but was used as an intermediary between the two sides in 1563 after the murder of the Duc de Guise at Orléans. By this time King Charles IX (r. 1560-74) was fifteen and with his mother Catherine de Medici went on a prolonged tour of France to try to enhance his popularity. Meanwhile the Dutch had rebelled against Spain and the Huguenots became alarmed at the Spanish Army with its Swiss mercenaries marching up from Switzerland through the Rhineland towards Holland. Their response was an attempt to kidnap the young king near Meaux (an event known as the *Surprise de Meaux*) and Condé with his army blockaded Paris, reducing it to a state of famine which aggravated the anti-Huguenot sentiment in the city.

The Huguenots, with an army of around 20,000, fought another indecisive battle at St Denis, but Condé now changed tack to try to link up with German Protestant troops in Lorraine and next besieged Chartres. By this time the king's more aggressive younger brother Henri (1551-89) Duc d'Anjou, at the age of seventeen was appointed commander in chief of the royal armies and there was something of a stalemate, exacerbated by the fact that neither side could afford to pay their foreign mercenaries for very long. Henri Prince of Navarre at the age of fourteen had managed to escape from St Germain to rejoin his mother, who promptly sent him to La Rochelle to be trained as a soldier by his uncle Condé. The training was soon put into practice. When the war (known as the Third War) resumed after a series of truces Anjou won a significant victory against the Huguenots at Jarnac in 1569. Condé surrendered again, was murdered soon afterwards on the orders of Anjou by one of his guards and carried off the field on a donkey to emphasise his humiliation.

Condé's son Henri (1552-88) was only sixteen and as yet too young to step into his shoes. The other Henri, his nephew the Prince of Navarre was also still a teenager and for the time being also too young to lead the Huguenot cause, so for the the next period that role went to Admiral Coligny, with the two young Henris ordered by Queen Jeanne of Navarre to assist him. The result was a bloody Huguenot defeat by the royal army under Henri of Anjou at Moncontour. Yet Coligny survived with a still substantial army and the royal side made some concessions to achieve a peace that lasted two years.

By 1572 Henri de Bourbon, Duc de Vendôme became on his mother's death, due to poisoning by some accounts, King of Navarre. At the age of nineteen he was head of the Bourbon clan with huge tracts of land including Navarre, Béarn, Albret and Vendôme. As a result of the machinations of Catherine de Medici he was also engaged to her daughter, the king's sister Marguerite. Their marriage on a special platform outside Nôtre Dame was conducted by his uncle, the rather feeble-minded Charles Cardinal de Bourbon (1524-90) – he had been made a cardinal in his early twenties as Archbishop of Rouen, where he was pelted by the Huguenots, and an Inquisitor in 1557. This royal wedding attracted a significant number of prominent Huguenots to the capital which still had a strong anti-Protestant bias. The combination of sectarian fault-lines, hot weather, paranoia and convivial drinking led to a volatile atmosphere in which one of the Huguenot guests, Admiral Coligny was wounded in an attempt on his life.

Perhaps this was engineered by his arch-enemy Henri of Anjou, brother of the King, but it was certainly condoned by his mother Catherine and feeble-minded brother Charles IX. Two days later mob violence took over, allegedly encouraged by Anjou who wanted the job finished. Coligny and several thousand Huguenots were massacred in cold blood on St Bartholomew's Day.

In this atmosphere of terrorism the two young Huguenot leaders, both Bourbons, Henri of Navarre and Henri Prince of Condé, were given the choice of reconverting to Catholicism or being shot. Neither chose martyrdom. The newly married Henri of Navarre was put under heavy guard and consoled himself not with his wife but with Charlotte de Sauve. Henri of Condé kept a low profile while their tormentor Henri of Anjou was surprisingly elected King of Poland and departed for Cracow.

Yet in 1574 the scene changed yet again as amazingly the Valois dynasty continued to self-destruct. Charles IX died at the age of only twenty-five, the second of Henri II's four sons to die without leaving a child. Apart from Henri of Anjou, the third son, there was still the fourth one, Alençon, alive, but the two hated each other. Only these two now stood between Henri of Navarre and the throne of France, though both of them were fully expected to produce sons. Meanwhile Henri of Anjou quickly abandoned his Polish crown and dashed back to Paris for the larger prize. As the author of several defeats of the Huguenots in battle and the probable instigator of massacres in Paris and several other towns his accession as Henri III (r. 1574-89) did not bode well for Protestants.

In this situation Henri of Condé who was a much more committed Calvinist than his namesake of Navarre, was the first of the two Bourbons once more to change sides. With money from England and mercenaries from Germany he even had the cooperation of the new king's maverick brother the Duc d'Alençon. They invaded Burgundy and waged a desultory civil war. Meanwhile Henri of Navarre seized the opportunity to escape from Paris while on a hunting trip near Senlis and he too went back to Protestantism in 1576, partly influenced by his sister Catherine. He abandoned his wife who preferred the sociability of court life and joined the Huguenots. Faced with this uprising, Henri III decided to make concessions and granted the Huguenots freedom of worship. Condé was given a royal appointment as governor of Peronne. However, this did not solve the king's problems for the hard-line Catholics objected to his compromising behaviour and he soon found himself in a triangular contest, condemned by both the Catholic and Protestant extremists.

Henri III was now blackened by the propaganda of both sides, portrayed as besotted with his mignons, but though he was a foppish dresser he may well not have been homosexual. He was an obsessive huntsman yet despite his military prowess prone to nervous disorders and abscesses. A highly complex character he was devoted to the Catholic cause. By 1579 the two other Henris were once more making war against him: Condé stormed the border town of La Fère while Navarre scored his first military success in sole command with the capture of Cahors, a campaign that took four days of intensive effort and proved his powers as a field commander. At this time he was quite enjoying life as King of Navarre with his little court at Nerac from which he would steal out incognito to mix with the peasants, find out what was going on and have some rough fun. Catherine de Medici was alarmed at his reversion and insisted on bringing her daughter back to him at Nerac in 1576 but Marguerite was allegedly just as promiscuous as he was and left him finally in 1578.

The self-destruction of the Valois continued in 1584 when the king's only surviving brother the Duc d'Alençon, once a suitor for Elizabeth of England, died of consumption. Thus there was now only one life between Henri of Navarre and the throne of France. While it was still to be expected that Henri III would have children Navarre must by this time have sensed the serious possibility that the Bourbons could acquire the crown. This naturally did not please the extreme Catholic party. The Guises backed by Philip II of Spain organised a campaign to exclude Henri from the succession, replacing him in that role with another Bourbon, his uncle Charles Cardinal de Bourbon, who though now in his late sixties had never taken the final vows of the priesthood. With an archbishopric and the additional income of more than twenty abbeys he was enormously rich. At some point he had fathered an illegitimate son but he was very much a Catholic. Thus in 1585 Pope Sixtus VI was persuaded by the Guises to excommunicate Henri of Navarre and declare Cardinal Bourbon heir to the French kingdom. It was this event which, according to Henri, made half his moustache turn white.

The two Bourbon Henris, Navarre and Condé, responded with their own alliance and defeated Henri III and Henri of Guise's army at the battle of Coutras in 1587, hence the War of Three Henris – it could have been four if they had included Condé. The Huguenots were helped by a third Bourbon, Charles of Soissons (1566-1614), who with Condé led a division at the battle. This victory was, however, offset when the Guises beat the Huguenots' German allies. Henri III found himself uncomfortably hemmed in by the Guises and decided to get rid of them. Their leader Duc Henri the Scarred, one of the veterans of St Bartholomew's Day and himself ambitious to succeed the king was murdered at Blois on his orders in 1588. The murder of his brother Cardinal Louis de Guise followed soon afterwards. Cardinal Bourbon was also imprisoned as Henri III seemed to align himself more towards the Huguenots – in vain. The next year the king was himself murdered by a fanatical Dominican friar who claimed to be doing the work of the Lord. Since he had no children this meant that the Capet/Valois/Angoulême dynasty had run out of direct heirs so Henri of Navarre who had a Capet ancestor from nine generations earlier could at long last claim the throne for the Bourbons. He was now in his mid-thirties and still had to face another five years of fighting before he could have himself crowned at Chartres.

Sadly the other Bourbon Henri, the Prince of Condé, who had shared many battles with his cousin Henri of Navarre as joint Huguenot leader, had also just died in mysterious circumstances. Latterly he had become something of a liability as his allegiance was with the extreme Protestants concentrated in Poitou and his numerous trips abroad to raise money and armies had been to little effect. He was wounded at the Battle of Coutras and the next year in 1588 at the age of thirty-six was poisoned, allegedly by his second wife Charlotte who had renounced her Catholic faith to marry him, and at the time was pregnant with his heir Henri II who was thus born whilst his mother was in prison.

Less controversial and even more convenient was the death in 1590 of Charles Cardinal Bourbon, the new king's uncle and the preferred candidate of the Catholic League as successor to the last Valois. On that basis they had acknowledged him as King Charles X of France, one of two Bourbon kings that were never kings, the other being the sad young Louis XVII who died in his cell in 1795.

6

FRANCE:
THE ANCIEN RÉGIME 1589-1789

'When Henry IV died France wept, when Louis XIII died they laughed,
when Louis XIV died they got drunk.' Mackinnon
'Apres nous le delugé.' Attributed to Madame de Pompadour or Louis XIV
'The Oedipus complex could scarcely be more dangerous than when its
effects are to distort the functioning of an absolute monarch.'
Philippe Erlanger, *Louis XIV*

Thus some six hundred years after it first settled in the north of Auvergne
the Bourbon family had clawed its way up to the throne of France. Centuries
of picking the right side in wars, managing ever larger estates and making
profitable marriages had helped the family's relentless climb up the social
ladder. Then had come the big breakthrough, the royal marriage to the son
of Louis IX. After that it had still taken another two hundred years for the
other branches of Capet and Valois to breed themselves into extinction. Even
the main branch of the Bourbons had died out sixty years too soon when
Charles Duc of Bourbon was shot on the battlements of Rome and with his
wife Suzanne left no living children. In the end it was the lesser branch of the
Vendôme Bourbons who had won through to the ultimate prize.

In their first two hundred years as a royal dynasty the Bourbons in France had
only five kings, thus managing an extraordinary average reign of forty years each.
They also within that period acquired two more thrones: Spain and Naples, so
that between the three branches of the family they controlled a huge portion of the
world's wealth and straddled five continents. Whilst towards the end of the period
they seemed suicidally incompetent they had many achievements to their credit.

HENRI IV

'He will have all the inheritance' Nostradamus of Henri IV
'Je veux que le dimanche chaque paysan ait sa poule au pot...' Henri IV
'He was a warrior but not a warmonger.' Shennan, *The Bourbons*

The religious wars had lasted more than thirty years and had cost France
around 800,000 lives, nine towns – which had been destroyed – and huge debt.

By 1589 Henri had won a significant number of battles against the Catholic League but had by no means defeated it. It still had substantial reserves of manpower, was still backed by Philip II of Spain and still at this point had its alternative king, the feeble Cardinal Bourbon or 'Charles X'. On his side Henri had an experienced army with effective cavalry and artillery, he had support from Queen Elizabeth of England and at times from the Protestant Germans of the Palatinate. Given that the two sides were relatively well-balanced and separated by a deep religious divide that had been accentuated by half a century of gratuitous violence it appeared that the Civil War could go on for a long time, resulting in further bloodshed and the possible permanent splintering of France. It was soon obvious that Henri could never capture or hold the big Catholic cities like Paris or Rouen, because although he was strong in cavalry such a task needed huge numbers for street fighting. The one hopeful sign was that some of the less fanatical Catholic supporters began to drift over to what was now the official royal side. For example, another Bourbon, also called Henri, his cousin the Duc de Montpensier brought Normandy into Henri's fold.

As we have already seen from Henri's childhood and early career he was like his father who had died when he was seven – hyperactive, ambitious, brave in battle and a serial adulterer – but perhaps unlike him he was highly intelligent and could see the bigger picture. These last two characteristics he may perhaps have inherited from his mother and grandmother, who were highly educated for their day, conscientious and in the mother's case adhered to a strict Calvinist code of ethics. At the same time he had grown up in the Bearnais countryside with an earthy appreciation of human psychology so that in an age of fanatics and sticklers for detail he had a commonsensical capacity to see both sides in any argument and was perhaps uniquely placed to be the potential unifier of a divided nation. He was to show remarkable lack of arrogance in his approach to the truculent *parlements* – 'Yield up to my entreaties what you would not give up by threats, for you will have none from me... you will be doing it not just for me but for the sake of peace.'

In his childhood he had been shuttled between his two parents, one moment a Calvinist, the next a Catholic and this was to be repeated in his adult life. The trauma of the Massacre of St Bartholomew happening so soon after his first wedding and followed by a long period of intimidation and house arrest left its mark. Being forced, albeit briefly, to live with a wife whose fidelity was no stronger than his own must have increased his cynicism about marriage. His early military career had been equally frustrating, yet once he emerged from the shadow of Admiral Coligny and his own uncle Condé he soon learned rapidly how to be an effective field commander, particularly of cavalry. In turn his closest associate the confirmed Protestant Maximilien Baron de Rosny, later Duc de Sully (1560-1641), was not only an able comrade in arms right from the first escape in 1576 but in due course became a brilliant organiser of artillery, builder of forts and finance minister.

Once declared King of France Henri enjoyed his status as Most Christian King and the full ritual associated with the French crown, including his newly acquired duty to cure people of scrofula, yet he was extremely careless with his own apparel – short, hook-nosed, notorious for a neglect of personal hygiene, passionate about oysters, gardens and hunting, a keen tennis player, a touchy-feely man so short-sighted that he had to wear glasses, constantly suffering from toothache, and regularly troubled by infections related to his venereal exploits. Nor according to Dumas did he ever quite lose his Bearnais accent.

In his first two years as king Henri won two important battles against the Catholic League, which was now led by the surviving Guise brother the Duc de Mayenne. The first was at Arques near Dieppe, the second at Ivry west of Paris. Thereafter by a mixture of force, bribery and compromise he won over most of his aristocratic opponents, both amongst the die-hard Catholic and extreme Calvinist factions. The ultimate compromises were his own dramatic reconversion to Catholicism in 1593 to appease the Catholic majority, particularly in Paris (though he probably never actually said 'Paris is worth a Mass') and to offset this the Edict of Nantes five years later which guaranteed freedom of worship for the Huguenots, who by this time amounted to around a million people, roughly 5 per cent of the French population. These acts of conciliation would never satisfy the extreme Catholics who kept up their treasonable liaison with Philip of Spain nor the extreme Huguenots who were bitter about Henri's religious relapse. Thus though the majority of the population settled down to enjoy a peace that had been absent for over forty years, there were still groups of aristocrats who persisted in plotting Henri's downfall and over the two decades there were at least twenty serious attempts to assassinate him. Nevertheless by 1594 he had been properly crowned at Chartres and had taken possession of Paris where he was to be based for the rest of his reign. Paris, according to a contemporary tract, had become 'a dark cavern of wild beasts, a refuge for robbers, murderers and assassins' so it too needed normality.

The most serious threat to the stability of the new régime remained Philip II of Spain who wanted to wipe out all traces of heresy from France and had numerous covert sympathisers amongst the French aristocracy as well as groups like the Jesuits who were committed to eliminating Protestantism. They were eventually expelled from France in 1594 for their complicity in murder plots against the king. This threat was all the more dangerous because the two halves of Philip's kingdom, Spain and the Spanish Netherlands, almost encircled the French, particularly if we add in the Burgundian lands still held by his Habsburg cousin, the emperor. In a desultory war against Spain Henri lost a number of towns north of the Somme but eventually regained most of them after the Treaty of Vervins in 1598. In the peace that followed Sully helped him create a fortified frontier to deter further Spanish encroachments. Sully also built up stocks of weapons and ammunition with depots to store them, roads to reach them and reserves of money locked up in the Bastille so that Henri wouldn't again be caught halfway through a campaign without the cash to pay his troops. He even created a new naval port in the south at Toulon with a new fleet of galleys. Thus between them they consolidated France as a defensible entity at the same time as the internal divisions caused by years of sectarian violence and civil war were gradually healed. Yet it was 1609 before Henri felt confident enough to integrate his own personal fiefdom of Béarn into his kingdom.

By the time of Henri's accession France had been economically on its knees with trade and agriculture disrupted by war, overuse of the soil to maintain a population that had grown too fast and since around 1550 there had been the beginnings of a miniature ice-age which resulted in a succession of poor harvests. In the 1590s there was the first of a series of peasant rebellions known as the *Croquants* brought on by food shortages. Henri had since his Navarre days earned a perhaps undeserved reputation for caring about peasant welfare – his famous chicken in the pot every weekend dictum – but he certainly understood that France depended on sound agriculture. In addition he and Sully encouraged a number of specific added-value industries such as silk, paper, fine glass and tapestry manufacture, encouraged road-building and new canals to improve water transport. This, plus the employment created in the armaments industry, undoubtedly contributed to enhancing the prosperity of France, even if extreme wealth was concentrated in a very small minority. He used his own wealth to make a major impact on the built environment with his famous construction of the Pont Neuf in Paris, the Louvre embankment and palace extensions, the new buildings at Fontainebleau, St Germain and the Hôpital St Louis.

In addition Henri was conscious of the long term potential of colonies and from 1594 onwards worked at the New France concept. He appointed Pierre du Gua as Lieutenant General of Acadie which led to the foundation of Annapolis in 1605 and of Québec in 1608. It was on the basis of these varied achievements that he began to encourage his propagandists to present him to the world as the 'Gallic Hercules'.

As a man not constricted by slavish obedience to any church Henri was more effective than many good Catholic kings in reforming the French Catholic Church. He appointed many more middle-class bishops, a policy which reduced corruption, he encouraged good preachers, patronised some of the newer, more pro-active monastic orders and even allowed the Jesuits back in 1603.

Latterly the one great problem left for Henri was that now in his mid-forties he still had no legitimate heir, so in 1599 his childless marriage with Marguerite de Valois was at last annulled after years of mutual infidelity and plentiful proof of his own fertility. At this point he was still in love with his long-term chief mistress, Gabrielle d'Estrées, Duchess of Beaufort, and to the concern of many of his advisers intended to marry her and legitimise their children as his heirs. From the political point of view it was almost certainly a blessing that she died of an aborted pregnancy just at the critical moment, so Henri in 1600 made a more politically sensible match with Marie de Medici, a Tuscan princess with a good dowry who a year later bore him the future Louis XIII. He had meanwhile consoled himself with a succession of new mistresses including Henrietta de Balzac, Marquise de Verneuil who was later involved in one of the many plots against the king, this time to install one of her sons by him as the next king. Meanwhile César Bourbon (1594-1665), Gabrielle's eldest son by the king became the new Duc de Vendôme, ancestor of the great general in the Spanish wars (see p.78).

Ironically it was Henri's insatiable lust after younger women that led to his final political escapade in 1609. He had been pursuing the fifteen-year-old Charlotte de Montmorency for two years and had her married off to his supposedly pliable nephew Henri II Prince of Condé who was expected to act the cuckold. But Condé refused to cooperate and eloped with the lovely Charlotte to Brussels where he received political asylum and sent defiant messages back to the king. As a Catholic, Condé was anyway a key political opponent of Henri's régime. Henri reacted as if Charlotte was Helen of Troy and planned a ridiculous invasion of Flanders backed up by a simultaneous attack on northern Italy. Just three days before he was due to leave Paris to lead the army in the north he was stabbed to death by a Catholic fanatic, François Ravaillac. He was fifty-seven, more than forty years older than the girl who had led to his besotted lack of judgement. He died just before the completion of his new townhouse in his magnificent new Place Des Vosges.

There were numerous conspiracy theories that associated Ravaillac with the Jesuits, with other European leaders or senior members of the French court or even with one of his disgruntled mistresses, but nothing was ever proved and Ravaillac may simply have been a lone fanatic as it appeared on the surface. For all his faults Henri Le Vert Galant left France a very much stronger and more prosperous country than he found it. He also left eleven acknowledged children, three by his wife, three by Gabrielle, two by Henriette, one by Jacqueline and two by Charlotte des Essarts.

The other senior surviving Bourbons of Henri's generation had varying fortunes. Condé's brother Charles Count of Soissons who fought for Henri IV in his campaigns from Coutras in 1587 to Savoy in 1600 was disappointed not to be allowed to marry the king's sister and soon afterwards was involved in a Spanish plot against Henri where Bourbon of Montpensier also played a part and was thrown into the Bastille. Soissons was also annoyed not to be included in the regency after Henri's death. He was made governor of Normandy instead and died two years later in Brandy en Brie. Overall therefore Henri had profited from the help of his relations, particularly the two Condés in the early days but after his death it was to be some of his spare children who were the greatest nuisance to the continuance of the dynasty.

LOUIS XIII, LE JUSTE

'He (Louis) is God.' *La Grande Demoiselle*
'I am dull and dispirited. Come let us be bored together.' Louis XIII
as recorded by Alexandre Dumas in *The Three Musketeers*
'Je voudrai bien voir la grimace qu'il fait a cette heur sur l'échafaud.'
Louis XIII on Monsieur le Grand
'... a reign destined to be a largely painful and joyless odyssey.'
Shennan, *The Bourbons*

Louis was only eight when he became the second Bourbon king of France
(*b.* 1601, *r.* 1610-43) also King Louis II of Navarre and even had he been older
his father, Henri IV, was a hard act to follow. Unlike him he was born a Catholic,
had an Italian Catholic mother and at an early age dedicated his life to the
Virgin Mary. Genetically he was half-French, quarter-Italian from his Medici
grandfather and quarter-Austrian from his Habsburg grandmother. Yet for all
that it was his father who had been present at his birth at Fontainebleau and
was much the more attentive and affectionate of his two parents, Henri perhaps
with the pride of an old man in his first healthy legitimate son and Marie perhaps
put off by her husband flaunting his mistresses in front of her, even after she
had given him what he most wanted from her. For some reason, she seems to
have preferred Louis's younger brother Gaston. According to some accounts
she never kissed Louis and he was always jealous of Gaston (1608-60) who in
his turn was to spend most of his life trying to destabilise Louis's government.
During his childhood Louis was forced by his father to accept equal status as
a child with his bastard siblings, was regularly whipped and often neglected.
As he grew up it suited the Medici favourites to try to spoil him and introduce
adult pleasures in the hope that he would lose interest in political affairs.

His mother Marie de Medici acted as regent for the first seven years of his
reign with the help of her Italian favourites, the Concini. In 1614 she arranged
his marriage to the Spanish princess Anne of Austria (1601-66) so that he was
even more aligned to the Catholic cause. Under pressure to make this political
match he had to reject his own choice of Louise de La Fayette. Despite their
religious affinity Louis's relationship with his wife was plagued by inhibitions
perhaps created by his father's flaunting of his sexual prowess and the couple
produced no living children during the first twenty-three years of their marriage.
It is suggested that Louis was humiliated when virtually forced into a public
consummation of their marriage when he was only fourteen, that he then refused
to touch her for five years until urged to do so by his stalwart falconer Charles
d'Albret, and thereafter his wife had four still-born babies in 1619, 1622, 1626
and 1631. He was probably bisexual or fundamentally homosexual, but there is
no proof of any form of extra-marital affairs. Rather he seems to have been prone
to platonic crushes on members of both sexes during which he was emotionally

dependent on and submissive to him or her but restrained himself on religious grounds, or other inhibitions, from any form of consummation. It is also believed that he suffered from a form of tuberculosis or what is now called Crohns Disease, an often debilitating condition causing intestinal problems which would be exacerbated by the then current medical fashion of blood-letting and by his alleged klismaphilia – in one year he had 215 enemas – nor helped by the latest imported luxury, chocolate. He escaped from his neuroses by campaigning with the army or hunting and when neither was available he busied himself in obscure hobbies like jam-making or trellis-making, he loved putting on fancy dress and little dancing displays, but found relationships difficult with his own class and was so aloof that he failed to make himself popular with them though he found it easier to mingle with ordinary people in the streets or countryside.

To emphasise the original purely political nature of his marriage his sister had on the same day been married to Philip (later IV) of Spain and the two young brides had been ceremonially swapped on the Isle of Pheasants on the River Bidassoa. Subsequently the wretched young queen was ignored by her mother-in-law as well as by her husband despite trying hard to learn French and French habits. Even when Anne did at last become pregnant she fell down stairs and suffered a miscarriage which her husband pompously blamed on her frivolity.

In 1617 when Louis was sixteen his friends Charles d'Albret, the falconer, now Duc de Luynes, Henri Prince of Condé (1588-1646) who had resented his exclusion from the regency and his bastard half-brother César Duke of Vendôme helped him organise the palace coup that freed him from the control of his mother Marie de Medici. His teenage rebellion coincided with the huge unpopularity of his mother's favourites Concina Concini and his wife Leonora the first of whom he arranged to have murdered on the steps of the Louvre and the second executed on charges of witchcraft. Meanwhile there was a new man rising in his councils, Armand Jean Duplessis (1585-1642), bishop of Luçon and later Cardinal Richelieu, who had become his mother's adviser and part of the regency team in 1614. He was out of favour till 1622 when he was made a cardinal and two years later the king's chief minister, no longer attached to the king's now exiled mother. She had managed to escape and staged an attempted counter-coup with the king's brother Gaston and his two half-brothers César and Alexandre, but Louis defeated their troops in a skirmish, Gaston escaped and Louis treated the culprits quite leniently.

Meanwhile Louis had developed a fixed idea about the state and would tolerate defiance neither from his relations, his grandees or separatist groups like the Huguenots who had been allowed to keep their 150 forts and whom he regarded as a potential fifth column inside the frontiers of France. He and Luynes first mounted an attack on his own Huguenot enclave of Béarn, which provoked a Huguenot backlash throughout the Midi that damaged the credibility of the new régime. Yet in the end Louis did wear down the Huguenots until he finally captured their last remaining fortress, La Rochelle in 1628.

From 1624 onwards Richelieu's was the dominant personality in the reign and it was Richelieu the 'scarlet courtier' who helped Louis to build up the Bourbon monarchy and the French nation to make it the dominant superpower of seventeenth-century Europe. By eroding the privileges of the aristocracy they strengthened the power of the Crown so that it could shortly be genuinely described as an absolute monarchy. By attacking the independence which the Huguenots had enjoyed under Henri IV they consolidated the French state so that there was no longer a state-within-a-state.

Next it was a question of dealing with potential threats from outside. Even before Richelieu's promotion Louis had already in 1624 shown that he intended to tackle the problem of encirclement by the Spanish and Austrian Habsburgs. In 1629-30 he twice crossed the Alps into Italy with his army to try to cut the supply route by which the Spaniards reinforced their army in the Netherlands. By ignoring religious affiliations to back the German Protestants against the catholic Holy Roman emperors during the Thirty Years War he and Richelieu outsmarted the Habsburgs. By creating a new Atlantic naval base at Le Havre and building an ocean-going fleet Richelieu put France in a much more favourable position as an imperial power. By subsidising the Swedish Army of Gustavus Adolphus he radically changed the balance in the Thirty Years War.

Above all Louis and Richelieu consolidated the physical structure of the kingdom by annexing a number of peripheral areas whose sovereignty had previously been in doubt: Navarre itself, northern Catalonia, Perpignan, Roussillon, Savoy, and part of Hainaut. In 1633 they invaded Lorraine, two years later declared war against Spain and three after that against Austria.

Louis himself though prone to bouts of lethargy, indecision and depression, all of which can be blamed on his medical condition or his stressful childhood, nevertheless took a great interest in military matters and according to Dumas was 'one of the best hands with a rapier in his own kingdom.' He was closely involved with the siege of La Rochelle and the Alpine passage to Susa at the very time when the fictional d'Artagnan joined the king's musketeers. Louis took part in the invasion of Lorraine in 1635, the siege of Artois in 1639 and of Roussillon in 1642. He was the last Bourbon king to lead his own troops in battle. In Wedgewood's words he 'had grown from an oppressed neurotic adolescent ready to fall under the control of the first affectionate and flattering friend into a secretive, moody, intelligent, critical young man with an acute judgement and a will of his own.' His favourite occupation, like so many monarchs of this era, was hunting and it was he who first fell in love with Versailles as an out-of-town base where he built the original relatively small hunting lodge later hugely expanded by his son. He showed remarkable will-power in fighting off the effects of his illness, riding with his men for seventeen hours without rest, marching twenty miles a day, standing to spread his curing hands on the heads of over a thousand subjects in a single session. This in particular appealed to his view of his kingship as a supernatural duty in which his exercise of power must also entail personal suffering.

He recognised in Richelieu a talent doubtless motivated by personal ambition but nevertheless dedicated to the promotion of France and the Bourbon monarchy. So sensibly he let Richelieu get on with it, but just occasionally played hard to get to make Richelieu realise that his power depended on the king.

It was very much Richelieu rather than Louis who first thought of supporting the Protestant side in the Thirty Years War as a means of reducing the threat of Habsburg encirclement – the Habsburgs at this time between their two capitals in Vienna and Madrid held Spain, the Flanders and much of the Rhineland so the threat was genuine. Louis being an ardent Catholic and married to a Habsburg had rejected the first cry for help from Frederick of Bohemia. It was perhaps Richelieu rather than Louis who pushed the idea of an alliance with protestant Great Britain when the king's sister Henrietta Maria was sent across to be the queen of Charles I, so that the next generation of Stuart kings were half-Bourbon, prone to be Catholic and prone to favour France. It was the autocratic ideas of this Bourbon Queen of Britain which through her influence over her husband played a not inconsiderable part in causing the English Civil War. Ironically it was Louis's wife Anne who caused scandal by her flirtation with the British envoy the Duke of Buckingham, who had been the bisexual favourite of James VI and I, the first Stuart king of England – having already been king of Scotland since 1666.

It was not until 1635 that Richelieu persuaded Louis to enter the war. It initially went badly for France with a defeat at Corbie in Picardy and the imperial armies threatened Paris itself. It was only by an intensive programme of administrative reform that replaced amateur aristocrats with professionals and massively increased tax revenue to support a much expanded standing army that France moved into the ascendant, in the process becoming a much more efficient totalitarian state.

The dominance of Richelieu obviously created tensions amongst those envious of his power, and it was easy to find popular dissatisfaction for taxes bore heavily on the middle and lower classes as the war effort damaged the economy. These rebellions regularly included the king's trouble-making brother Gaston who was also his heir until the birth of the future Louis XIV in 1638. Despite marrying the heiress of the Montpensier Bourbons and being given the dukedom of Orléans Gaston was never happy. In 1626 he joined the Chalais conspiracy along with the king's mother, his wife, his two bastard half-brothers César and Alexandre and his cousin Condé with the aim of removing Richelieu and probably Louis as well. If it had succeeded Gaston would have become king, eliminated Louis and married Queen Anne. It failed and both César and Alexandre were put in prison where Alexandre died. Gaston escaped again and Condé became a reformed character, was given a series of high profile governorships and his sons were to play a major part in the victories over the Habsburgs at the end of Louis's reign.

The next crisis came in 1630, the so-called Day of Dupes. The king's mother and brother Gaston were involved in yet another conspiracy to get rid of Richelieu. Louis wavered but ultimately swung to support Richelieu, so Gaston fled to

Lorraine and their mother to permanent exile in Brussels. However, Gaston never gave up for he tried invading France in 1632, and then, both in 1635 and 1642, he was involved in other failed plots to overthrow the Richelieu régime.

Another inveterate Bourbon plotter associated with this group was the king's cousin Louis de Bourbon (1604-41) Comte de Soissons who planned to murder Richelieu in 1631 and had also joined the Chalais conspiracy of 1626. Ultimately he went over to the Habsburg side and was killed in the moment of victory fighting with a Spanish army near Sedan. Also in that plot was the king's half-brother César de Bourbon, Henry IV's son by his mistress Gabrielle, who had been given the family dukedom of Vendôme. He was imprisoned for conspiracy 1626-30, exiled, but eventually reconciled with the king and supported Anne of Austria after his death. Overall it appears that Louis throughout his reign was most worried about the loyalty of his closest relations: his wife Anne who was suspected of wishing to replace him as her husband with his brother Gaston, Gaston himself and until 1626 Henri Prince of Condé.

With the Duc de Luynes out of the picture it is suggested that Richelieu procured a new male favourite for the king, Henri d'Effiat later Comte de Cinq Mars. The extent of the friendship is hard to judge and on the count's side it turned out to be a false one for like Gaston and others he joined in one of the many plots. There was an atmosphere of upper-class rebellion against the new professional breed of government officials. The radical Jesuit philosopher René Descartes (1596-1650) had finally left Paris for Holland in 1628 but many free-thinkers remained, as did the group of *Libertins* which included the squashbuckling Cyrano de Bergerac (1619-55). Even Richelieu's favourite playwright Corneille offended by his ultra successful *Le Cid* in 1636.

There was also mention of at least two potential mistresses of the king's, Louise de La Fayette who later retired to a nunnery and Madame d'Hautefort, but the nature of these relationships was peculiar in that they played the role of confidante and dominatrix without apparently any overt sexual contact. Yet it seems according to gossip to have been an accident of fate when in December 1637 Louis who was on his way from Versailles to stay with the now rehabilitated Condés at St Maur was caught in Paris by a storm and persuaded against his will, for there was no other suitable accommodation, to spend the night with his wife at the Louvre, the first time he had done so for several years. Since the idea of such a rapprochement seemed at the time abhorrent, there may have been some possible behind-the-scenes plotting by the queen and the king's guard commander Guitaut to lure Louis into her bed after such a long gap. Whatever the circumstances this famous one-night stand resulted nine months later in the unexpected birth of the future Louis XIV immediately called *Dieudonné*, because of such a long wait. The palace dolphins spouted wine and there was a huge firework display to greet the news. The birth not only preserved the dynasty from some kind of succession crisis but provided Anne of Austria with a potential political career should her husband, as expected, die relatively young.

Meanwhile Richelieu and Louis XIII continued with the support of the colonies of New France and the more lucrative plantations in the West Indies. Guadeloupe was conquered in 1635. The Princess of Condé (1594-1650) endowed a Jesuit mission to the Petun Indians of Ontario at Port Royal, Acadia.

In his final years Richelieu picked out a young Bourbon aged only twenty-two as new commander in chief of a revitalised, highly disciplined new French army. This was Louis de Bourbon, (1621-86) Duc d'Enghien eldest son and heir of Henri the Prince of Condé and of the famous Charlotte who had been so arduously pursued by Henri IV but were now settled in Chantilly. The price d'Enghien had to pay for his sudden promotion was marriage to Richelieu's niece, Claire Clemence de Maille at a time when he was in love with Marthe de Vigean and besides regarded Richelieu's family as socially inferior. Claire was to bear him four children and be an aggressively supportive wife despite appalling treatment from her reluctant husband, particularly after his victories started going to his head. On grounds of alleged adultery he later had her locked up in Châteauroux.

In 1642 there had been one final anti-Richelieu plot involving Queen Anne and the king's current favourite, the dashing Cinq Mars, who was promptly executed. As the terminally ill Richelieu lay on his death bed Louis XIII personally spooned egg yolk into his mouth to try to keep him alive a little longer, having once more backed the old cardinal against young pretenders like the treacherous Cinq Mars. Louis himself was far from well and after Richelieu's death in December 1642 he was himself confined to bed in the early spring as Enghien began his new offensive on the Flemish border. Yet the strategy was unaltered for Richelieu had primed his successor Cardinal Mazarin. It was a question of '*Le Cardinal est mort, Vive le Cardinal*'.

Louis XIII whose body had wasted away almost to a skeleton told his elderly cousin Condé that he had had a dream that Condé's son Enghien would win a great victory. The king died at last on 15 May 1643 aged forty-two, and leaving a son of four to take over. Three days later, Enghien who had just heard the news from Paris formed up his army of 22,000 men against a larger Spanish force outside the frontier fortress of Rocroy. The next day he achieved a remarkable victory which Wedgewood describes as 'the gravestone of Spanish greatness'. It was certainly the climactic triumph for the dead cardinal and at least in terms of dynastic power politics it justified the faith that Louis XIII had placed in him. It was largely because of this effort and Enghien's military skill that France five years later in 1648 was to do so well out of the Treaty of Westphalia that ended the Thirty Years War and subsequent treaties, which made France and the Bourbons much less vulnerable to Habsburg encirclement. It was to the credit of Louis XIII that he recognised the abilities of Mazarin, the humbly born Italian Jesuit who was to make sure that the period of royal minority that followed his death saw no weakening of policy.

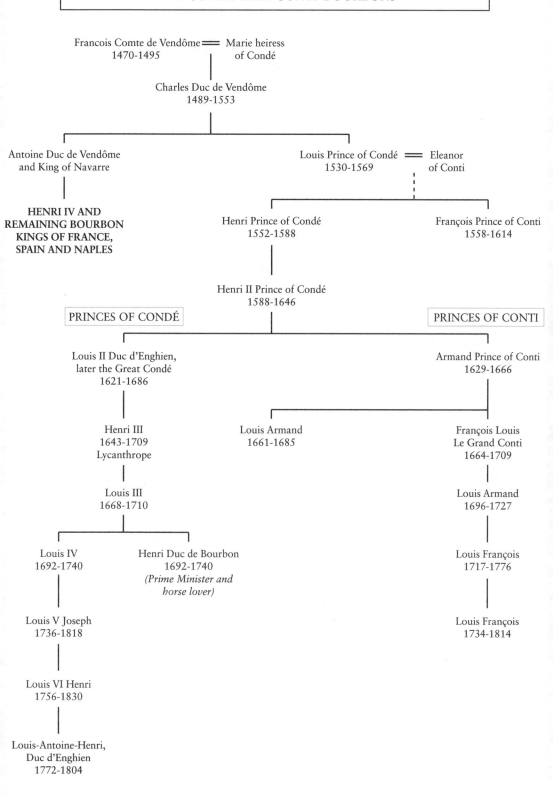

THE CONDÉ AND CONTI BOURBONS

Francois Comte de Vendôme === Marie heiress
1470-1495 of Condé

Charles Duc de Vendôme
1489-1553

Antoine Duc de Vendôme
and King of Navarre

**HENRI IV AND
REMAINING BOURBON
KINGS OF FRANCE,
SPAIN AND NAPLES**

Louis Prince of Condé === Eleanor
1530-1569 of Conti

Henri Prince of Condé
1552-1588

François Prince of Conti
1558-1614

Henri II Prince of Condé
1588-1646

PRINCES OF CONDÉ

PRINCES OF CONTI

Louis II Duc d'Enghien,
later the Great Condé
1621-1686

Armand Prince of Conti
1629-1666

Henri III
1643-1709
Lycanthrope

Louis Armand
1661-1685

François Louis
Le Grand Conti
1664-1709

Louis III
1668-1710

Louis Armand
1696-1727

Louis IV
1692-1740

Henri Duc de Bourbon
1692-1740
*(Prime Minister and
horse lover)*

Louis François
1717-1776

Louis V Joseph
1736-1818

Louis François
1734-1814

Louis VI Henri
1756-1830

Louis-Antoine-Henri,
Duc d'Enghien
1772-1804

LOUIS XIV

'Henceforth you must have courtiers who know how to amuse you
– madmen who will get themselves killed to carry out what you call your
great works.' D'Artagnan to Louis XIV in *The Man in the Iron Mask*,
Alexandre Dumas
'No longer satisfied with mere success, but must also enjoy it exclusively'
Mitford, *Louis XIV and Versailles*
'After mass the king felt ready for sin' Philippe Erlanger, *Louis XIV*

Louis XIII had been forty-two when he died and his heir Louis was only four, so France was set again for an awkward period of regency with once again a queen dowager in charge who was not a Frenchwoman. Whereas Marie de Medici had been an Italian, Anne of Austria was a Spanish Habsburg. There was, however, one key element of continuity for Cardinal Mazarin had stepped into the shoes of Richelieu and was well-entrenched with Anne, allegedly her lover, perhaps even her new husband, but the probability is that she just used her flirtatious wiles and both of them had far too much to lose by such a risky liaison, whether sanctioned by the Church or not.

Louis XIV was born in St Germain en Laye in 1638, the first healthy child of a marriage that had already lasted twenty-three years – there had been four stillborn babies – and even then his birth was attributed to the fact that Louis had been forced by a storm to spend a night with his wife. The more charitable said he was a gift of God so he was nicknamed *Dieudonné*. Subsequently this man who was directly responsible for five wars, three of them extremely bloody, was to reign for a total of seventy-two years, longer than any other European monarch and to acquire new names such as Le Roi Soleil, Le Grand Monarque and Louis Le Grand.

Genetically it has been calculated that Louis was 25 per cent French, 25 per cent German 20 per cent Spanish, 12 per cent Italian with the remainder split fairly evenly between Portuguese and Slavic with perhaps also a tiny proportion of Moorish and Jewish genes from his ancestors in Aragon. He had Habsburg genes on both sides, but his most important ancestor in image terms was the saintly Louis IX. He had one brother Philippe Duc d'Orléans (1640-1701) the bisexual rake driven to libertinism by enforced unemployment for most of his life and through his marriages to Henrietta Stuart (1644-70) of Great Britain and Elizabeth-Charlotte of Bavaria (1652-1722) reputed to be the ancestor of almost every surviving royal family in Europe.

Anne of Austria had already before her husband's death been involved in several plots against Richelieu, often aided by the arch intriguer Madame de Chevreuse and motivated also by Richelieu's war against her native country of Spain. Hardened by years of neglect she now seized her moment for power. She escaped from the Louvre to the Palais Royal with her two sons and with

Mazarin's help overturned the section of Louis's will which said she would only play a junior part in the regency team. Cardinal Mazarin (1602-61), originally Giulio Mazarini, a Jesuit from the Abruzzi, who had never taken the full priestly vows, had been groomed as his successor by Richelieu and had a relationship with the dowager queen so close that it has sometimes been suggested that they had secretly married, but this is unlikely. Certainly they were able between them to dominate France for the next eighteen years.

Meanwhile the period of regency saw further major victories by the French under Louis's cousin the Duc d'Enghien who was now in his mid-twenties and had fulfilled the early promise shown at Rocroy. Together with Turenne he achieved a bloody and devastating defeat of the Austrians at Nordlingen in 1645, but was himself wounded and had to return to France to recover. When he came back to Flanders he had to accept demotion to serve as second in command to the king's uncle, Gaston of Orléans, but when Gaston was out of the way had further success with the siege and capture of Dunkirk in 1646. This resulted in Spain making peace and was the beginning of the end of the Thirty Years War. At about the same time d'Enghien's father died and he succeeded to his title as Prince of Condé, but his reputation was now so high that Mazarin felt threatened and arranged for his appointment to a potentially disastrous campaign round Barcelona where even Condé proved a failure, just what Mazarin wanted. Condé, however, wriggled out of the Spanish campaign before his reputation was irreversibly tarnished and forced Mazarin to give him back the command in Flanders. There in Artois at Lens in 1648 he won another stunning victory against the Austrians which effectively brought an end at last to the Thirty Years War, with France in a dominant position to negotiate its new frontier along the Rhine.

It was at this point that Mazarin was so supremely confident that he thought it the right moment to press the Paris *parlement* to register a new value-added tax to be imposed on all goods brought into the city. The *parlement* rejected the new tax at the same time launching an attack on the increase in tax farming and the spread of the hated intendants. Anne of Austria with her autocratic Spanish background thought the measure should be put through by force, using the now ten-year-old King Louis to make the announcement. It did not work and the *parlement* instead threatened to turn itself into a proper legislative assembly, more like the British model. It was a confrontation that bore some resemblance to what had happened in London a few years earlier and was potentially as dangerous for the monarchy. When the news arrived of Condé's victory at Lens Mazarin seized the moment to send the troops in to arrest the leaders of the rebellion. This simply made matters worse and spread the appeal of the rebellion to the general populace.

Thus developed the first period of attempted revolution known as the Fronde, so called because the catapult or fronde symbolised the amateurish status of the rebels who now erected barricades in the streets of Paris. Years of poor harvests and heavy taxation for the war effort had come to a head as Mazarin tried to extend taxation to the nobles and high clergymen who were in the *parlement* and to the trading classes beneath them. He felt so confident after Condé's victories in 1648 that he decided to arrest the recalcitrants and the Parisian mob took to the streets in protest.

Soon afterwards Louis de Bourbon d'Enghien, now aged thirty and since his father's death known as the Grand Condé and France's most successful general, returned to Paris from the front to find the beginnings of a civil war. He was so pleased with his victories that he wanted also to be appointed chief of the fleet as well as the army and to add the Franche Comté to his already huge estates in Berry, Lorraine and Burgundy, but for the time being used his reputation to broker a truce between the two sides. He soon lost patience with the unruly mobs and sided with Mazarin to suppress them. Queen Anne fled with her children as the rebels erected 1,200 barricades and attacked the Palais Royal. Though it had started as an aristocratic rebellion against Mazarin's dictatorship it soon attracted support from other dissatisfied groups, just as later happened in 1789. It also had affinities with the similar upsurge of feelings in England and Scotland which climaxed in the execution of Charles I early in 1649. Condé used his army to suppress the rebels and starved them into submission. Houses were burned, many were stripped of their clothes and left to die of hypothermia. Yet the *parlement* was also raising an army and its command was given to Condé's brother Armand de Bourbon (1629-66) the diminunitive and unstable Prince of Conti. Condé scored a victory against the rebels at Charenton, killing two thousand of them.

The monarchy at this point depended very much on Condé and he knew it. Even his fellow general Turenne had changed sides to help the Fronde, though, soon afterwards Mazarin bribed him to change back again. There was a sense that Condé's habitual arrogance and apparent love of danger, the grudge he had against Mazarin for sending him to Catalonia plus his lingering resentment at his forced marriage to the niece of Richelieu seven years earlier seem to have been enough to turn him against Anne of Austria and Mazarin a year after the brutal siege of Paris. He was at one point reputed to have boxed Mazarin's ears. He had a feeling for his fellow aristocrats who were being squeezed into submission by the relentless centralisation policy pursued by Mazarin. Thus he became potentially the military leader of the second Fronde uprising. He was backed by several other members of the Bourbon family, his brother Prince of Conti, Gaston of Orléans, François Duc de Vendôme, son of the inveterate conspirator César, and Gaston's formidable daughter Anne Marie Louise (1627-93) the Duchesse de Montpensier, known as the virgin warrior or *Grande Mademoiselle* who at the age of twenty-three seized Orléans. There was also Condé's able sister the Duchess of Longueville and his wife the indomitable Claire.

At this juncture in 1650 Condé and Conti were both arrested as traitors on the Queen's orders and not even released when Condé's neglected but feisty wife Claire raised an army to rescue him, backed by Condé's rival Turenne with Spanish troops. In the dungeons of Vincennes his brother Armand of Conti who had been an early patron and friend of Molière who is said to have used him as a model for his *Don Juan* had something like a nervous breakdown and besides nursed an incestuous passion for his sister Longueville, buying all kinds of potions from the alchemists in hope of wooing her. François de Bourbon, Duke of Vendôme, managed to escape and died later defending Candia in Crete against the Turks.

When Condé was at last released from his cell in Le Havre he met with less than his usual military success for he had to fight the royal army at Faubourg St Antoine on the outskirts of Paris and by this time Turenne had changed sides back to the crown. Condé was nearly beaten at Faubourg St Antoine but could have taken the city, yet held back because neither he nor Gaston of Orléans really wanted to become involved in the daily grind of politics. Condé himself just enjoyed the adrenalin-rush of professional soldiering. In the aftermath he was saved when the virago Duchesse de Montpensier organised the guns of the Bastille to fire on his opponents, apparently firing some of the cannons herself. Condé escaped to Spain where he became a general again with considerable success against his own country, mirroring the career of that other great Bourbon general, Duke Charles III who had also gone over to the Habsburgs. He was, however, defeated by Turenne at the Battle of the Dunes in 1658, the battle which effectively ended the Fronde.

It was only when peace was made with Spain and Louis XIV married a Spanish princess in 1659 that Condé was at last pardoned and allowed to return home. He then had another fifteen years as a successful French general for Louis XIV, an intuitively brilliant field commander completely oblivious to his own safety. At his home in Chantilly he became a major patron of artists and writers such as Molière and in 1668 was very close to being crowned king of Poland, but for the international prejudice against the Bourbons having another throne. Plagued in his later years by gout he died at the age of sixty-five. His brilliant but somewhat unstable brother Armand was also rehabilitated as a general and commanded the French Army in Italy till defeated at Alexandria in 1657.

Louis XIV meanwhile had had a somewhat perfunctory education, learning some Italian and Spanish, riding and arms drill and how to be a good Catholic but missing out on some of the academic basics, according to some because Mazarin wanted to keep him ignorant. It was also reported by his valet La Porte that at the age of fourteen he was sodomised by Mazarin's nephew Paul Mancini who was soon afterwards killed at the front. If not by this, Louis was certainly traumatised by his experiences during the Fronde and by the disloyalty of his own relations. He thus grew up reserved, secretive and self-controlled, soon acquiring the ability to dominate those around him through the power of his personality.

Louis made no effort to seize real power from his mother and Mazarin when he came of age in 1651 at the height of the Fronde. For another decade until Mazarin's death in 1661 he let the cardinal carry on, but then at last at the age of twenty-three decided to end the powers of his mother Anne of Austria who died of breast cancer five years later. Clearly the terror induced by the Fronde, coupled with the disillusionment brought on by the desertion of Condé and other members of his own family combined to harden the young king's attitudes and make him realise that he could trust no one. Unsmiling, pockmarked, wearing a long peruke, methodical, aloof and dedicated to the task he set himself a six hour working day, appointed no new first minister and made all his own decisions convinced in his own infallibility, determined already to make his mark on history. In a way he responded to the demands of the Fronde by ruling himself and no longer relying on one pre-eminent minister. In Antonia Fraser's words 'he was marked as much by his industry as by his hedonism.' As Fisher put it he was the first French king 'to make monarchy a serious profession.' Later he was to tell his son 'My natural authority, my hot faith and my violent desire to augment my reputation impelled me to a strong feeling of impatience. Luxembourg, Mons, Ghent and Brussels were ever before me.' To project his personality he had himself hailed as the new Apollo or the Roi Soleil, he emphasised his commanding presence by insistence on the minutest details of court protocol to the point where courtiers of both sexes would suffer near bursting bladders rather than risk asking to leave the room or stop a coach.

A year earlier, as organised by Mazarin with whose nieces Olympe and Marie Mancini Louis had had his first real romances, he had for reasons of state married his first cousin Maria Theresa, daughter of Felipe IV of Spain and his Bourbon queen Elizabeth (daughter of Henri IV), so there was yet another dynastic link between the Bourbons and Habsburgs and one that was to prove of enormous importance in the continued rise of the Bourbons. To make it even more competitively incestuous Maria's sister was married to the Austrian emperor and in previous centuries the Viennese Habsburgs had been hugely successful in expanding their empire through marriage. Now by the same technique they could be about to have it seriously contracted, for Maria's brother, Carlos, the heir to the Spanish throne was mentally defective and not expected to live. Maria did very soon give birth to the Dauphin Louis (1661-1711) but all their five subsequent children died soon after birth. Not only did she have that misery but she also soon had to suffer the serial infidelity of her husband, her teeth were blackened by chewing garlic and chocolate, she never learned to speak good French, he spoke no Spanish and she had to settle for being a largely neglected wife.

Louis's assumption of power coincided with the start of his extraordinary passion for Versailles. There had been a small hunting lodge there used by his father Louis XIII who was also a dedicated huntsman. Young Louis was an excellent shot and all round sportsman who also liked to follow up the hunt with a good party. Hence Versailles needed to be expanded to accommodate guests and this was to motivate one of the most extravagant architectural creations of modern history. The other factor influencing Louis was a visit he paid, just before this, to the new country house built by his finance minister Fouquet at Vaux le Vicomte. It was so stylish and magnificent that Louis wanted to outdo it, sacked Fouquet in a jealous rage, stole a thousand of his orange trees and permanently borrowed two of his main artistic advisers, the sculptor and architect Bernini and the painter, Le Brun. Thus began the new palace of Versailles with a new town to support it. By 1682 it became the official centre of government and its building cost around 5 per cent of France's entire national income, much to the disgust of the urban taxpayers. Yet its chimneys did not work, so the rooms were cold but full of smoke, no shutters were allowed for aesthetic reasons, the toilet facilities were abysmal and courtiers lived there in huge discomfort but at great expense.

Meanwhile Louis also had an additional country mansion at Marly, rebuilt the Louvre, where in 1662 Le Brun redecorated the Gallery of Apollo with the sun-king as his theme. Louis gave Paris its first boulevards instead of walls, built Les Invalides, the Place Vendôme, the Observatory and founded the Comédie Française. He also took over from his cousin Condé the patronage of Molière about whom he said 'this man suits me; he is amusing and clear-sighted', so like Racine he was added to the pay-role as a subtle propagandist for the régime. So was the Italian composer Lully, for apart from architecture Louis's favourite art-form was undoubtedly music.

Louis's first passion for Versailles also coincided with the acquisition of his first regular mistress, Louise de la Vallière, who was to bear him five children of whom two survived to adulthood. Louise was dropped in 1668 and died in a nunnery in 1710. Apart from flirtations with his cousin and sister-in-law Henrietta Stuart, Duchess of Orléans, which were regarded as indiscrete, his other two main mistresses were the Marquise de Montespan (relationship from 1668-78) who bore him six children and Madame de Maintenon, the oldest of the three who bore him none. Ironically for a man who acknowledged seventeen children as his own he had only one legitimate child who grew to adulthood, Louis the Dauphin, and even he was to die before him.

The first seven years of Louis's reign saw the groundwork for expansion being planned by Jean Baptiste Colbert (1619-83), an apprentice minister from the Mazarin period, who came to be the financial driving force of the new régime. This non-drinking workaholic with his meticulous sense of detail and obsession with central control paid special attention to the infrastructure; roads, canals, the building up of both the merchant and military fleets, the encouragement of colonies, business and the more efficient collection of taxes.

From the fisheries of Newfoundland and the plantations of the West Indies to the depots of Louisiana and Madagascar and the factories in India everything was regulated from Paris. Colbert also continued the encouragement of industry, particularly the production of luxury items such as silks and tapestries, so it was no coincidence that it was in this reign in 1693 that Dom Perignon according to legend discovered the process for making Champagne. Colbert's notion of economics was pre-Liberal for he believed in protecting France with high tariffs, so he failed to tackle the archaic exemption from taxes still enjoyed by the aristocracy, but by the standards of the time he created a very sound base for the king's ambitious plans. He even began work on the codification of laws which was completed by Napoleon. Unemployment was reduced to a minimum as beggars and vagrant criminals could be condemned to the galleys. Paris was given a proper police force and parents were encouraged to have large families.

All this efficiency on top of the improvements already achieved by Richelieu and Mazarin meant that Louis could exercise absolute power without having to consult anyone or gain any parliamentary approval for his taxes. From 1614 the Bourbons summoned no Estates General till compelled to do so by impending bankruptcy in 1789 and no Assembly of Notables after 1626. The Church too was gradually reformed, partly to remove the justification for Huguenot non-conformity, partly to keep the Pope in Rome from having too much control. France began once more to breed its own saints. The future St Vincent de Paul had done time as a galley slave and founded various hospitals till his death in 1660. Two years later Armand de Rancé became the abbot of La Trappe and established a new order of silent self-denial. Even the former reprobate, the King's cousin Conti was now in charge of the Company of Holy Sacraments.

It was in this atmosphere that Louis first started more overtly using the sun image, though he was not the first French king to do so. Despite relying on Colbert he was his own book-keeper at least in matters of royal income if not expenditure for he trusted no one, allowed no ministers to issue orders without his express approval and spent hours each day updating himself on each aspect of government, a task he seemed to enjoy. In the spring he moved the entire court to Compiègne so that he could keep a close eye on military exercises. He made sure that none of his family or other senior aristocrats except Condé and later Vendôme had meaningful posts in government and began to show signs of barely controlled megalomania, ready for example to risk a serious diplomatic incident to ensure that British and Spanish warships dipped their ensigns to his when passing at sea.

Thus six years after assuming sole power Louis was in a position to launch the first of the five wars by which he was to set about expanding Bourbon influence. This was the War of Devolution (1667-8) which was prompted by the death of his father-in-law Philip IV of Spain, in 1665, and the succession of his mentally retarded son Carlos who was only four. The justification for the attack on the Spanish Netherlands was that under the law of Brabant it could be argued that Louis's wife Maria was the true heiress. In real terms Louis wanted to consolidate his northern frontier and mop up the French-speaking areas of the Netherlands. The attack was made easier by the fact that the king's cousin Charles II of Britain was at this time his ally and did not object to the northward extension of French power. So Turenne captured a series of towns like Lille, Charleroi, Armentières and Tournai which were added to France. It was the reinstated Condé who again beat the Spaniards in the Franche Comté. Things went less well when Britain for a while became hostile and Louis agreed to evacuate the Franche Comté but soon managed to bribe Charles back on to his side, using his sister-in-law, the flirtatious Henrietta Stuart, as the go-between.

There then followed a six year war against the Dutch (1672-8) during which the last ditch efforts of William of Orange made things much more difficult, but despite horrendous casualties Condé famously crossed the Rhine in 1672 at Tolhuis, helped by the introduction of a new weapon, the bayonet. He fought his last great battle in 1674 at Seneffe where he had three horses shot from under him, so by the end of this war Louis was able to absorb Luxembourg, Alsace and the Franche Comté in 1678. However, the closer Louis got to the Rhine the more alarmed other powers became and a coalition was organised to put a stop to his expansion. Yet thanks to the now huge standing army of 200,000 men which had been organised and equipped for him by Louvois and his fleet, which now had around 200 ships, he was able to hold his own. So in 1681 he formally added Alsace to his empire and occupied Strasbourg. It was during this war that the highly efficient Colonel Martinet introduced several improvements to the army but was so unpopular with his own men that he died in what is today referred to as a 'friendly fire incident'. At least Louis wisely rejected a new invention of chemical warfare suggested by one of his boffins.

At this point Louis was probably at the peak of his power, already from 1680 referring to himself as Louis the Great on his own coins, and should have consolidated, but he was not content. After 1681 he began an internal war against the Huguenots whom he disliked intensely and every means of intimidation and considerable brutality were used to persuade the million or so that remained to become Catholics. This was not an unpopular move with the other 95 per cent of the French population who also disliked Protestants, partly because many of them were wealthy middle class and flaunted their different clothing and alternative lifestyle.

This new policy of religious intolerance coincided with a change of direction in the king's life style. His relationship with the liberal and increasingly obese Montespan was cooling off and once past the age of forty he had a period of serial promiscuity with one lady-in-waiting after another. Yet at the same time he was coming increasingly under the spell of Madame de Maintenon, the virginal and staunchly Catholic governess of his favourite bastard, the Duc du Maine. His much neglected wife died in 1683 and at the age of forty-five he secretly married Maintenon despite the fact that she was three years his senior. This in some ways uncharacteristic behaviour perhaps reflected the fact that he had no longer any need to produce an heir, for his only son the Dauphin Louis had with his Bavarian wife provided him with two healthy grandsons Louis Duc de Bourgogne (1682-1712) and Philippe (1683-1746) the future first Bourbon king of Spain.

This change of mood had to some extent been brought on by a series of poisoning and witchcraft scandals that afflicted Paris society from about 1670 and climaxed in trials that implicated Montespan amongst others high up in court circles. In the background was the increasing demand from courtiers including the near middle-aged king himself, for aphrodisiacs such as Spanish Fly to help them maintain their exhausting schedules of extra-marital affairs and the rising trade in bath-house brothels.

One of the fringe Bourbons accused and subsequently banished was one of Louis's short-term mistresses, Olympe the Comtesse de Soissons – the last count, a Savoy Bourbon, had died in battle against the king in 1641 –and her son Eugene (1663-1736) appeared to Louis to be a transvestite fop, so was not allowed a comission in the army. This was unfortunate for Eugene joined the imperial army, turned out to be a brave and brilliant officer, rose to be a field marshal and was, along with Marlborough (who himself had served in French employ till 1675), the general who did most damage to France during the last period of Louis's reign. The exiled Olympe was involved in subsequent poison rumours in 1680 about the death in Madrid of Queen Marie Louise (1612-80) daughter of Louis's brother Orléans, the miserably lonely Bourbon wife of the impotent Carlos II. Another influential court personality implicated in the poison scandal was the dramatist Racine (1639-99) who had allegedly procured some potions for an unsatisfactory abortion for his mistress.

As it happened the king, along with his attempt to clean up the poison scandals, also had a homophobic drive which was all the more difficult for him as his heavily made-up brother, Philippe Duc d'Orléans (he was given the title after the death of his uncle Gaston), was the most noted bisexual in Paris, having been lured into a life of unbridled sensuality by his brother's minders who wanted to lead him away from active involvement in politics. His Condé and Conti cousins, his cousin and billiards partner Louis Joseph, Duc de Vendôme (1654-1712 – grandson of Henri IV's bastard son César his name conveniently rhymed with sodom), were all flagrantly promiscuous in their habits with either sex – Vendôme was also involved in a suspected attempted poisoning of his mistress's husband – and the king's own bastard son Louis Comte de Vermandois (1667-83, son of La Vallière) died in disgrace for early transgressions when he was only sixteen in 1683.

The death in 1670 of Henrietta Stuart, Orléans's first wife and a favourite cousin of the king as well as being sister of the half-Bourbon Charles II of Britain had been another break with the past and this crucial period saw other significant deaths; Colbert in 1683, Charles II in 1685 and the Great Condé, the senior Bourbon outside the immediate royal family, in 1686. After years of persecuting his wife whom he locked up at Châteauroux the aging Condé took to religion in his last years at Chantilly. The new Prince of Condé, Henri III (1643-1710) had been a general on his father's last Rhine campaign but was less able and even less amiable, suffering from the delusion that he was a wolf so that he had to be declared insane and died in 1709. His cousin Louis Armand, the younger Bourbon Prince of Conti (1661-85) had, in 1685, just come back from fighting the Turks in Hungary, caught smallpox from his wife and died, leaving his younger brother François Louis (1664-1709), who had also been fighting in Hungary as the new Prince of Conti, who was also known for his 'Italian habit'.

It was in this morbid atmosphere of death and scandal that Louis decided to rid himself of the diehard remainder of Huguenots. So in 1685 he revoked the Edict of

Nantes which his grandfather Henri IV had passed to give freedom of worship to the Huguenots. The non-conformist Vaudois people in Savoy were ethnically cleansed. Not only did the disastrous attack on the Huguenots result in the emigration of some of France's most entrepreneurial craftsmen but it also created shockwaves in Britain where the half-Bourbon James II had now taken over as king, and was manipulating for a Catholic take-over. Thus Louis's revocation of the Edict of Nantes indirectly contributed to the revolution by which William of Orange, Louis's most persistent enemy, was invited to become King of Britain, in the longer term creating a nemesis for Louis. Significantly there were around a thousand Huguenot army officers including the excellent Huguenot general Marshal Schomberg helping William to win the battle of the Boyne against James II.

The arrogant self-confidence of Louis's act against the Huguenots had also been evident in a number of his other unprovoked but carefully targeted attacks designed to strengthen the frontiers of France. He had captured Strasbourg on the Rhine and Casale on the Po in 1681 as he gradually extended the frontiers of France. Other cities like Metz and Besançon he acquired by employing good lawyers when other nations were too busy to notice. His invasion of the Palatinate in 1688 on a fairly feeble legal pretext was conducted with great brutality and cities like Heidelberg and Mannheim were devastated. He encouraged the Turks to invade Austria and planned to have his son made Holy Roman Emperor instead of the next Habsburg. He used the latest invention of sea-borne mortars to destroy most of Algiers and the Barbary pirates, and then gave Genoa the same treatment for refusing to comply with his policies.

One of Louis's most serious errors of judgement was to underestimate the ability of his old enemy William of Orange to manage two campaigns at the same time and to overestimate the will of his own cousin James II to regain his kingdom. He expected them to be embroiled in another British civil war and so failed to concentrate his own efforts or to realise just how unpopular he had become with every other European ruler. He offended by still showing favour to the exiled James II and his bastard son the Duke of Berwick, despite the fact that both had been embroiled in a plot to murder William. The resulting war against the Grand Alliance or Nine Years War or Orléans War (1689-97) included many victories for Louis like Mons (1691) and Steinkirk (1692) on land but he lost La Hogue (1692) at sea and in the end Louis was forced to concede most of his gains, so the huge expenditure of life and money had been to no purpose. The threat to invade Britain came to nothing. Considering the French had a total population at this time of around twenty million, the British five or six and the Dutch less than three it was hardly impressive.

The next great crisis began in 1700 when at long last the imbecilic Carlos II of Spain, brother of Louis's late wife, died with no direct heir and on his deathbed was persuaded by the French ambassador to bequeath his entire empire to Louis's and his sister's grandson, Philippe of Anjou. If accepted this meant that the Bourbons would acquire not only Spain and the Spanish Netherlands but also half of Morocco, Milan, Naples and Sicily, Sardinia, the Balearics and Canaries, Cuba, Mexico, Florida, California, the Antilles, Panama, virtually all South America except Brazil and the Guianas, plus the Philippines.

Other states in Europe had already recognised the enormity of this expansion and from 1798 had been negotiating for various different splits of the inheritance. Louis had previously offered various concessions which would have allowed the Spanish inheritance to be split up and was well aware that for the Bourbons to get all of it would provoke a war in which he would have to face virtually every other nation in Europe. Now he was faced with an all or nothing choice, made slightly easier for him by the fact that if he refused the entire legacy would transfer to his arch rivals the Habsburgs in Vienna. He made it, accepting on his grandson's behalf and Philippe headed for Madrid as Felipe V. His father Louis the Dauphin and his elder brother Louis de Bourgogne stayed behind as the heirs to France.

At this point Louis might have avoided war simply because of the inertia of his enemies, none of whom particularly wanted a general war at this time, but he overplayed his hand or was insensitively arrogant in ignoring the feelings of the rest of Europe. Without warning he sent troops to occupy the Spanish Netherlands and took over the Dutch barrier towns. He also demanded for himself the *asiento*, the Spanish quota of the highly profitable slave trade to central America and a year later in a final act of tactlessness when the exiled James II, ex-king of Britain died at Saint Germain he ostentatiously recognised his cousin James Edward Stuart, the Old Pretender, as the new rightful king of Britain. It was enough to persuade an apopleptic William of Orange to rehabilitate Marlborough and to send him to Holland to organise a new coalition against France. The War of Spanish Succession (1701-13) which ensued was to be a serious disaster for Louis even though William died before it really got started. For by this time the numbers of troops on both sides had seriously escalated, as had the expense. Moreover both Britain and Holland had developed sophisticated new banking systems whilst France had not.

One of the extraordinary facets of this long and very expensive war was the number of Bourbon relations involved on both sides. Of the principals on the other side, Queen Anne of Great Britain had a Bourbon grandmother as had the Holy Roman Emperor Leopold, while one of Leopold's most successful generals was the half-Bourbon exile Prince Eugene of Savoy (1663-1736), son of the scandalous Olympe de Soissons and her late husband. On the French side two of the principal generals were the king's cousin the Duc de Vendôme and an illegitimate cousin James Fitzjames, Duke of Berwick, bastard son of James II and Arabella Churchill, sister of their arch-opponent the Duke of Marlborough. Towards the end of Louis's reign four out of the eight ablest generals available to him were Bourbon relations and three of them he was stubbornly reluctant to promote: the eccentric but brilliant Vendôme whom he used grudgingly, the future Regent Philippe Duc d'Orléans (1674-1723), a popular and dashing officer to whom he briefly gave half-hearted command in Italy, and the brilliant

Conti who had set a new fashion trend with his jaunty cravat in the thickest of the fighting at Steinkirk but to whom Louis gave no decent appointment until he (Conti) was on his death bed in 1709. Only the relatively poor and landless Berwick was allowed to develop his career without reverse nepotism.

Louis was in his early sixties by the time the war began, more authoritarian than ever and no longer served by any ministers or generals who could think of questioning his decisions. Having stoically undergone a painful and very dangerous anal operation without anaesthetic in 1686 he must have had considerable confidence in his body, despite having lost part of his jawbone earlier to an over-enthusiastic dentist when red-hot coal was used to cauterise the abscess in his mouth. His gargantuan eating habits if not his twice-daily obsession with sex were perhaps attributable to the fact that, as shown by his post mortem, he had an exceptionally large stomach and gut. Yet his exhausting schedule of work and play, plus perhaps the strain of his unshared responsibilities, led to occasional fits of the *vapeurs* for which the fashionable treatments were bleedings and enemas.

The Dauphin Louis was by this time forty and overweight, uninspiring and bisexual but apparently in good health. The next in line, his son Louis Duc de Bourgogne, was twenty and recently married to another half-Bourbon, partially Stuart, Marie Adelaide of Savoy, so that soon the king might expect to become a great-grandfather. Meanwhile the Dauphin's middle son Philippe having been dispatched to rule Spain at the age of seventeen had also married another of the half-Bourbon Savoy sisters. So dynastically the Bourbons appeared impregnable, yet Louis was always adding to the pool by getting his illegitimate children to marry legitimate Bourbons. It was one of these matches of his daughter Françoise Marie (1677-1749, daughter of Montespan) to the Duke of Orléans' heir which produced years later the infamous Philippe Egalité but also Louis Philippe, the last French king.

Meanwhile another series of deaths somewhat changed the picture. That of James II in 1701 had been followed by Louis's impetuously offensive recognition of his 'heir' James Edward Stuart as James III of Great Britain. That of his old adversary William III in the following year had brought in Queen Anne who might seem less formidable, but was equally offended by the recognition of her Stuart half-brother. 1701 had also seen the death of the king's brother, the old roué Philippe Duc d' Orléans after a stroke brought on by a quarrel between the two of them over the failure to give Orléans's son Philippe (1674-1723) a senior post in the army. In 1703 also came the death of 'The Man in the Iron Mask' who had spent the previous sixteen years in the Bastille and whose identity (some had suggested Fouquet) was supposedly only known to the king and his brother, Orléans who had just died.

The war went badly for France in Italy and Spain, commerce was paralysed and the treasury began to empty. Though there was no reduction in the number of balls at Versailles Louis had to increase his working day to nine or ten hours, yet hampered his generals by obsessive control and arrogantly not opening the mail from the front until he had been out hunting. Of the two main generals with Bourbon blood Vendôme and Berwick were both very able but did not get on with each other. Vendôme's nose was eaten away with syphilis and he had what Winston Churchill calls 'filthy habits': he was also arrogant and brave, surprisingly popular with his men but preferred to be involved himself in the thick of the fighting rather than making strategic decisions. Berwick was more of a parvenu, equally brave and a better strategist. The Dauphin also was a popular officer, regarded as much fairer to subordinates than his father, but was too important to let near the front.

The heir to the princedom of Condé Louis III de Bourbon (1668-1710) was dwarflike, yellow-faced, suffering from delusions and married to Louise Françoise (1673-1743) one of the king's illegitimate daughters by Montespan. He died of a brain tumour soon after his vulpine father. Similarly his cousin François Louis de Bourbon Prince of Conti (Le Grand Conti 1664-1709) whose father was the model for Molière's *Don Juan* had done well in battles like Steinkirk and fought the Turks in Hungary but was overlooked for command by Louis perhaps because he had a a trace of jealousy or bore a grudge for a letter opened by his spies in which Conti described him as '*Le Roi de Theatre*'. Instead he was for a while rusticated to his château at Chantilly and pushed in 1694 as the candidate for the crown of Poland which he did not want as it would mean leaving his mistress, the wife of his cousin. Conti sadly died in his mid-forties in 1709 frustratingly just after the king had at last offered him the post of commander in chief.

Meanwhile Marlborough had made his famous dash to the Danube in 1704 which gained him the co-operation of Prince Eugene of Savoy, the officer dismissed as a fop twenty years earlier by Louis XIV. The battles of Blenheim and Ramillies were major setbacks for France and were sufficient to allow Britain to demand its original objectives from Louis: that the Spanish and French crowns should be separate entities even if both Bourbon and that neither should control the Netherlands. However, the British now wanted more: the use of Lisbon and the annexation of Gibraltar and Minorca so the war had to continue for another seven years.

Next came Vendôme's attempt to win back Flanders which resulted in his defeat by Marlborough at Oudenarde. Vendôme blamed this on the king's grandson Louis Duc de Burgogne who was technically in command and in his opinion failed to pursue the attack and ordered a premature retreat. The outcome was the loss of Ghent and Lille.

Meanwhile Louis's grandson Philippe was twice ejected from his new throne in Madrid and twice restored thanks to memorable victories by Vendôme at Brihuega and by Berwick at Almansa. Since the double throne was Louis's main objective in the war this had been achieved and was to last till the revolution. It also fulfilled the Spanish ambassador's dictum that there would be no more Pyrenees and France could or would not be invaded from the south. Britain had failed to conquer Spain for the Habsburg claimant Charles and by 1711 when his brother Joseph I died of smallpox Charles had succeeded him as emperor so he no longer had any interest in Spain. Besides it was reasonably clear that the Spaniards themselves much preferred a Bourbon to another Habsburg. The one downside to the Spanish inheritance was that for the time being virtually all of the Italian components had been lost, but that was a modest price to pay.

In the meantime Marlborough had continued his inexorable aggressions in Flanders and Northern France with the hugely destructive battle at Malplaquet in 1709 where the French retreated in good order having inflicted more damage than they received, but technically defeated because of their withdrawal. Louis facing total annihilation was ready to make peace on reasonable terms. His army was defeated, his treasury empty, his people close to starvation. Two desperately cold winters had meant very poor harvests and disease was rife. However, the British terms for peace were unacceptably humiliating and the despotic king for once addressed his own people, publishing the outrageous peace terms from every pulpit and town square. The result was remarkable with an extraordinary outburst of patriotic indignation which brought in new recruits to his army and a new will to fight. This plus the successes in Spain and the withdrawal of the Habsburgs as contenders there narrowed the scope of the war and removed some of the motivation of the British to keep it going. Having borrowed gold from the Spanish-American banking system Louis was back in the fight.

Meanwhile even the extraordinary willpower of Louis XIV was to be tested by one further major crisis in his family. In 1711 his only legitimate child Louis the Dauphin died at Meudon at the age of only fifty-three when on the verge of recovering from smallpox but weakened by unnecessary blood-letting and purging by the court doctor – doctors were particularly dangerous at this period as demonstrated in Molière's play *Le Médecin Malgré Lui* which had first appeared in 1666. Life expectancy in the court was lower than that of the ordinary peasant. The Dauphin had never appeared a charismatic character: he had been withdrawn and devoid of most emotions except the lust for hunting wolves and an apparent preference for fat ugly women although he was much less callous with regard to human life than his father. He might have made a reasonable if much less ambitious king.

The new Dauphin was his eldest son Louis Duc de Bourgogne (1682-1712) who had been a small and violent child that grew up disapproving of his father, less sporty, more academic, ostentatiously pious, proud and thin to the point of anorexia. Of his two brothers Philippe had already renounced any claim to the throne of France when he went off to take over Spain and Charles Duc de Berri (1680-1714) was at twenty-four still something of an unknown quantity.

Tragedy soon struck again, this time the new Dauphin's wife, the highly popular Marie Adelaide died at twenty-six of measles in an outbreak that cost over 500 deaths in Paris alone. She was followed soon afterwards by the

Dauphin himself who also caught measles and was hastened on his way by the court doctor. This left their sickly baby son Louis (1710-74) as the heir to France and the third dauphin in twelve months. The only senior Bourbons left were Philippe of Orléans (1674-1723) who had recently been accused of molesting his own married daughter and his son-in-law the Duc de Berri who as it turned out was to die after a hunting accident, too afraid of the ministrations of the court doctor to dare to ask for treatment.

Thus just when the war seemed to be going more the way of France the Bourbon dynasty itself was decimated and Louis himself at seventy-five could not have long to live. Thanks partly to the withdrawal of Marlborough and the victories of Villars in Flanders, such as Denain in 1712, France regained some territory in the north and the Treaty of Utrecht which at last ended the war was much more favourable than the terms offered in 1709. There was no erosion of France's hard won new frontiers in the north and east, only minor losses in Newfoundland and Nova Scotia for France and Gibraltar, the Spanish Netherlands and Minorca for Spain which kept its entire overseas empire. Britain got the main thing it wanted which was separate controllers of its three neighbours across the Channel, (Spain, France and the Netherlands) but the cost had been very high.

The cost of Louis XIV's achievements had also been very high and in concentrating on his frontier wars he had failed to make many reforms, which might have made his monarchy more sustainable for the future. But at his death France was undoubtedly much stronger and considerably larger than it had been at his accession. His family albeit technically divided now controlled vast territories over four continents. The only trouble was that as at the age of seventy-seven he at last faced death his heir was his tiny great grandson. He died as stoically as he had lived, refusing to let the doctors amputate his gangrenous leg just to give him a few extra painful days of life.

Louis had without doubt enhanced the territorial integrity of France and its potential prosperity, but at a great cost in money and lives. Cobban describes him as 'the greatest postmaster general' because of his workaholic obsession with processing paperwork and his minute attention to detail that sometimes frustrated his generals and ministers. Shennan sums him up as 'above all he was a great self-publicist' and certainly the image was greater than the reality. In reducing the entire aristocratic class to the status of unemployed and unemployable courtiers he had paid for it by leaving them their ridiculous tax privileges and had done little to tackle the basic corruption of the tax collection system despite the fact that the national debt had risen tenfold since 1683. Thus he had made the Bourbon monarchy absolute but left its financial foundations totally inadequate. He had made the crown appear so omnipotent that its wearers could not see through the fog of pomp to its underlying weakness. Sadly since neither of his two successors were to be geniuses they failed to tackle the flaws which he left them and sooner or later the edifice was bound to collapse.

THE BOURBONS AFTER HENRI IV

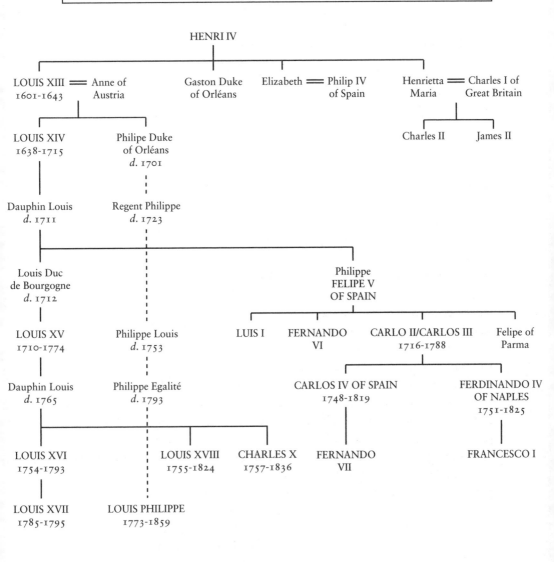

HENRI IV

LOUIS XIII = Anne of
1601-1643   Austria

Gaston Duke
of Orléans

Elizabeth = Philip IV
of Spain

Henrietta = Charles I of
Maria   Great Britain

Charles II   James II

LOUIS XIV
1638-1715

Philipe Duke
of Orléans
d. 1701

Dauphin Louis
d. 1711

Regent Philippe
d. 1723

Louis Duc
de Bourgogne
d. 1712

Philippe
FELIPE V
OF SPAIN

LOUIS XV
1710-1774

Philippe Louis
d. 1753

LUIS I   FERNANDO
VI

CARLO II/CARLOS III
1716-1788

Felipe of
Parma

Dauphin Louis
d. 1765

Philippe Egalité
d. 1793

CARLOS IV OF SPAIN
1748-1819

FERDINANDO IV
OF NAPLES
1751-1825

LOUIS XVI
1754-1793

LOUIS XVIII
1755-1824

CHARLES X
1757-1836

FERNANDO
VII

FRANCESCO I

LOUIS XVII
1785-1795

LOUIS PHILIPPE
1773-1859

Family tree continued on page 100

LOUIS XV

'Pick it up and throw it back at them, Monsieur le Dauphin' Louis XV's
alleged remark to his son when a cannon ball landed near them in 1744

Louis XV (1710-74) became king at the age of five and was an orphan, for
both his father and mother had just died of measles. Both his elder brothers
had also died as infants and his own life was probably only saved by the
presence of mind of his nurse Madame de Ventadour who kept him away
from the court doctors. Thus with both his father and grandfather dead the
crown skipped two generations and he stepped into the shoes of his formidable
great-grandfather. At the time his own prospects of survival looked bleak and
he was hardly expected to live to adulthood.

To remedy the sudden dearth of legitimate male Bourbons Louis XIV had
legitimised two of his own bastard sons: his favourite the spoiled Louis Auguste,
Duc de Maine (1670-1736), and Louis Alexandre, Comte de Toulouse (1678-
1737), sons of Montespan and protégées of Madame de Maintenon's. In his
will he decreed that they should serve in prominent roles alongside the official
chief regent his nephew Philippe Bourbon Duc d'Orléans (1674-1723).

Born in his father's palace at St Cloud the forty-year-old Philippe of Orléans
had shown himself an able soldier at Mons and Steinkirk but then been denied
employment until at last given command in Italy in 1706. He had then done
well in Spain in 1707 but once more incurred his uncle's jealousy by appearing
to have ambitions for himself on the throne of Spain instead of the king's
grandson Philippe. So he had spent the final years of Louis XIV once more
out of favour. His reputation for orgies, his penchant for acting, his avowed
atheism, his hiding of Rabellais in the covers of a bible, his love of the *Fêtes
gallantes* painted by Watteau all made him seem an unsuitable candidate for
power in the staid last days of Louis XIV.

However, in 1715 there was no question of his right as senior prince of the
blood to be regent for the old king's great grandson, Louis XV. Nevertheless he
had ideas of his own and favoured a revival of aristocratic power which had
been eroded by the totalitarian style of Louis XIV with his thousand nobles
kicking their heels in Versailles. Thus he had the will overturned so that he did
not need to treat the two former bastards as equals and proceeded to become
something of an autocrat himself, albeit with the intention of reforming the
autocracy. He reduced taxes, cut the size of the army, and introduced a more
consensual form of government called *Polysynodie* though sadly most of the
aristocrats had become so accustomed to idleness that they were not interested.
He shifted the centre of government back from Versailles to Paris and installed
the young king in the Tuileries. He expanded the university at the Sorbonne and
encouraged the new colony of Louisiana where the city of New Orléans was
founded in his name with a new port in Brittany, Lorient to service it.

In 1717 he had to fend off an attempted coup in which Cardinal Alberoni plotted to have him replaced by his cousin Philippe/Felipe V the King of Spain, a serious attempted breach of the Treaty of Utrecht.This resulted in a war between the two Bourbon kingdoms. The Duke of Berwick, his even more distant cousin led the French armies to success and Felipe of Spain made peace. However, the government was now short of money and Orléans tried a bold experiment, helped by one of his former gambling colleagues, the Scotsman John Law. The objective was to increase the money supply by creating plenty of credit through a new royal bank of France, similar to the Bank of England developed so successfully in London in 1694. Unfortunately this coincided with Law's heavy involvement in the new Mississippi Company founded to handle the Louisiana and Senegal monopoly. Shares boomed to a ridiculously high price and then collapsed, just like those of the similar South Sea Company in London the same year, 1720. At least one Bourbon, Louis Armand the new Prince of Conti (1717-76), sold out at the top of the market and made a fortune. But by withdrawing his cash in three cartloads of silver, he precipitated the run on the bank, which turned it into a disaster for nearly everyone else. The failure to provide France with a reliable system of credit combined with the régime's lack of the courage to impose taxes on the rich were to be its undoing seven decades later.

In the end Orléans stayed on an extra six months as chief minister after the young king came officially of age and was crowned at Reims in 1723, then died soon after retiring.

The next chief minster was also a Bourbon, but less popular. Louis Henri, Duc de Bourbon (1692-1740), was the son of Louis de Bourbon, Prince of Condé and Louis XIV's illegitimate daughter Louise Françoise. Hunched-up, uncharismatic he had lost one eye but like his Conti cousin had made a lot of money out of the Mississippi Company for he knew how to exploit La Systeme. As chief minister he introduced much more virulent anti-Huguenot measures. His most significant act, however, was to break up the engagement of the teenage king to the even younger Spanish Infanta Maria Anna – a Bourbon herself as she was the daughter of Felipe the first Bourbon king of Spain – because of the expected delay before she would be old enough to produce an heir. Instead he organised an uninspiring marriage for Louis with Maria Leczynska, daughter of the former Polish king. She was seven years older than Louis, neither bright nor rich, pious and not very fashionable, but he found her attractive and allegedly made love to her seven times on their wedding night. By the time he was twenty-seven they had ten children of whom six daughters and one son survived to adulthood. Not content with this Louis had his way with a succession of maidservants laid on for him by his valets. All this was easier when they moved back to Versailles in 1723.

After three years in power the Duc de Bourbon made the mistake of trying to get rid of Cardinal Fleury (1653-1743), the king's aged tutor who responded by outwitting him, had the king sack him and himself took over effectively as prime minister but without the title in 1726. Bourbon retired to his castle at Chantilly and his obsession with hunting. His mistress Madame de Prie was so bored that apparently she committed suicide. He meanwhile had become convinced that he would be reincarnated as a horse and built the magnificent stable block – Grandes Ecuries – at Chantilly which could house 250 horses with one stall saved for his own use in the next life.

Louis XV was by this time approaching adulthood. He turned out tall and handsome with a sensual moodiness that was allegedly irresistible to women, but then he was a king, and apparently also incapable of resisting pretty women. He was intelligent and conscientious, an early riser who often lit his own fire to avoid disturbing the servants, though perhaps not so much because he cared for their welfare as because his inherent secretiveness and shyness made human contact at that level difficult for him. He had the usual passion for hunting and was somewhat addicted to masked balls and to gambling like his uncle Orléans, so it suited him to delegate the work of government. However, his tutor Fleury had given him an interest in the sciences and he did encourage the founding of several technical colleges.

For the next seventeen years the cardinal who was already in his seventies dominated the French government and provided as stable and effective policies as were possible within the limitations of the *ancien régime*. His preference for peace helped considerably and the economy boomed. Though the colonies in America and India failed to break-even the West Indies were a big commercial success as was the slave trade based mainly in Nantes which sent out more than 400 ships each year to West Africa. Also significant was the fishing industry, which trawled the Grand Banks off Newfoundland and supplied cheap food for the slaves on the West Indian plantations. While French industry lagged behind British, hampered by guild conservatism and internal tolls, the state-run luxury industries of Gobelin and Sèvres did well. Road building was impressive as was the network of canals and rivers for water transport. The population rose by some twenty per cent during the eighteenth century and until overtaken by Russia in 1789 France was the most populous nation in Europe. Sadly, however, due to the conservative methods of the average peasant and the fact that most of the more significant landlords were attending the perpetual party at Versailles, agriculture remained small-scale and its productivity failed to keep up with increasing demand. There were many rural unemployed who took to brigandage to survive.

Thanks to having a Polish wife Louis felt obliged to join in the war of Polish Succession in 1733 despite the objections of Fleury. The fighting was mainly in Italy and achieved little except that the Spanish Bourbons gained Naples so that they were able to acquire the dynasty's third crown and the Infante Carlos Borbon became King Carlo IV of Naples (see p.108). Much more for the French Bourbons was achieved by Fleury at the conference table when by an ingenious ploy he was able to procure Lorraine as a kingdom for the queen's father in exchange for the Austrian emperor getting Tuscany. This was on the understanding that France would take over Lorraine officially as soon as the ex-Polish king died.

The War of Austrian Succession proved a much more dangerous affair as French hotheads seemed determined to have a war. Fleury now ninety and close to death was ignored and Louis was persuaded to back the fickle Frederick of Prussia which because of Hanover meant a clash with Britain. The French under Marshall Saxe won Fontenoy against the Duke of Cumberland but had lost at Dettingen. When Fleury retired, dying soon afterwards, Louis decided to do without a chief minister, but had neither the will nor ability to supervise the departmental ministries himself. He was inconsistent, uncommunicative and dabbled in secret diplomacy, for example in his attempt to get the Polish crown for his cousin Louis François de Bourbon, Prince of Conti (1717-76) who had done well as a general in Italy during the war of Austrian Succession, winning a significant battle at Corni in 1744. Conti's grandfather had reluctantly accepted the crown of Poland back in 1697 but been perhaps deliberately too slow in going to collect it (see above p.80) – all this was against official French policy which supported the Saxon family's claim to Poland partly because the Dauphin's new wife was a Saxe. So for a second time the Conti Bourbons missed out on the Polish crown, Louis François fell out of favour with Madame de Pompadour and was given no more military commands, so he retired, supported the aristocratic opposition in the *Parlements* and became a patron of Jean Jacques Rousseau. His son Louis François Joseph (1734-1814) later did well in the Seven Years War but was to be the last of the Bourbon Contis for he lost all his property in the Revolution and died in exile in Barcelona.

Even more half-baked was King Louis's support for his distant cousin Bonnie Prince Charlie when he set out to reconquer Britain for the Stuarts in 1745 and at the last minute was deprived of support. At Fontenoy Louis had enjoyed a brief fling at being commander-in-chief, allegedly joking to his son the Dauphin when a cannon ball dropped near them 'Pick it up Monsieur le Dauphin and throw it back at them' but this is at odds with the fact that he seems to have been genuinely shocked by the horrific number of casualties. He was at this time in 1744 at the peak of his popularity for when he nearly died of an illness at Metz in his mid-thirties his recovery was greeted with joy and he was given the nickname '*Bienaimé*'.

By this time he had had serial love affairs with three sisters one after the other. Now at one of his balls he met the ambitious and sophisticated Jeanne Antoinette Poisson (1721-64), fell in love with her and gave her the title Marquise de Pompadour. The affair was to last twenty years and Madame de Pompadour certainly had a major influence on fashion and the arts if perhaps not quite as much on political affairs as is sometimes suggested. She organised the patronage of Voltaire, Couperin, Boucher and others. She set new fashions and new styles.

That same year there was a double marriage between the French and Spanish Bourbons when the Dauphin married Maria Theresa while his elder sister married Felipe the heir to the Spanish throne. Louis did not take to his new daughter-in-law but then he had not had much of a relationship with his son either for he was overweight, priggish and lazy. As it turned out Maria Theresa was to die quite soon and be replaced with the Germanic Marie-Josephe de Saxe who bore him eight children, three of whom were destined to be highly unsatisfactory kings, while the Dauphin like his grandfather and great-grandfather was destined to die young without ever reaching the throne.

In 1756 when Louis was in his mid-forties he found himself caught out by a change of alliances and was pushed into a war on the side of Austria and Russia against Britain and Prussia. This was to prove disastrous, especially when initial success in invading Hanover was negated by the defeat at Rossbach inflicted by Frederick of Prussia. As the French Navy had been neglected the British under the elder Pitt used the Seven Years War as a means of detaching some of France's main colonies: Canada, some of the precious West Indies, Senegal, Gorée in West Africa and the trading depots in India. Even Louisiana had to be handed over to Spain. Yet though the defeat was humiliating the lost territories seemed insignificant in an atmosphere where most of these colonies were just distant risky enterprises of little consequence for the bulk of the opinion-forming class in France. The French had only 70,000 settlers in North America compared with the British half-million and the network of Indian depots set up by Dupleix was not to be compared in profitability with Martinique and the other French Antilles where there were around 50,000 French settlers and ¼ million slaves working for them, providing 20 per cent of all French trade.

Coincidentally the worst period of the war was followed by an attempt to murder Louis XV by a fanatic called Damiens who was tortured to death to see if he would reveal some sinister plot.

In the aftermath of the war Louis appointed a new chief minister Choiseul who brought more order to affairs, improving both the French navy and army ready for the next confrontation with the British. France saved face by finally taking over control of Lorraine in 1767 and then acquiring Corsica the following year by purchase from the Genoese. New colonies were attempted in Madagascar and Guiana to replace the ones that had been lost.

In 1765 the Dauphin had died in his thirties having suddenly shrunk from his former obesity and in 1770 the new Dauphin, Louis's grandson Louis (1754-93) had a marriage arranged for him to the Austrian princess Marie Antoinette. However, Choiseul went too far for the king when he wanted to join in another war against the British to help Spain keep the Falkland Islands. Louis had lost his taste for war and Choiseul was dismissed.

Meanwhile there was the usual financial crisis as once again the aristocratic members of the *parlements* obstructed reforms in the tax system that would have turned them into taxpayers. Expedients like forced loans and the cancellation of debts did nothing to help, nor did an effort to replace the *parlements* with new royal courts that would do the bidding of the administration. But resentment of the autocracy continued amongst the upper classes, many of whom were now infected with the ideas of Diderot and Voltaire. A new 5 per cent tax, the *Vingtième*, was introduced but resisted as the monarchy as usual shrank from the ultimate difficulty of forcing its own upper class to accept its share of the tax burden. Certainly the tax farming system was tightened up but the government's finances remained on a very fragile footing, especially when extra war expenditure was required. And even in his sixties Louis still had a desire for revenge against Britain so that he dreamed of a seaborne invasion.

Louis's personal behaviour in his later years did nothing to revive his popularity. His reaction to complaints about the extravagance of the royal family was to dismiss eighty gardeners. Even when there was peace the taxes on the lower orders remained high and food was often scarce. There were rumours that little boys were being kidnapped and sent to the colonies. As Madame de Pompadour had lost her physical charms – and she never was very keen on the physical side – she had arranged for him to be provided with a succession of young women until he made the transition to Madame du Barry. He was sulky and self-absorbed. Within a few years he had lost his wife, his only son, two of his grandsons and Madame de Pompadour. Finally at the age of sixty-four he caught smallpox and died an agonising death. He was refused absolution by the priests until his whole body was black with the disease and he had publicly confessed his sins.

Louis XV left France weaker than it had been when he first took over nearly seventy years earlier but he did leave Paris the Champs Élysée and the Place Concorde, originally the Place Louis XV. He had at last in his final years appointed a minister in Maupeou willing to tackle the problem of the rich people in the *parlements* who paid no taxes, but he left it too late and died before it could be completed leaving a grandson who was too immature and too nervous to take over such a potentially dangerous mission. In his own life he had spasmodically tried to emulate his great-grandfather Louis XIV without having the personality to carry it off, nor the intelligence to realise that he was trying to imitate a badly outdated formula.

LOUIS XVI

'*C'est donc une revolte?*' Louis XVI. '*Non, sire, c'est une revolution.*' Duc
de Lioncourt on the fall of the Bastille
'*Fils de Saint Louis, montez au ciel.*' Abbé Edgworth
'That rare thing, a pacific monarch who did not relish going to war.'
Antonia Fraser, *Marie Antoinette*

Louis XVI (r. 1774-93) succeeded his grandfather at the age of twenty and had already been married for four years though it was to be another three before a minor operation enabled him to consummate their relationship. He was tall, shortsighted and as rumours of his impotence were circulated he developed a not surprising inferiority complex. In Fraser's words with 'his heavy-lidded eyes and thick eyebrows he looked equally awkward... already quite portly', so he found it hard to look regal.

In the meantime he replaced the tough-minded Maupeou with the emollient and nearly senile Maurepas so that the nobles in the *parlements* were able to reassert their refusal to accept a fair tax system. Anne Robert Turgot was added to the team as comptroller general and did quietly begin to achieve some tidying up of the financial mess. He tried to cut out the large number of highly paid sinecures, began a reform of the army and with the help of the great chemist Lavoisier made sure that France had the best gunpowder and artillery in Europe – an asset that was to prove very useful in the Revolutionary and Napoleonic wars a few years later. He also made it possible for middle-class officers to work their way up by merit, a factor that made possible the career of Napoleon. He reformed the postal services but as soon as he tried, as others had before him, to cut down internal customs barriers, get rid of restrictive practices in the towns and to introduce taxes payable by the rich landowners, the *parlements* started their obstructive tactics and Louis did not have the character to support him against such opposition. In 1776 he was dismissed.

After Turgot's fall a new talent emerged, Jacques Necker, first director of the treasury. He was a successful Swiss banker and a Huguenot but he too managed a number of useful if superficial reforms such as the abolition of *mainmorte*, a relic of serfdom. Torture was abolished despite objections from the *parlements*, most political prisoners were released and a decision taken to demolish the Bastille. Louis also cancelled the usual military drill displays at Compiègne. Even the Church was reformed and a number of uneconomic monasteries closed down. The streets of Paris were widened and the water supply improved, but overall Necker's attempts to balance the books by cutting back expenditure made him unpopular with the nobles and the queen.

Louis himself was turning into a conscientious, kindly and devout king but lacked the steel that was necessary by this time to force through a reform of the tax system against the will of the privileged classes who used the *parlements* as their focus for obstructing progress, particularly after their recall in 1774. So Louis escaped the pressures of a job that was beyond him and of his humiliating impotence by eating voraciously, by taking to the hunting field or retreating to his foundry and his locksmith's workshop where he spent hours making intricate locks.

His wife Marie Antoinette had grown bored with the monstrous head-dresses and elaborate gowns that had been fashionable, with the endless rounds of formal parties and with seven years of sexless marriage. So she started a new fashion of simple pastoral clothes and left the vastness of Versailles for the simpler pleasures of the expensive new Petit Trianon. Having played the piano with young Mozart in her youth and studied under Glück she pushed new musical fashions and spent a lot of time on amateur dramatics. She had a number of both male and female friends that provided gossip material which was later turned into obscene pamphlets accusing her of both heterosexual and gay relationships, including in the former category her friendship with her playboy brother-in-law Charles Comte d'Artois (1757-1836), later Charles X.

She was also fond of gambling and ran up considerable debts. Even her amateur theatricals at Petit Trianon involved huge expenditure. Like her husband she was probably a reasonably intelligent and sensitive person but brought up to enjoy extremes of luxury and subservience, thrust into a political land-slide that only a superhuman effort might have stopped. She had the talent to be a trendsetter yet that same talent soon led to accusations of extravagance. Moreover she was constantly under pressure from her mother and brother to push pro-Austrian policies, so she was open to accusations of meddling in political affairs. She also made powerful enemies like Madame du Barry whom she usually cut dead and Philippe Duc d'Orléans (1747-93) whose incompetence as a naval officer she had made jokes about. In many respects she had the charisma to be a popular icon and once Louis's sexual problem was solved she became an affectionate wife and mother, yet as the number of her enemies increased she was an easy target for hostile publicity. The legend of her saying 'let them eat cake' was a recycled story that had been applied to earlier queens, but though probably untrue in her case it was unfortunately credible.

Meanwhile the American War of Independence, which had begun in 1776, seemed suddenly to offer a great chance for France to get its own back on the British for the losses sustained twenty years earlier. It began with volunteers like La Fayette going out to help Washington, but by 1778 it was official. French troops helped the Americans humiliate the British Army at Yorktown after the French Navy had thwarted Admiral Hood in Chesapeake Bay. Philippe of Orléans returned from the fleet and its victory at Ushant covered briefly in glory, only for gossip (encouraged probably by Marie Antoinette) soon to circulate that he had been cowardly and incompetent.

The results of this war for the French were fourfold: the satisfaction of seeing Britain lose three quarters of its overseas empire, France regained St Pierre Miquelon, St Lucia, Tobago, Senegal and Gorée but the expenses of the war caused another acute financial crisis and many of the soldiers who had fought in America came back infected with liberal ideas. Of these by far the most significant was the financial crisis, for despite Turgot and Necker the underlying problem of a tax-exempt and aggressively conservative aristocracy had still not been tackled.

The cultural climate too was changing as more and more writers challenged the concept of absolutism and class inequality. One example was the royal banning but subsequent clandestine performances of the play *The Marriage of Figaro* by Beaumarchais which challenged the feudal rights of the landlord, particularly the ancient *Ius primae noctis*. Its very banning served to make it more popular.

A series of events now began to aggravate the post-war crisis. First in 1785 came the diamond necklace scandal, the climax of a monstrous confidence trick aimed at using the queen's name and forged letters to steal a huge haul of diamonds from a Paris jeweller. It was not the queen's fault but because she had the reputation for extravagance the mud unfairly stuck to her and in Napoleon's words it was 'the start of the revolution.' If nothing else as an example of conspicuous consumption it harmed her image at a time when she, her friend Charles of Artois and others were also being accused of profiteering from grain sales during a food shortage.

The second event was the revelation two years later of a secret correspondence from Necker in which he criticised the *parlements*. As a result they stopped the government from borrowing cash at a time when the national debt was abnormally high and Louis had no choice but to dismiss him. By this time Louis was in the grip of something approaching clinical depression, weeping frequently in his wife's room, escaping to the hunt, eating and drinking too much so that he was even more obviously obese and sometimes visibly drunk.

Over the next two years there were a number of attempts to call together some of the various assemblies of aristocrats who might be persuaded to allow taxation of themselves and confirm the creditworthiness of the government. One after another it proved impossible to have a tame assembly of notables, tame *parlements*, tame substitute *parlements* or even tame church assemblies. Louis wanted a reform of the tax system, the aristocrats wanted reform of the monarchy. Even the king's own relations were amongst those who stood in his way, particularly his cousin Philippe Duc d' Orléans the would-be naval hero who later adopted the surname Egalité to demonstrate his revolutionary credentials, but was really planning to replace Louis. He provided a useful base for agitators at the Palais Royal and probably had the ulterior motive of snatching the crown for himself as soon as Louis could be dethroned. Other Bourbons who made the crisis worse rather than better included the king's brother Charles of Artois and distant cousin Condé who both adopted an unhelpfully reactionary stance. Meanwhile Louis and Marie Antoinette had their own personal tragedy as the eight-year-old Dauphin died a painful death from rickets.

In the end after a gap of nearly two centuries Louis was forced to call the Estates General in May 1789 and it proved just as unco-operative but with an added dimension. There were now representatives not just of the aristocracy or second estate and the clergy or first estate, the two groups which had caused most of the trouble so far, but also from the middle class or third estate which had grown hugely over the previous centuries and on the basis of its size now demanded a greater say than the other two. Necker who was by this time back in office agreed to this and thus at a stroke nullified the aristocratic obstruction which had bedevilled affairs for so long. However, the great problem for Louis was that he had failed to appoint chief ministers who had any experience of coordinating a credible government strategy let alone persuading an assembly of intelligent people that it was worthwhile. Certainly Louis himself was incapable of taking the lead personally and probably thought it was beneath his dignity anyway.

So the initiative was lost and the amorphous Third Estate – *Tiers Etat* – began to articulate its demands. Louis made other mistakes, as for instance letting the Third Estate be kept waiting outside for hours in the rain and sending in troops who gave the impression that he was planning a lock-out of the Third Estate which now transmogrified into the National Assembly and in response to the perceived threats swore the epoch-making Tennis Court Oath.

By this time it had turned into a three cornered struggle with the king, the first two estates and the third, intensified when the more liberal members of the first two moved over to join the third. Louis in this crisis was even less capable of taking a meaningful lead and still did not seem to grasp the direction in which events were moving. He was more concerned that his relations Orléans, Artois and Condé were plotting to replace him as king than that the monarchy itself needed to adapt or perish. When he once more dismissed the still quite popular Necker things rapidly got out of control. Orléans and others who had been aiming at a coup d'état rather than a revolution failed to realise the combustibility of the atmosphere in which they had begun to play with fire.

After the bad harvests of 1787-8 there was a scarcity of cheap food, prices had risen, many rural workers were unemployed and had wandered into the cities. This had been made worse by a glut in wine production, the spread of cattle disease, a trade recession and the pressure of high taxes due to the American war. It was in this atmosphere that sudden revulsion against authority began to spread rapidly down the social scale and soon there were unruly mobs on the streets. Some of them raided the royal armouries for weapons and stormed the Bastille. It had no great political significance and Louis in his own diary for 14 July wrote 'Nothing' but it turned out to be the turning point in the revolution. The sacking of Necker and rumours, perhaps half-true, of royal troops being mustered to put down the Third Estate had created a mood of desperation and hysteria.

Philippe of Orléans was still stirring up trouble and it is probable that it was he who inspired the raid that forced Louis to come back from Versailles to Paris as a virtual prisoner, but Louis's brother Provence and Condé fled abroad while the king's youngest brother Artois had been sent earlier as an ambassador to keep him out of harms way. Louis had been out hunting as usual when the Paris crowd stormed into Versailles. The National Assembly became the Constituent Assembly. Soon the red and blue colours of Paris were put either side of the white of Bourbon to create the *Tricolor*, a flag that also happened to bear a close resemblance to that of the Orléans branch of the Bourbons.

Louis was still king, a reluctant constitutional monarch, and could have survived as such, but it was perhaps too much of a change for him to manage and he was hampered by the fact that there were no ministers who combined the skills needed to manipulate the assembly and form a working relationship with the king. Neither he nor Marie Antoinette found it psychologically easy to adapt their styles to the change in standards. The final mistake that Louis made was either to leave it too late to escape or to try to escape so late in the day in 1791 that it was bound to look like an act of treachery.

Meanwhile Louis's position was made more difficult by the mass emigration of aristocrats and their threats to organise a counter-revolution, not so much for his benefit as their own. Their absence also triggered a further trade recession in luxury goods, the sugar islands rebelled, and Paris was swamped with inflammatory propaganda made more hysterical by the both real and imagined threats of foreign invasion. The king's cousin Louis Comte de Narbonne (1755-1813), an alleged bastard son of Louis XV who had joined the revolutionary government, saw the war as a means of restoring the king. Reluctantly Louis gave his blessing to war with Austria yet was still blamed for the defeats the army suffered in its early stages. Once the extremist *sans culottes* took over the monarchy was doomed. In August 1792 France was officially declared a republic and as fear of invasion intensified Louis was brought to trial in December. On 21 January 1793 he was executed and ten months later Marie Antoinette after enduring considerable brutality followed him to the guillotine in October. Their surviving son and heir Louis XVII, turned by his new guardians into a foul-mouthed street urchin, died of unknown causes in 1795.

Amongst the other members of the French Bourbons the number of executions was fairly modest. The king's sister went to the guillotine but his two brothers Artois and Provence both survived to become somewhat unsatisfactory kings after the fall of Napoleon. His cousin Philippe of Orléans who had contributed so much to the start of the revolution because he hoped to win the crown for himself was even rumoured to have dressed up as a woman to add muscle to one of the female street demonstrations. He had famously voted at the Assembly for his cousin the king's death yet was nevertheless himself shortly arrested along with two of his sons and Conti, then sent to the guillotine. He left a son who nearly four decades later at last won the crown of France for this trouble-making branch of the family.

Three generations of the Condé Bourbons had emigrated and joined in the invasions which tried to put down the revolution, playing such a large part that their force was known as Condé's Army. The grandfather Louis Joseph (1736-1818) who had done well in the Seven Years War, particularly at Johannesburg, had led his own army, paid for partly by the British, against the revolution till 1797, then did time with the Russian Army in Poland in 1800 and served in Bavaria before a period of exile in England. He survived to recover all his wealth after the restoration and die in his bed. His son Louis Henri VI (1781-1830) fought with him in the 1790s but then for a time led his own army, but was to die in very controversial circumstances in 1830 (see p.120) while his grandson Louis Antoine Henri de Bourbon Condé, Duc d'Enghien (1772-1804) became the scapegoat for Napoleon's fury at the attempted plot to murder him by Cadoudal. He was almost certainly innocent but Napoleon sent his dragoons over the German border to Ettenheim, kidnapped him and had him shot in March 1804. Tolstoy's version of the story in *War and Peace* was that Napoleon and Enghien shared the same mistress, both met accidentally in her house, Napoleon had a fainting fit, Enghien did not use the opportunity to kill Napoleon and Napoleon wanted to make sure that the story never leaked out. It is not too plausible. What is certain is that Napoleon used the panic caused by Cadoudal to have himself declared emperor instead of just Consul for Life and that the judicial murder of Enghien sent shock waves through Europe, particularly to Russia. It thus was at least partly responsible for Russia abandoning its alliance with France and for the first period of war between the two countries, which ultimately led to the retreat from Moscow in 1812.

In retrospect it would have taken a man of much greater ability than Louis or any of his brothers and cousins to avoid some radical change in France after 1789. The primitive finances of the state and the intransigent attitude of the richest subjects towards paying any tax had made some kind of change inevitable. Yet if he had been more adaptable and energetic Louis XVI could certainly have survived as a constitutional monarch. It was his tendency to vacillate and procrastinate, to avoid facing up to difficult problems that thrust the revolution down a more radical route than any of the first rebels had envisaged. That in turn led to his own and his wife's execution, to the Terror, to the rise of Napoleon and therefore to the deaths of several million people.

7

SPAIN:
THE SPANISH BOURBONS 1700-1808

'The story assumes the character of a historical tragedy.' Gwyn Williams in
Hargreaves-Mawdsley's *Spain under the Bourbons*

FELIPE V

'Be a good Spaniard: that is now your first duty.' Parting advice of Louis
XIV to his grandson Philippe
'… an efficiency in administration previously unknown.' Hargreaves-
Mawdsley, *Spain under the Bourbons*

Philippe Duc d'Anjou (1683-1746) was the second grandson of Louis XIV and
therefore deliberately educated to be non-assertive, self-indulgent and unambitious
so that he would not be a threat to his elder brother. On that basis his education was
quite successful but it turned out that at the age of seventeen he was unexpectedly
summoned to take over as king of Spain, so a different training régime would
have been more helpful. For a young man of his age and sheltered upbringing it
was a traumatic shock to move suddenly to a strange foreign city, whose people
he could not understand. Even though his predecessor the childless Carlos II, the
last of the Habsburg dynasty in Spain, had been mentally subnormal it was still
hard for the newcomer, now known as Felipe V, to make an impression.

Carlos had unexpectedly lived till he was thirty-nine, sadly handicapped
as a result probably of years of Habsburg in-breeding and some Bourbon
in-breeding too. He had been the only legitimate son of Felipe IV who had
left at least thirty healthier royal bastards. Unsurprisingly Carlos had failed
to make either his Bourbon queen or her successor pregnant. His assertive
mother had led a chaotic regency so that the economy was in a poor state, the
army's wages were often unpaid. The French were allowed to annex Flanders,
Captain Morgan got away with storming Panama. Generally Spain's prestige
was low and the Spanish Habsburg's dynasty increasingly unpopular.

In this situation Louis XIV had spent years trying to manipulate the Spanish
crown into the clutches of the Bourbons using the claims of both his Habsburg
wife and his Habsburg mother. Aware of the fact that other European leaders
would not tolerate a single king ruling both the Spanish and French empires

1. The three remaining towers of the fortress at Bourbon l'Archambault.

2. *(left)* The ruins of the Bourbon château at Lavardin.

3. *(right)* The cathedral at Moulins.

4. Charles, Duke of Bourbon who died capturing Rome in 1527.

5. The entry of Henri IV to Paris.

6. Louis XIII crowned by Victory after the capture of la Rochelle.

7. Louis XIV.

8. A bust of Louis de Bourbon, the Great Condé.

9. The execution of Louis XVI in 1793.

10. King Felipe V of Spain.

11. King Carlo IV of Naples who became Carlos III of Spain.

12. *(left)* King Fernando IV of Spain.

13. *(above)* King Alfonso XIII of Spain.

14. The Notorious Queen Isabella.

15. King Ferdinando I of the Two Sicilies.

16. Louis Philippe at the barricades.

17. Pau, the birthplace of Henri IV.

18. The palace of Versailles.

19. The Palacio Real at Aranjuez south of Madrid.

20. The façade of Caserta, the Bourbon palace north of Naples.

at the same time he had been willing to let the Spanish one be chopped up so there had been a series of compromise agreements, culminating in 1699 when it was agreed to let a Bavarian succeed as king of Spain. But the Bavarian died, the French ambassador was unexpectedly successful in persuading the dying Carlos to leave a will favouring France. The Austrian Habsburgs were less popular and less competent, the Pope backed France and to his astonishment when Carlos at last died in 1700 Louis was offered an all or nothing deal for his grandson to take over the Spanish empire. If he refused it would go to Austria and he would be encircled, so he had no choice but to accept, though he knew it would mean war.

Thus at the age of seventeen Philippe was packed off to Spain. He was accompanied to his new kingdom by a large staff of French civil servants, for though Louis XIV had accepted international pressure which said that no one man could be king of both the Spanish and French empires at the same time he had managed to keep them both in the family and had every intention of making sure that the Spanish kingdom would be centralised and modernised in the same way as France. Thus Philippe/Felipe V moved from being El Rey Animoso to Un Rey ilegitimo and un Rey Frances as the Spanish grandees like their French counterparts found absolutism hard to take.

Felipe, was genetically 25 per cent Spanish, 50 per cent German and 12.5 per cent French with the usual mixture of dynasties, especially Bourbon and Habsburg. Warned on leaving France to watch out for poison plots he soon became paranoid and later suffered from long bouts of clinical depression that perhaps went back to his Spanish ancestress Juana the Mad. Like his father the Dauphin he was lethargic, non-talkative, easily bored, obsessed with hunting, fair-haired and timid.

Meanwhile he was given a warm welcome in Madrid and settled into the Bon Retiro Palace, but not for long as the Austrians invaded Northern Italy. Felipe was told by his still manipulative grandfather, Louis XIV, to take an army to defend his sub-kingdom of Naples in 1701, but found it depressing and shot birds from the palace windows. The following year the British destroyed his treasure fleet in Vigo Bay. In 1705 along with his cousin the Duke of Berwick he invaded Portugal but failed to hold it, then lost Gibraltar and the Battle of Malaga while his Austrian rival Archduke Charles (Carlos III) established himself in Catalonia. Things were so bad that Felipe had to abandon his capital and suggested moving to America. Luckily for him, however, his own Castilian subjects hated his Aragonese subjects so much that they helped to restore him and Berwick recaptured Madrid in October 1706. Felipe had meanwhile married Maria Luisa of Savoy (half a Bourbon) who encouraged him to fight on and added to his popularity by providing a male heir, Luis in 1707. She and her lady-in-waiting the Princess of Ursins, effectively an agent of Louis XIV, now managed affairs between them and Berwick with the French Army won a good victory against the Austrians at Almansa. The only problem was that Felipe became convinced, perhaps justifiably, that his cousin Philippe Duc d'Orléans, the French commander in Spain was plotting to replace him.

Then things took another downward turn. Louis XIV's armies were doing badly against Marlborough in the north and the Austrians once more forced Felipe to abandon Madrid. His grandfather who was near to despair told him to abdicate but Felipe had a stubborn streak and refused. As a last resort Louis sent his hated cousin the Duc de Vendôme who took over the army and saved Spain for the Bourbons with a victory at Brihuega. Soon afterwards the Austrian would-be Carlos III withdrew because his brother's death had led to him becoming the emperor and he no longer had ambitions in Spain.

As a result of the War of Spanish Succession, Spain lost Gibraltar and Minorca to the British, the Spanish Netherlands and Naples to Austria and Sicily to the House of Savoy, but with difficulty kept the rest of its huge empire. In 1713 Felipe was at last able to take the initiative with an attack on the Catalans who were forced to accept his rule, many of those who resisted being sold as slaves, so most of the old divisions of the Spanish kingdom were got rid of, administration was centralised on French lines and the finances reformed.

Felipe turned into a rather weak-minded manic depressive, with a penchant for religion and slightly offbeat sex. When his first wife died he was so crazed that he wanted to marry the geriatric Princess Ursin, forty years his senior. Instead he was persuaded to take as his second wife Elizabeth (translated Isabella in Spanish) Farnese the heiress of Parma who came to dominate his life by withholding her sexual favours whenever she wanted a change of policy. She brought in her henchman Alberoni and set about a programme of rearmament and further reform designed to recover Spain's Italian possessions as a potential inheritance for her children. This aggression led to a Spanish invasion of Sicily which was thwarted by the British fleet at Passaro in 1718. In retaliation Alberoni organised an invasion of Britain which in the end turned out just to be the landing of a small Spanish force in north-west Scotland that failed to help the cause of the Old Pretender.

The French under the regent Orléans were angered by this intransigence and sent an army under Berwick to invade Spain. Felipe who had had a severe breakdown in 1717 carried on hunting at El Pardo but was growing increasingly eccentric. Now in his late thirties, slightly hunchbacked, drinking too much, eating erratically he had to be constantly watched by Isabella. She busied him with building the new palace of San Ildefonso at Granja near Segovia. It was the Spanish Versailles with twenty-six fountains. Yet in 1724 when he was forty-one Felipe suddenly abdicated in favour of his son Luis. It was a mixture of guilt, religious vocation and neurosis.

The new King Luis was sixteen, tall, thin, good at sports but intellectually timid and poorly educated. His wife Elizabeth de Montpensier was a French Bourbon aged fourteen, a daughter of the Regent Orléans with a liking for enormous feasts, doing her own laundry and nude frolics with her chamber maids which offended Luis. However, within a year Luis died of smallpox and his queen returned to France where she died of dropsy nearly two decades later.

Since the king's younger brother Fernando was only ten Felipe V had little choice but to resume his reign, his reluctance overcome by the ever-manipulative Queen Isabella. However, he was far from well and Isabella decided to move the court to Seville for five years so that fewer people would be aware of his oddities. These included a refusal to cut his nails, to get out of bed or to wear new clothes, even the assertion that he believed he was a frog. He started renewing his wish to abdicate and Isabella had to keep so close an eye on him that she had a double privy built for them. However, he had a habit of reviving if there was the stimulus of a new challenge and in 1729 there was for a while a renewal of the dream that he could be king of France as well as Spain. He was also keen on the rebuilding of the Madrid Alcazar as the Oriente Palace, the new palace at Aranjuez and the Madrid Opera.

Isabella, meanwhile, realising that her stepson Fernando would soon inherit Spain was desperate to find royal careers for her own two sons. In 1731 the first of Felipe's children with Isabella, the Infante Carlos, was sent with an army to invade her old home, the Duchy of Parma, where he was ensconced as heir. A Spanish force also recaptured Oran in Morocco, and three years later a larger army went to drive out the Austrians and install Carlos as King in Naples. A similar effort to get Isabella's younger son, the dandyish Don Felipe, fixed up in Parma failed but was to be resumed after the old king's death.

Meanwhile Spain had become embroiled in war with Britain again in 1739 over the maltreatment of British rogue traders like Captain Jenkins. Isabella had been so desperate for money to support the ambitions of her two sons in Italy that Spanish coast guards had been encouraged to act with unexpected severity against British ships even vaguely suspected of illicit trading. Spain suffered the humiliating capture of Portobello by the British and several other losses but eventually staggered through this war without any major disaster.

Felipe V was over sixty when he died of apoplexy in 1746. Despite his flaws he left Spain much more unified and more efficiently governed than it had been under the later Habsburgs. New roads had been built. Ports like Seville had lost their damaging trade monopolies in America, so there had been an overall expansion in the economy.

FERNANDO VI

'... remembered as a man who could see nothing beyond his obese wife and had only one virtue, he loved peace.' Hargreaves-Mawdsley, *Spain under the Bourbons*

Fernando (1714-59), the second surviving son of Felipe and his first half-Bourbon wife succeeded to the throne of Spain in 1746 at the age of thirty-two. Brought up by an increasingly unstable father and a voraciously ambitious stepmother who largely ignored him, he would have had a struggle whatever his temperament.

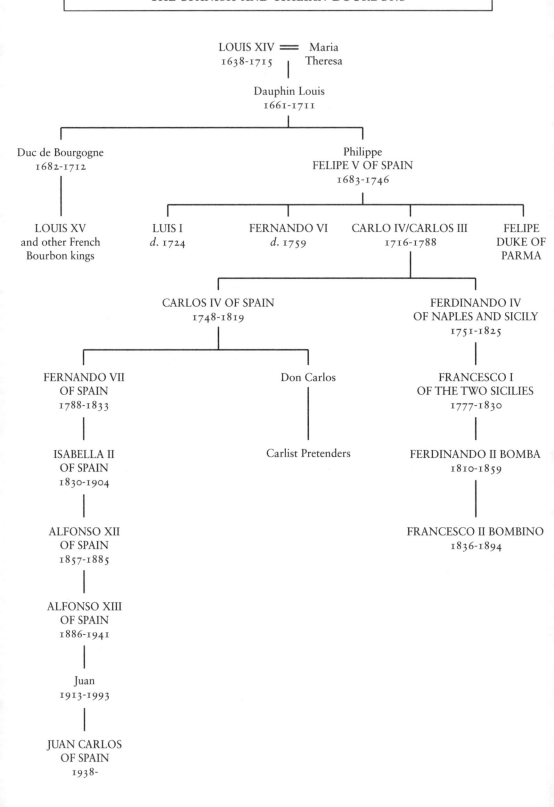

THE SPANISH AND ITALIAN BOURBONS

LOUIS XIV ═══ Maria Theresa
1638-1715

Dauphin Louis
1661-1711

Duc de Bourgogne
1682-1712

Philippe
FELIPE V OF SPAIN
1683-1746

LOUIS XV
and other French
Bourbon kings

LUIS I
d. 1724

FERNANDO VI
d. 1759

CARLO IV/CARLOS III
1716-1788

FELIPE
DUKE OF
PARMA

CARLOS IV OF SPAIN
1748-1819

FERDINANDO IV
OF NAPLES AND SICILY
1751-1825

FERNANDO VII
OF SPAIN
1788-1833

Don Carlos

FRANCESCO I
OF THE TWO SICILIES
1777-1830

ISABELLA II
OF SPAIN
1830-1904

Carlist Pretenders

FERDINANDO II BOMBA
1810-1859

ALFONSO XII
OF SPAIN
1857-1885

ALFONSO XIII
OF SPAIN
1886-1941

FRANCESCO II BOMBINO
1836-1894

Juan
1913-1993

JUAN CARLOS
OF SPAIN
1938-

It is uncertain when he first began to show signs of similar neurosis, but for the time being he appeared kindly, not very intelligent but anxious to do the right thing. Married by arrangement to Barbara Braganza of Portugal he and his new wife were 'bound together by mutual ugliness' (Bergamini) and never showed any signs of producing an heir. Like nearly all Bourbons in all three of their kingdoms he was obsessed with hunting, but also adored musical evenings on their miniature fleet sailing on the ornamental lake at Aranjuez – the court musician was Domenico Scarlatti.

Meanwhile his chief minister Zenon Ensenada continued the work of restoring the Spanish economy. The bullion trade from America was tidied up and the surplus used to pay for famine relief, build roads and enable the abolition of tax-farming. The public burning of heretics (there had been 728 *auto da fes* under Felipe V) was brought to an end, astronomy, botany and other sciences were greatly encouraged.

Fernando was totally opposed to war and kept out of the Seven Years War. However, by peaceful means his younger half-brother, the dashing Don Felipe was at last established in Parma as its prince so that the Bourbons now had four independent monarchies. In 1748 Felipe was also put up as potential King of Poland, as had several previous Bourbons, but to no avail.

Then Queen Barbara died and Fernando went completely to pieces. He retired to the monastery in Villaviciosa, attempted suicide and willed himself to death smothered in his own excrement. He and his wife were both buried in the convent of Las Salsas Reales which they had founded in Madrid – now the law courts.

CARLOS III

'He never touched another woman after his wife's death' Harold Acton

Carlos III (1716-88) the elder son of Felipe V and Isabella Farnese had already been a king in Naples (see p.108) for more than two decades when he had the summons to return to Spain so it was nearly thirty years since he had last seen his mother. He was now in his early forties, a mature and confident ruler whose reign in Naples and Sicily had been remarkably successful (see p.108). He had inherited the big pointed nose of a Habsburg and the slightly drooping mouth but was also very much a Bourbon, a great-grandson of Louis XIV. Like him he was a passionate hunter, an early riser and a hard worker, unlike him he never strayed from the marriage bed.

It was clearly a wrench for Carlo IV of Naples to turn himself into Carlos III of Spain, but Spain was a much bigger kingdom, duty called and he could at least now speak both languages. He had to leave behind two of his sons: the eldest Felipe was mentally retarded, perhaps the same genetic link with his grandfather Felipe and his uncle Fernando, and had to be locked up by his minders in Naples though he occasionally ran amok with the servant girls. The third son Ferdinando was also left behind as the new king of Naples (see p.110). His second son Carlo had to go with him as the new heir to the kingdom of Spain. His German wife Maria Amalia also came, though somewhat reluctantly. She did not like the climate in Madrid, died soon after the move and left him disconsolate, though he never tried to replace her but paced the corridors of the palaces at night to try to dismiss sensual longings.

In terms of the domestic achievement King Carlos through his ministers continued the work of enlightened improvements organised by his half-brother. Canal and road building helped the infrastructure. Customs barriers were used to help the Catalan cotton industry so that it nearly caught up with the British. Other trade restrictions were removed and trade with the Americas rose fivefold. The new Banco de San Carlos gave Spain a sound credit system which France still lacked. The Jesuits were expelled and an attempt was made to reduce the vast number of the clergy – Spain had 200,000 monks and nuns to serve a population of 10 million.

In 1760 some of Charles's modernisation plans went too far for the conservative population of Madrid who disapproved of his new streetlights and an order that they should abandon their traditional big hats and cloaks which were used to conceal weapons. The unrest was aggravated by inflation due to the extra gold coming from America and bad harvests. The rising was put down and Carlos temporised, but wisely left the capital for Aranjuez until things calmed down. It was foretaste of revolution, and he deflected it by not over-reacting. Subsequently he much improved Madrid by giving it a police force, creating boulevards like the Paseo al Prado, building the Prado itself as a centre for botanical research and other major new buildings.

In foreign affairs Carlos had more mixed success. He was more belligerent than his half-brother and more belligerent than he had been himself during his rule at Naples. Particularly he had a prejudice against the British for their threat to bombard Naples back in 1749 which he never forgave. So he rashly went to war with them in 1762, losing Havana and a large fleet to the Royal Navy, then also Manila in the Philippines. He invaded Portugal without achieving much and in the end lost Florida temporarily and gained Louisiana which was a dubious benefit.

Similarly he had to back down in a confrontation with the British in 1770 when his governor in Buenos Aires rashly evicted British whalers from the Falkland Islands.

His war effort in 1778 was more successful for the British were severely weakened by the American revolution and he made sure that Portugal was on his side before the new war started. Together with his French allies he threatened the invasion of Britain. That was prevented by the Royal Navy but he captured Mobile in 1780 and as a result of the war regained Florida and Minorca for Spain.

At this point the Spanish empire was at its geographical peak but already beginning to show signs of weakness. In 1781 there was the first *communeros* revolt in New Granada and in 1783 there was a rebellion by Inca descendants in Peru. In some ways the liberal reforms of Carlos, such as expelling the Jesuits from the American colonies, were potentially disastrous, as religion was one of the few genuine building blocks of loyalty that bound New Spain to Old. More constructive was his colonisation of California which was threatened by Russian encroachments and where he organised a chain of twenty-one forts, the Camino Real and a number of mission stations including the first settlements of Los Angeles and San Francisco.

When he died in 1788 Carlos had been a widower for twenty-eight years. Of all the so-called enlightened monarchs of the century he was the one most people regard as being the least hypocritical.

CARLOS IV

'Curse the day
When first Spain's queen beheld the black-eyed boy
And gore-faced treason sprang from her
Adulterate joy.'
George, Lord Byron *Childe Harold*

The extent to which Carlos IV (1748-1819) was made a fool of by his wife Maria Luisa may have been exaggerated by the propaganda of the day and Lord Byron, but even his father pointed it out to him, so it is probable that at least for a period the king was cuckolded by his queen and that, and his grotesque portraits by Goya, are the aspects of his life for which he is most remembered.

Born in Naples when his father was still king there he had come to Spain with him when he was eleven. Genetically he was half-German through his Saxon mother and quarter-Italian from his Farnese grandmother. Mentally sluggish but compensating with a big show of piety he was tall, inclined to fat, rather timid but at least physically energetic, ruddy-complexioned and fit. As a boy he enjoyed wrestling and was good at it. He outdid even some of the keenest hunters in his dynasty by regularly spending six hours a day in the saddle. For company he preferred gossip with the court servants to competing with his aristocratic peers and his other hobby was to play his violin in the palace quartet.

In 1765 Carlos had married his Bourbon first cousin Maria Luisa (1751-1819) daughter of Felipe the Duke of Parma so the habit of near-incestuous inbreeding was to continue, for he was himself on his mother's side a first cousin of Louis XVI of France. Whether Maria Luisa was a nymphomaniac, just a manipulative flirt or something in between it is hard to tell. Certainly she found life in the Madrid court boring and sadly for her rather rapidly lost the good looks which she so treasured. She continued well into middle age dressing like a much younger woman. Several of her male friends were sent packing by Carlos III, her father-in-law, who warned his over-tolerant son to keep more of an eye on her but to no avail. The fact that she bore fourteen children in two decades and that half of them failed to survive to adulthood indicates that her life was far from easy.

The longest and most politically serious of her alleged (probably correctly) affairs began in 1785 when in her mid-thirties she met the eighteen-year-old guards officer Manuel Godoy. This unlikely pair, along with her injured husband, became an amazingly inseparable trio for the next three decades. Three years later Carlos III died and Carlos IV, already into his forties, took over as king with Godoy already ensconced as his closest adviser. He was rapidly promoted up the ranks and by 1792 to the disgust of many was chief minister. Both Godoy and the Queen had other lovers by this time, but he could if necessary use the threat of exposure to blackmail her into acquiescence. So their relationship survived numerous crises – he allegedly once slapped her on the face and she covered up the incident rather than make a fuss. Certainly Godoy was no mere gigolo for he worked hard, but equally he was no more than a second-rate statesman and was responsible for many of the failures that were to mark the reign of Carlos IV. The royal couple and Godoy came to be known as the Holy Trinity and the rapid promotion of the young guardsman caused huge offence amongst the Spanish grandees.

Luckily we have a revealing artistic impression of this strange ménage because from 1775 Francisco Goya (1746-1828) was working in the royal tapestry factory on the decoration for the El Pardo Palace. By 1789 he had become chief court painter and has left remarkably honest portraits of all the family.

It is not surprising that the seven surviving children of this extraordinary marriage – and some were alleged to have been fathered by Godoy rather than the king – should turn out devious if not seriously eccentric. The hypocrisy and sadistic tendencies of Fernando, heir to the kingdom will be dealt with later as will the dangerous machinations of his brother Don Carlos who was to be responsible for three civil wars. Carlotta, their sister, became queen of Portugal and as promiscuous as her mother despite being crippled due to a hunting accident and another sister Mari Josefa was also disabled.

In 1788 soon after Carlos became king there were food shortages in Barcelona that caused riots, which might well have been a warning of things to come. At the same time Spain's armed forces were too weak to manage any response when there was a row with the British over the Nootka Sound off British Colombia. Three years later Carlos interrupted his hunting for long enough to sack the chief minister Floridablanca and Godoy soon afterwards replaced him with the challenging brief to save the king's cousin Louis XVI from the Paris mob. The task was impossible but Godoy's promotion created scandal and his uncouth diplomacy resulted in France declaring war on Spain two month's after Louis was guillotined.

The Spanish army invaded France but was soon pushed back and a French army retaliated by invading Catalonia early in 1794. The Spanish objective now was to save the life of the Dauphin but he died the next year, the war went badly and Spain changed sides, joining the French against their old enemy the British. The price of this change was handing over the Spanish half of San Domingo to the French. Godoy was named Prince of Peace and given huge financial rewards. Yet the new war, this time against the British, was almost as disastrous as the previous one, for Nelson won the battle of St Vincent in 1797 and Spain lost another valuable colony, Trinidad, to the British. Godoy was reluctantly sacked by Carlos but was soon back in office in 1799.

Napoleon had by this time taken power in France and the next ten years were to see a battle of wits between him and the Spanish Bourbons, which with Godoy as chief adviser they were unlikely to win. With a mixture of gifts and threats Napoleon wooed them to do as he wanted. To please Napoleon Spain invaded Portugal, despite its queen being Carlos's daughter, and handed Louisiana back to France, in return for France allowing an increase in the size of Bourbon Parma so that its duke became King of Etruria and Carlos's daughter Maria Luisa its queen – two of his other daughters became queens, one of Portugal the other of the Two Sicilies. So this naive arrangement resulted in the Bourbons briefly winning their fourth crown though they had just lost their first and were shortly about to lose the second and third.

The next price Spain had to pay for supporting Napoleon was the loss of eleven out of its fleet of fifteen battleships defeated alongside the French by Nelson at Trafalgar. This meant the virtual end of Spain as a naval power and signalled to the South American colonies that they could no longer be protected by a Spanish fleet nor need they fear Spanish reprisals if they wanted independence. The following year Venezuela staged its first rebellion and the British captured Montevideo. The Spanish Empire was about to disintegrate.

The most significant of the Spanish grandees to be annoyed by the promotion of Godoy was the King's eldest son, the unpredictable Fernando (1788-1833). Excusably he could not understand his parents' joint infatuation with the incompetent minister and deeply resented their failure to consult him on major matters. He offended the Holy Trinity by refusing to take Godoy's daughter as his second wife – his first, Maria Antonetta from the Naples Bourbons, had just died. In the end Fernando was to have three more wives; the first three marriages produced no surviving children, the last gave him two daughters and of his four wives two were first cousins. The coincidence of three of his wives dying prematurely was eventually to arouse suspicions that he had deliberately engineered their fate.

Meanwhile Fernando, who was now twenty-three, was so frustrated with his situation that he even sought the help of Napoleon and clearly already had in mind the idea of usurping his father's throne. Though deep down he was as reactionary as any of the family, he liked to play the liberal and had an increasing following amongst those disgusted Spaniards who were distressed by the flagrant immorality of Godoy and his lack of military success. Unluckily for him Godoy's spies found a copy of a letter written by him to Napoleon so he was arrested for treason. He was acquitted and emerged from his trial even more of a hero than he had been before.

Napoleon had by this time expelled the Bourbon dynasty from Naples and now made up his mind to deprive 'this family of cretins' of their last remaining crown. He sent an army under Murat to threaten Madrid. Carlos and the queen contemplated escaping to South America but Fernando rallied opinion to prevent them. He orchestrated a military coup during which Godoy hid sweating under a pile of rugs for two days. Carlos abdicated in Fernando's favour, then retracted his abdication, appealing to Napoleon. Fernando continued to strut his stuff as king and the triangular battle of wits continued with Carlos and his wife in one corner, their hated son in the second and Napoleon in the third. Murat meanwhile took control of Madrid, so it was an almost bloodless conquest.

Napoleon now invited the entire Spanish royal family to a conference over the French border in Bayonne. Extraordinarily all of them took their coaches into the trap. Napoleon commented that Carlos was a 'nice man' and Fernando 'very stupid'. All of them were made prisoners and Napoleon wrote to each of his brothers in turn asking them to take over as king of Spain. In the end Joseph reluctantly accepted. Fernando who had heard how his cousin the Duc d'Enghien had been made to face a firing squad was easily persuaded to abdicate his claims.

Extraordinarily the people of Madrid strongly resented the virtual kidnapping of their ineffective royal family, particularly the still popular Fernando. On 2 May 1808 – *Dos de Mayo* – there was a popular rising in the city by both men and women which was brilliantly portrayed by Goya, especially in his well-known painting of a firing squad *Tres de Mayo*. There were several hundred casualties. As news arrived that Carlos and Fernando had both signed Spain over to the French the rebellion spread to other cities like Valencia, Cartagena and Cadiz. Joseph Buonaparte, Jose I el Re Intruso, was not welcome. But by 1809 the French had driven the British troops out of Spain at Corunna, had brutally sacked Burgos to set an example and for the time being had extinguished all opposition. King Jose started to introduce reforms which could have been popular such as the abolition of the Inquisition, but Napoleon interfered too much and Spanish resentment was soon to be rekindled into a massive revolt.

Carlos IV and his wife spent the first period of their exile with Godoy and his entourage in Compiègne, then moved to the Bourbon château of Chambord, then to Marseilles and finally to the Barberini Palace in Rome. Maria Luisa died in 1819 followed very shortly by Carlos. Fernando lived in comfort for five years at Valençay, noticeably making no effort to escape or to help the brave Spanish resistance movement until he was quite sure that Napoleon had fallen from power. Then he was summoned back to Spain and at last emerged from the safety of Valençay. Godoy lasted till 1851 when he died in Paris in his mid-eighties.

8

ITALY: NAPLES AND SICILY UNDER THE BOURBONS 1733-1805

CARLO IV

'One of the best kings in Europe... ' Harold Acton, *The Bourbons of Naples*

Don Carlos (1716-88), a great-grandson of Louis XIV, was born in Madrid the son of Felipe V of Spain and his second wife Isabella Farnese, so since Felipe already had two sons by his first marriage there seemed no likelihood of him succeeding to the Spanish throne. However, his ambitious mother was determined that he should be a king somewhere and in 1731 took advantage of her Parmesan connections and some British help to make sure that at the age of fifteen this rather unattractive, slightly hunch-backed boy should at least inherit her family's Parma dukedom and become the potential Grand Duke of Tuscany. A Spanish force under Montemar beat the local Austrians at Britanto and Parma was his. So he left Spain and never saw his father again nor his mother for the next twenty-eight years.

His sole passion at this age was hunting and when he moved into the Pitti Palace in Florence he took to shooting the birds in the tapestries. Two years later his mother nagged her pliable husband Felipe to become involved in another war with the Austrians and 30,000 troops were sent to conquer Naples, a former Spanish Habsburg possession, which had been lost in 1713 to their Austrian Habsburg cousins. The Austrians were not popular in Naples as their régime had been both greedy and incompetent, so the Neapolitans were glad enough to see the return of the Spaniards. Don Carlos, at least in theory at the head of his troops, had a relatively easy victory and was welcomed by his new subjects. At the siege of Gaeta he met young Bonnie Prince Charlie for whom it was his first experience of war and a misleading one at that which gave him unwise ideas of how easy conquest could be. Thus the Bourbons acquired their third Kingdom when Don Carlos was crowned in Palermo as Carlo IV of Naples and Sicily. The price of recognition was that Spain and Isabella Farnese had to concede any claim to Parma and the duchy of Tuscany which went for the time being to the Habsburg empress's husband.

Carlo turned out to be one of the most efficient and sensible European kings of his day during the twenty-four years of his reign. For the first decade he was very much under the postal management of his father and mother who dictated policy and supplied the troops when necessary. Even when Felipe died in 1746 Isabel still tried to be manipulative. Carlo had lost his French Bourbon fiancée in a tit-for-tat exchange – the French Regent had sent back Louis XV's child fiancée because he needed an heir in a hurry so eventually at the age of twenty-two he married the fourteen-year-old Maria Amalia of Saxony, an unattractive girl to most but not to Carlo who promptly fell in love with her, thereafter never looking at another woman. It was a period of fountains running with wine, mock sieges, make-believe castles and galas.

Despite his lack of interest in music Carlo had rapidly rebuilt the San Carlo Opera house, famous for its composers and castrato singers. In Naples he built a library and the National Museum to house the great Farnese art collection. He built new royal palaces at Portici, Caserta and Capodimonte, all three of them unhygienic but ideal for hunting trips. He used spare galley slaves to do some of the work and began excavations at the buried Roman city of Herculaneum, later also in 1748 for the first time uncovering the long lost city of Pompeii. Of his new palaces Caserta in particular was modelled on Versailles and required a twenty-five mile aqueduct to feed its fountains.

King Carlo began his working day at 5am but finished around 8 after which his main activity was hunting and he left the detail to his able long-term minister, Tanucci. He had an underlying worry provoked by the eccentric, if not abnormal, behaviour of his father and of his unstable half-brothers Luis, who died in 1724, and the suicidal Fernando who became King of Spain in 1746. So he became convinced that plenty of exercise would ward off any inherited mental problems. In later life it became more obvious that he was prone to depression.

Despite his building projects he managed to keep taxation lower than it had been under the Austrians and Naples boomed, its population rising to 300,000. Capodimonte was developed by his German wife as a china factory like the one in her native Meissen. There he ran a campaign to discourage gambling, built an *Albergo* for the poor and was within his limits a relatively benevolent monarch, a policy designed to prove that monarchies in Italy did better than republics. Unusually amongst kings of that century he had a real aversion to war and unlike most of them did not even like wearing military uniforms. He did, however, acquire a lasting dislike of the British when one of their admirals threatened to bombard Naples. The one notable military event was an Austrian attack in 1745. After what Acton calls 'an unusually tedious war' there came a six-week confrontation at Velletri, notable for the number of Irish mercenaries fighting on both sides. When the Austrians eventually tried a surprise attack Charles was caught in bed, but he soon showed courage and leadership, his troops rallied and achieved a useful victory. In Rome he was hailed as a liberator, was embraced by Pope Benedict XIV and took the opportunity to ask for a reduction in the large number of religious holidays in Naples as they were a severe impediment to productivity.

The one problem was that his eldest son Felipe was mentally retarded and incapable of taking over. Then suddenly in 1759 Carlo's half-brother King Fernando of Spain died leaving no children, so Carlo was summoned back to take over as Carlos III of Spain where he spent the last twenty-nine years of his life with almost equal distinction. He had to take his second son Carlo with him as his potential heir in Spain but his third son Ferdinando (1751-1816) was left behind at the age of eight as the new King of the Two Sicilies. He took with him his queen, Maria Amalia, but sadly she was to die at the age of thirty-six within a year of her move to Madrid and he never remarried. Their retarded (in most respects other than his huge appetite for the opposite sex) eldest son Felipe was to live another seventeen years.

Meanwhile Carlo's younger brother Don Felipe had had to wait much longer for his inheritance. After the end of the War of Austrian Succession in 1748 Parma was handed back to the Farnese dynasty by the Habsburgs and Don Felipe took over as Duke, thus founding the house of Borbone-Parma which held the duchy on and off till 1860. Under Felipe's rule his leading minister Guillaume de Tillot tried to turn Parma into an enlightened court, a 'miniature Paris of philosphers' as Condillac put it, with a magnificent library and expanded university, but he was always short of cash to pay for the new dynasty's expensive weddings and disproportionately large army. However, he did reform taxation by getting rid of the French tax farmers, and he tried to stop the drain of cash out to the Vatican.

Felipe ruled Parma till his death in 1765 though he was dependent on subsidies and military support from Spain. So its claims to genuine sovereignty are open to doubt, though they were sufficient to justify a number of further inter-dynastic marriages with the three main Bourbon lines and also their cousins the Habsburgs, so the inbreeding intensified. Felipe himself married Louise Elizabeth de Bourbon and their mathematically gifted daughter Isabella became the wife of the Holy Roman Emperor Joseph II. Felipe's son Ferdinando (1751-1802) took over as the second Bourbon duke in 1765 (see below) His daughter Maria Luisa became the scandal-ridden wife of Carlos IV of Spain (see p.103).

FERDINANDO IV 1751-1816

'This rascally court of Naples.' Queen Maria Luisa of Spain.

Ferdinando (1751-1835), the third son of King Carlo and his German wife was left a lonely little boy-king aged eight, never to see his mother again. At least Tanucci was there to manage affairs during the minority and for some time afterwards. When he came of age in 1767 he was neither good-looking nor particularly fit, was addicted to gambling, loved, like so many princes with German blood, to drill his own pet régiment of soldiers, yet was so afraid of the dark that he insisted on attendants being present even when indulging in prolonged bowel movements. Beckford put it kindly that 'he had the boldness to prolong his childhood.' The circumstances were, however, far from promising for there had been acute food shortages and plague, which had cost 30,000 deaths in Naples alone.

Ferdinando became engaged to one of the Empress Maria Theresa's daughters and when she died of smallpox he was given her sister Maria Carolina, also a sister of the French Queen Marie Antoinette and of the Emperor Joseph II. Ferdinando was therefore tied very much to the Austrian cause in Italy and against their only Italian rivals the House of Savoy and Piedmont. The couple's first child in 1772 was a daughter but in 1775 Maria Carolina produced a son Francesco who became his heir. One of their daughters was later to marry the last Holy Roman Emperor Francis and therefore to be empress and the mother of Napoleon's second wife Marie Louise.

The history of Naples was for this period fairly uneventful. The Jesuits were expelled just as they were from Spain. Smallpox inoculation was introduced despite Church objections. Otherwise there was none of the drive for improvements that had been undertaken in the previous reign. Mercifully there was also peace for the first decades of the reign, for Naples was really too small a kingdom to act on its own. The worst catastrophe was the Messina earthquake of 1783 after which that city had to be virtually rebuilt.

Meanwhile Ferdinando became, in Acton's words, 'partial to country wenches' as well as hunting and as an excuse for his prolonged absences from his wife he had a new silk works built at his hunting lodge of San Leucio, the start of what was supposed to be the huge new Ferdinandopolis. It was an extraordinarily ambitious project perhaps partly provoked by the tragic death of his son Carlo in 1778 and was similar in scope and intention to David Dale's New Lanark begun in 1784. Its silk mills were still operational in the twenty-first century. He also built a new palace at Villa Reale and life in Naples continued, 'a mixture of magnificence and squalour' (Acton). Queen Maria Carolina not to be outdone, reminded people of her Viennese origins by her flirtatious behaviour, encouraged freemasonry, swore a lot and allegedly screamed like an eagle. Generally life at court was self-indulgent and promiscuous.

In some respects Naples at this time was more famous for three celebrity visitors than for its own inhabitants. The first was the Venetian adventurer Giacomo Casanova (1725-98) who exploited the gaming tables by cheating to make extra cash to compensate for his recent spell in prison. The second was Emma who arrived as mistress of the British ambassador Hamilton, then married him and became one of the leading lights of the city. The third was the British sailor Horatio Nelson for whom Naples became a regular anchorage with Emma as one of its special attractions.

In 1793 everything started to go wrong for Ferdinando and Maria Carolina. First came the devastating news of her sister Marie Antoinette's execution in Paris, which was perhaps more of a shock than that of Ferdinando's distant cousin Louis XVI. The next year there was an attempted revolution in Naples as French ideas spread dangerously across Europe. The year after that there was an earthquake and an eruption of Vesuvius. War too was on the horizon and in 1796 Napoleon began his campaigns against the Austrians in northern Italy. Rome fell and was turned into a republic in 1798. It was too close for comfort and Nelson obliged by evacuating the royal couple to their safer residence in Palermo, the Colli Palace and the new Chinese Villa. Ferdinando remained more concerned about the woodcock shooting than the revolution and Naples, even when it was turned into the Parthenopean Republic. This did not last long. Within the year Ferdinando was back in the Bay of Naples, his kingdom re-conquered with the help of Sicilian criminals released from prison and Neapolitan gangsters of the Camorra under their leader the bandit Fra Diavolo who commited numerous atrocities. Luckily Napoleon was busy elsewhere, besides Naples was not really wealthy enough to be worth Napoleon's efforts. Ferdinando chose to go back to Palermo as he had grown so fond of the hunting there. Of the 8,000 republicans arrested in Naples 105 were executed, 300 deported and 500 kept in prison.

The war soon resumed with a changed scenario. The Russians came to help Italian resistance to Napoleon but after the battle of Austerlitz found it much harder. Ferdinando who 'did not let military preparations interfere with his sport' (Acton) found himself the grandfather of Napoleon's new wife, Marie Louise. Napoleon was unimpressed and pronounced 'the dynasty of Naples has ceased to reign.' So he sent his brother Joseph to take over. The British general John Stuart saved Sicily for Ferdinando at the battle of Maida and soon Joseph was promoted to be King of Spain in place of Ferdinando's cousin Carlos. In Naples his place was taken by the dashing Marshal Murat who had married Napoleon's sister.

Ferdinando, the quintessential survivor, held on to the other half of his kingdom in Sicily but granted a constitution to ward off the threat of revolution. He handed over some of his powers to his son Francesco who was not bright but was slightly more in tune with the idea of constitutional monarchy. Ferdinando's last significant action was to have the San Carlo Opera House rebuilt in a single year after a fire so that it could stage Rossini's *Lady of the Lake*. After taking part in the disastrous Russian campaign Murat tried to return to Naples and proclaimed himself King again but was captured and shot. Ferdinando was to survive his restoration for ten inglorious years (see p.140) and died at the age of seventy-four.

Even more erratic were the fortunes of the other Italian Bourbons, the house of Borbone-Parma. Don Felipe's son Ferdinando (1751-1802) whose mother was another Bourbon took over as duke in 1765 but his duchy was occupied by French troops in 1796 and soon incorporated in Napoleon's Cisalpine Republic. However, it suited Napoleon in 1801 to make friends with the Spanish Bourbons, so he bribed the family by turning the Duchy of Tuscany into the Kingdom of Etruria which was given to Ferdinando's son Don Luis (1773-1803), thus creating the fourth crown for the Bourbons at a time when they had already lost one and were about to lose the other two. Don Luis was sadly an epileptic and had other health problems so he died very soon after his investment in Paris by Napoleon. He had lived briefly in his new capital of Florence with his Spanish Bourbon wife, Maria Louisa, who had earlier in Madrid produced a son for him Carlo Luis (1799-1883). Thus the child became briefly King Carlo of Etruria with his mother as regent until Napoleon tired of the Spanish Bourbons in 1808 and decided to scrap the Kingdom of Etruria which he had so arbitrarily founded. There was a plan to make Carlo king of another fantasy realm, northern Lusitania, but that did not materialise. After the fall of Napoleon in 1814 he was not even restored to Parma, for the allies gave that to Napoleon's wife Marie Louise who lived there until her death in 1847. Carlo had to content himself for the time being with the much smaller duchy of Lucca but he had the consolation of two fine castles in Austria, Uchendorff and Weisstropp.

9

FRANCE:
THE RESTORATION, 1815-48

It was extraordinary that having lost two and a half kingdoms and an independent duchy along with two substantial empires in the brief period of 1793 to 1808, the main three Bourbon dynasties bounced back after the fall of Napoleon in 1814 and recovered all of them. The big question was had they learned anything from their period in the wilderness? One version applied to Louis XVIII said 'they had learned nothing and forgotten nothing.'

LOUIS XVIII

'He occupied the throne like an old idol, self-sufficient in divinely sanctioned egoism.' Cobban, *History of Modern France*

Louis-Xavier Bourbon (1755-1824), Comte de Provence, born in Versailles, was the younger brother of Louis XVI so like him was genetically a mixture mainly of German, Polish and Bourbon Habsburg ancestry. Well-educated and pious but with an admiration for Voltaire he developed a lasting interest in literature and himself dabbled in poetry. He was given the Luxembourg Palace for his home in Paris and Château Brunoy in the country and was in his late thirties when his brother lost the throne of France.

He grew up a good-looking man of indeterminate sexuality, if not actually impotent (it will be remembered that Louis XVI was impotent for the first seven years of his marriage – the phrase sexual impediment was used about both brothers). He had oddly shaped hips, was already showing signs of putting on weight and was possibly diabetic. In 1771 he was made to marry Marie Josephine of Savoy (1753-1810) who allegedly had a very low standard of personal hygiene and later evinced lesbian tendencies. So it is generally understood that the marriage was perhaps never consummated and was consistently unhappy, but she may have had a couple of miscarriages. For whatever reason Louis-Xavier loathed his sister-in-law Marie Antoinette and unlike his younger brother Charles Comte d'Artois, did not join in the amateur dramatics and other frolics of Petit Trianon. He was clearly also jealous of his elder brother the king and doubtless imagined that he could do the job better, particularly as for the first seven years of the reign when the king had no son, he was the heir to France. Thus during the run-up to the revolution he often impeded sensible reform and gave Louis the impression that he was plotting to replace him.

Perhaps for form's sake he acquired a mistress the witty Comtesse Albi but it is probable that their relationship was intellectual rather than physical. After 1795 nearly all his companions or favourites appear to have been men: the Comte d'Avaray and after 1811 when his wife had died the Comte de Blacas.

During the early stages of the revolution he damaged the prospects of his own dynasty by dabbling in politics and standing in the way of fiscal reform. In 1789 he opposed the revival of the *parlements* but later was one of those advocating the doubling of representation for the Tiers Etat, so he appeared a supporter of the revolution. Then as things later in 1789 began to spiral out of control he became involved in a plot to extricate Louis XVI and Marie Antoinette from France, apparently for their own or the country's good but probably also with the ulterior motive of himself becoming regent in their absence. The plot also involved the murders of Necker and Lafayette. It failed and he lost credibility with both sides in the impending struggle.

In 1791, when he was in his mid-thirties, he escaped from France to Westphalia and was to be a wandering exile for the next twenty-three years. When his brother was executed he proclaimed himself from a safe distance in Belgium as regent for the boy prisoner Louis XVII who died two years later at the age of ten. He then declared himself King Louis XVIII from his newly established court in exile at Verona. Soon afterwards the Venetians expelled him from Verona and a grovelling letter to Napoleon asking for his help to restore the monarchy was dismissed with scorn. For the next twenty years he moved around various places of exile: Warsaw, Mittau (then in Russia, now Lithuania) and Britain.

He was thus approaching sixty when Napoleon first abdicated in 1814 and at long last he had the chance to return to France. There was no certainty that the Bourbons would be restored but the master manipulator Talleyrand (1754-1838) and Napoleon's former police minister Fouché changed sides in the dying moments of the Empire so it suited them to restore the Bourbons and themselves stay in power. Thus Louis XVIII regained the crown for his dynasty with little personal effort thanks to the self-preservation of the Napoleonic infra-structure and to the general dread both at home and abroad of a new French republic. The tsar of Russia, the first of Napoleon's conquerors to reach Paris, was particularly keen to see the restoration and most of the Paris press was controlled by royalist interests. At the same time the advancing British army under Wellington in the south was impressed by the pro-Bourbon crowds in Bordeaux, which had almost always been a royalist city.

Thus Louis arrived in Boulogne and headed for Paris promising to be a constitutional monarch and not to inflict reprisals on those who had opposed the Bourbons over the previous two decades. However, his first measures as king were hardly reassuring. He did not appoint a prime minister as such but presided himself over severe redundancies in the army which caused dissatisfaction. Moreover he did not make the promised reductions in tax yet somewhat ostentatiously revived the extravagant court ceremonial of the *ancien régime*.

News of the dissatisfaction reached Napoleon on the Island of Elba and such was Louis's weak hold on his new kingdom that Napoleon took it from him again with just a handful of supporters. Louis departed rapidly for the safety of Ghent.

A hundred days later after Waterloo came the second abdication and the second restoration with Fouché this time taking the lead and Louis being allowed a second chance mainly because there was no acceptable alternative. This time the whole country was punished for Napoleon's impetuous arrogance. There was a massive indemnity to pay and the frontiers were cut back to those of 1789, meaning significantly that the Saar was no longer part of France.

Louis now made no more real effort to adjust to constitutional monarchy than he had before. He condoned the White Terror, brutal reprisals against the Bonapartists. He retained much of the recent Napoleonic infrastructure and the Civil Code but kept too much executive and legislative power for himself, making sure that the numbers allowed to vote were extremely small to ensure a compliant, conservative assembly, but in the end it was too right-wing even for his comfort. The Catholic Church in France also made an aggressive recovery from its decline under the Revolution and began to regain control of all French education. Louis made one of his new favourites, Decazes who was more to the left, his chief minister, so the situation was flawed.

Ironically it was the murder of another Bourbon that brought matters to a head. In 1820 the Duc de Berri, the king's nephew and son of his brother Charles of Artois was stabbed outside the opera. This was an excuse for the Assembly to force Louis to dispense with Decazes and lurch further to the right. This continued when Louis came under the influence of a young woman the Comtesse de Cayla who persuaded him to promote the ultra-royalist Villèle.

By this time Louis was in his mid-sixties, obese and hardly able to walk. He left the government increasingly to ministers and to his brother Charles of Artois who since Louis had no children was the heir to the throne. The final adventure was to send an army to Spain in 1823 to help restore the Bourbon cousins to Madrid. Led by Artois's surviving elder son, the diminutive but self-assertive Louis Antoine Duc d'Angoulême it won an easy victory, reinstalled Fernando in Madrid and returned in such a blaze of glory that work recommenced on the Arc de Triomphe. Otherwise trade was recovering, the population beginning to grow once more and there was peace. Louis died just before he became seventy.

CHARLES X

'It is not necessary to change; survival is not mandatory.' Charles X in 1824
'An old blockhead' Napoleon
'Toujour le dernier' Louis XVIII about his younger brother's school
performance

Charles Philippe, the Comte d'Artois (1757-1836) who became Charles X in 1824 was the third of Louis XV's grandsons to be king of France. He was already in his late sixties when he took over and during the lifetime of his two brothers had always shown himself an extreme conservative. He was now at last in a position to pursue his dream of restoring Bourbon autocracy.

Born like his brothers at Versailles and like them genetically a mixture of German, Polish and French he was more extrovert and charismatic than either Louis or Louis Xavier. Better-looking – he was known when young as the Beau Artois but later in life he had problems shutting his mouth as his upper lip was too small to meet the lower – and more articulate, he became an accomplished theatrical performer in the plays put on by Marie Antoinette at Petit Trianon. Unlike his elder brother he was so friendly with her and generally at this point so notorious as a womaniser that a scandal developed. He was involved in a duel with his cousin Condé in the Bois de Boulogne after he had cheekily flicked up the veil of Condé's wife at a masked ball. A lover also of fast horses he was notoriously extravagant, the most flagrant example being when he bet Marie Antoinette that he could have a small palace built, the Bagatelle in the Bois de Boulogne, in sixty-four days. However, he offset this extravagance with a very strong loyalty to the Catholic faith that was ultimately to damage his prospects as a ruler.

In 1773 when he was sixteen a marriage was arranged for him with Marie Therese of Savoy and two years later they produced the first of two sons, Louis of Angoulême (1775-1844). The marriage pleased neither of them and Marie Therese ultimately became very unpopular at court. Their daughters died young and it was to be the murder of his second and favourite son Charles Ferdinand Duc de Berri which sparked off the penultimate phase of his career.

His long-term mistress Louise de Polastron (1764-1804) was to be the love of his life and when she later died of consumption the former playboy took an oath never to touch another woman for the rest of his life, so that his religious life came to be even more important for him. His unhappy wife anyway died soon afterwards in exile in Graz, Austria where she was buried.

Before he was twenty he was a colonel of the Swiss Guard, then in 1782 saw brief service with the army at the attempted siege of Gibraltar. On his return to Paris he began to take an aggressive interest in politics, which embarrassed both his brothers. In 1786 he led a monarchist group that wanted to strip the aristocrats of their tax exemption, yet he was also involved in a plot to oust Necker whose policies were much the same.

Once the revolution began he stood out against the increased representation of the Third Estate and was so reactionary that Louis XVI sent him abroad to act as an ambassador and organiser of the émigrés, partly because Louis thought he had made himself a target for assassination by his reactionary stance. In this role he used his charms successfully on Catherine the Great of Russia in St Petersburg but after the king's execution continued to disagree with his surviving brother, Louis Xavier of Provence and callously refused to send him money when he was later living impoverished in Russia. Meanwhile he had more than a year in Turin, was based briefly in Brussels, Koblenz and Liège before heading to Britain where he organised in 1795 an armed landing on the Ile d'Yeu to back up a royalist rising in the Vendée.

The rising failed and having been put ashore at Leith by a British warship and welcomed with a twenty-one gun salute on the orders of George III he spent most of the next twenty years in Scotland at Holyrood Palace. This was a major advantage to him as by this time, like his elder brother, he was bankrupt, owed around two million francs, and Holyrood was a traditionally recognised asylum for debtors. The only problem was that he had to stay within the grounds except on Sundays or he could be dunned by his creditors. He had a large entourage of émigrés living in the Canongate. He found the Edinburgh Presbyterians hard to cope with though he was warmly welcomed by the Edinburgh fish-wife who supplied him with fresh fish. Years later he remembered his debt to Edinburgh by sending money after the great fire of 1824.

With the restoration in 1814 he became heir apparent to his childless elder brother Louis XVIII, but they still did not agree on politics. Charles was some way to the right of Louis, they did not trust each other and Charles thought Louis too weak. As we have seen it was the brutal murder of Charles's favourite son the Duc de Berri, an extrovert like himself, which provided the atmosphere for him to push Louis towards a firmer stance. Yet four years later when he had the crown himself he found the task harder than it looked. At the age of sixty-seven he was in Cobban's words 'still youthful in manner and child-like in mind.'

Charles certainly did not modify his monarchist stance when he at last became king. He was crowned with the most elaborate ceremonial at Reims and even went so far as to try curing the scrofula sufferers, the way his ancestors had done – such was his belief in his divine status. The problem was that it was not easy for him to deliver the programme that his émigré supporters had been waiting for, the return of their old lands to the pre-1789 owners, some 70,000 people. Instead he tried a financial arrangement but that did not satisfy.

His other great problem was the Catholic Church of which he was a devoted servant, yet many in France felt that the revival of the Jesuits and their increasingly tight control over education and the press were excessive. Charles could please neither the moderates nor the extreme supporters.

In 1827 he resorted like all struggling monarchs to a foreign war, the successful use of the French fleet against the Turks at Navarino, which helped free Christian

Greece from rule by Muslims and had the aura of a liberal crusade. Yet the 1827 assembly elections left the two main opposing parties evenly balanced with the ultra right wing holding the balance. Charles at seventy was too old to modify his policies. With what Cobban calls 'almost inconceivable imbecility' he messed around with different, ill-directed cabinets. He totally failed to appreciate that the rival branch of the Bourbons, now represented by Louis Philippe, Duc d'Orléans, which had been trying to outmanoeuvre the main branch since 1780, was at long last on the verge of triumph. The old manipulator Talleyrand who had engineered the restorations of 1814 and 1815 had now changed sides again and was plotting the Orléans take-over. At the same time an economic crisis combined with a sharp population increase meant that there were large groups of unemployed in Paris ready to man the barricades.

In a last effort to keep the initiative Charles tried the foreign war ploy once more. The search for a new empire in Senegal and Madagascar followed by the conquest of Algiers, the beginning of a new North African empire, was meant to confound his critics. Though his supporters lost the 1830 election Charles tried to exploit his military triumphs by staging a right wing coup of his own. But the Orleanists had their newspaper, *Le National* and issued a manifesto urging resistance. Like a true Bourbon Charles was away hunting while the crowds came out into the streets. His son the recent military hero swore to die at the head of his troops rather than give in, then promptly ordered a disastrous retreat. *Les Trois Glorieuses* was a very short-lived three-day revolution and the Orleanists as in 1789 were just using the crowds to create a mood of panic so that they could take over. Too late Charles abdicated and the ex-hero, his now middle-aged elder son the Duc d'Angoulême (Louis XIX) followed suit in favour of his nephew, the king's ten year old grandson, 'Henri V' the Count of Chambord (1820-83). This was the posthumously born son of the murdered Duc de Berri, hence his nickname Dieudonné. He was the only surviving grandson from the three brothers who had been kings, Louis XVI, Louis XVIII and Charles X. Thus with the abdication of both his father and uncle the boy became the third king of France in a single day but the political cards were stacked against him and there was to be a fourth ten days later, Louis Philippe of Orléans.

Soon ex-King Charles X was heading for Cherbourg and once more living in Holyrood, Edinburgh, where he stayed for two years with his surviving son the dwarf-like Duc d'Angoulême and his wife who had no children, but took to Scotland, travelling the Highlands incognito and occasionally sporting a kilt. Charles himself became a passionate gardener at Holyrood, shot snipe on Arthur's Seat and attended the Catholic church in Broughton Street. His period of ease was shattered due to the machinations of his other daughter-in-law, the widowed Caroline Duchesse de Berri, herself an Italian Bourbon, who was desperate to revive the cause of her son 'Henri V'. She was trying to organise a campaign in the Vendée but was imprisoned. This all led to a diplomatic crisis with Louis Philippe, so Charles and his family had to be expelled from Britain. At the same time the widowed duchess tarnished her own image with an ill-judged second marriage. Charles moved to Prague and died at the age of seventy-nine of cholera in Goriz, now Nova Gorica in Slovenia, where he was buried.

One of the great Bourbon survivors from the old days was Louis Henri (1756-1830) the last Prince of Condé who had fought under his father in the so-called Condé Army against the revolutionaries till 1797 and whose only son and heir, the Duc d'Enghien had been famously and rather unfairly shot as a traitor on the orders of Napoleon in 1804. Back in 1770 at the age of fourteen, at this stage still known as the Duc de Bourbon for his father was alive, Condé had succumbed to an arranged marriage with an Orléans Bourbon, Louise Mathilde, but been regarded as too young to consummate the union. However, two years later the ill-fated Duc d'Enghien was born. The marriage was unhappy and the couple moved in the fast set where as we have seen the future Charles X had insulted Louise Mathilde by flicking up her veil at a masked ball, the offence which led to them arranging a duel. The marriage broke down soon afterwards and Bourbon had his first affair with an opera singer Marguerite Michelot. Then came his period of fighting in his father Condé's army and for a while also his own force based at Liège, before heading for exile in London. He also led an attempted rising in the Vendée against Napoleon during the Hundred Days.

It was during his period in London that he met fifteen-year-old Sophie Dawes (1798-1840), a servant in a Piccadilly brothel brought up in a Portsmouth workhouse, the daughter of a drunken fisherman on the Isle of Wight. She became his Eliza Doolittle for he was so infatuated that he had her taught French, Latin and Greek so that she could be introduced in aristocratic society. Returning to France in 1814 Condé was one of the few emigrés to have regained all his massive wealth almost immediately, though his great château at Chantilly had been destroyed. To provide cover for his relationship with Sophie Dawes he arranged a marriage for her with an unsuspecting aide, Baron Feuchères, who thought she was his daughter. She was by this time an accomplished bilingual wit and charmed Louis XVIII until her real relationship with Condé came to light and she was temporarily disgraced. However, under Condé's former adversary, Charles X, she bounced back to favour as the 'Queen of Chantilly' and in 1829 persuaded the now elderly and childless Condé to leave her two million francs and several châteaux in his will. The rest of his massive fortune – 66 million francs – was to go to the eight-year-old Duc d'Aumale, a younger son of the future King Louis Philippe.

Within a year, shortly after the coup that brought Louis Philippe to the throne, Condé was found hanging from the window of his château at Saint Leu. His confessor argued credibly that he would not have committed suicide, so Sophie Dawes was suspected of the murder and because of the huge legacy to his son there was even suspicion that the king himself might have been involved in the plot. However, no charges were pursued and there is the possibility that neither explanation was correct. Instead Condé may have accidentally strangled himself in pursuit of sexual stimulus. Either way it was a sad end to a branch of the Bourbon dynasty which had been arrogant, eccentric and occasionally brilliant.

LOUIS PHILIPPE

'C'est moi qui mene le fiacre' Louis Philippe

King Louis Philippe (1773-1850) was the son of the notorious Philippe Egalité (a name he adopted in 1792 when titles were abolished) Duc d'Orléans and Louise de Bourbon Penthièvre. Thus he was descended from the brother of Louis XIV the roué Duc d'Orléans and his son who had acted as regent for Louis XV.

In 1785 on the death of his grandfather when he was twelve Louis Philippe became Duc de Chartres and his father Philippe, the failed naval officer and bête noire of Marie Antoinette became the new Duc d'Orléans. Already he was imbibing liberal ideas from his tutor Madame de Genlis and his father was plotting stratagems to undermine Louis XVI so that he might succeed him. In 1787 he was put under house arrest at his château of Villers-Cotteret. An opportunist political manipulator he had a long-term reputation as a drinker, womaniser and founding patron of the French horse-racing circuit.

In 1788 at the age of fifteen Louis Philippe was so enraged by conditions that he broke down the door of a prison cell on the Mont Saint Michel and during the early years of the revolution was part of his father's team at the Palais Royal in Paris, helping to push along the revolution with a view to taking over. In late 1789 he was trying to get English help to make him king of an independent Austrian Netherlands (Belgium). Philippe senior was now at the peak of his popularity, referred to as *Père du Peuple* but he lost many allies when he voted for his cousin the king's execution in 1793 and was shortly further tarnished by a series of scandals.

Meanwhile young Louis Philippe had joined the Jacobin Club and by 1791 at the age of eighteen was already a colonel in the revolutionary army. In 1792 according to legend, embellished by himself, he saved two priests from armed brigands and a day later dived into a river to save an engineer from drowning, so his reputation spread. He fought well at Boussu and Quievrain, then was promoted brigadier for Valmy where he also did well. However, he was fairly or unfairly implicated in the counter-revolutionary plots of his general Doumouriez and one of his letters to his father was intercepted by spies. Though old Orléans condemned his son's supposed activities he was still arrested and executed later in 1793, an ironic end for a man who had voted for his cousin's execution and been willing to disown his own son.

Louis Philippe now had no choice but to desert and headed for the Austrian camp. Unlike other émigrés, whom he avoided, he was still basically pro-revolution and had no desire to join the counter-revolutionary army under his cousin Condé. So for some time he wandered round Europe incognito, spending some time as a schoolteacher in Reichenau, Switzerland where he met his first mistress, a cook, and had his first child. He then had a spell at Miconio in Lapland where he had another mistress and another child. Next he headed for the United States where he spent four years in Philadelphia and taught French in Boston, at what later became the Union Oyster House restaurant. Finally after an eventful trip to Cuba and Nova Scotia he spent fifteen years in Britain where he became a friend of the Duke of Kent, later the father of Queen Victoria.

By the time of the restoration in 1814 he was a mature forty-two who had seen more of the world than any previous Bourbon. During the reign of Louis XVIII he resumed the old Orléans habit of joining the opposition to the main Bourbon line. Under Charles X he found himself becoming increasingly popular as a possible alternative to the right-wing king and the backing of Talleyrand was crucial in making his prospects of succession realistic, as were the funds provided by the banker Lafitte. His party included good propagandists and the economic downturn provided the crowds to intimidate the old king. The relatively bloodless July Revolution, *Les Trois Glorieuses*, saw the collapse of the main Bourbon line with the abdication in quick succession of Charles X and his son in the vain hope that Charles's grandson 'Henri V' would be acceptable. He was not and Louis Philippe who had been waiting at a safe distance from Paris initially stepped in as lieutenant general of the kingdom. Even his choice of name was shrewd for to be Philippe VII or Louis XIX would have sounded old-fashioned whereas in renouncing the divine right of kings he was aiming, at least in theory, to create a new kind of monarchy. The *tricolor* was back instead of the Bourbon flag but in reality the government was far from democratic since less than 3 per cent of males were wealthy enough to have the vote and the majority of them were therefore landowners, survivors from the *ancien régime* or men who had made themselves rich during the revolution and empire. The resultant very conservative assembly therefore had to put down the workers whose earlier violence had made the new régime possible. Eight hundred were killed by the National Guard during the Paris riots of 1832, and the weavers of Lyon had to be suppressed several times.

There was one brief attempt by the legitimist wing of the Bourbons to forestall Louis Philippe when the widowed Duchesse de Berri travelled in disguise from Marseilles to the Vendée to try to raise support for her son 'Henri V', but it failed and embarrassingly she was found to be pregnant by a low-ranking replacement husband, so her romantic image was shattered. Similarly any faint hopes of a revival of the Bonaparte dynasty were damaged by the death of Napoleon's only son the Duc de Reichstadt in 1832 and the two attempts to win support by his nephew Louis Napoleon in 1836 and

1840 were totally ineffective. Fear of a Napoleonic revival was so minimal that in 1833 his statue was put back on the Vendôme column and in 1840 his body was brought back from St Helena to be buried in Les Invalides.

Louis Philippe was shrewd enough to turn down yet another crown for the Bourbons when his son was invited to be King of Belgium after its revolt from the Netherlands. He knew the British would not tolerate Belgium and France under one dynasty, so opted instead for the treaty that guaranteed Belgian neutrality, a document that was to have huge consequences eighty-four years later. At least he had some consolation when his daughter married the first King of Belgium, Leopold of Saxe Coburg, in 1832.

With this success behind him the well-travelled Louis Philippe decided to manage all his own foreign policy and for that reason like his predecessors tried to avoid having strong chief ministers, so the first decade of his rule was characterised by frequent changes of cabinet and he always tried to play off one minister against another which, should there be a crisis, would put him in a very vulnerable position. But having endured years of impoverished exile he loved wealth and power and with success came complacency. This was emphasised by his exemplary wife, the Bourbon Marie Amelie of the Two Sicilies, and five healthy sons, all serving in the army. He was fussy, not as dignified or charismatic as some of his predecessors and had a pear-shaped face that made him the butt of cartoonists now that censorship had been relaxed.

The one slightly risky venture undertaken by Louis Philippe in foreign affairs was his intervention to help the rebellion led by Mehmet Ali against the Turks in Egypt. This was rather too successful and so alarmed the British, who had their own interests in the Middle East, that there might have been a war had Louis Philippe not backed down. The brutal war in Algeria, on the other hand, was not one of his ideas but did by the end of his reign see the establishment of a new French empire in North Africa and his son the Duc d'Aumale who had fought there installed as governor general of Algeria. The French also survived a confrontation with the British in Tahiti.

One other foreign adventure was more the idea of Guizot, the minister who dominated during the king's last decade in power. This was the devious plot to win the Spanish crown for the Orléans branch of the Bourbons. It centred round the plan for a double marriage in which the Queen of Spain, Isabella, would be palmed off with an impotent cousin, while her sister would marry one of Louis Philippe's other sons the Duc de Montpensier and produce a son who would inherit Spain. The plan failed largely because Isabella, despite her husband's misogyny (see p.129) did manage to produce a son herself, but the ambitious Montpensiers kept trying to snatch her throne and managed to cause trouble for the Spanish Bourbons for several years.

Meanwhile Guizot, as the nearest to a strong prime minister ever appointed by Louis Philippe began to acquire an unpopularity so malignant that it would ultimately take the king down with him as he fell. There were corruption scandals and ostentatious self-indulgence amongst the wealthier classes at a time when the economy was declining. The bad harvests and potato blight of 1846 caused a rise in the cost of living and French industry, which was anyway somewhat backward, suffered an acute crisis. To save himself Louis Philippe should have dismissed Guizot but he left it too late. When he called out the National Guard to put down Parisian street demonstrations in February 1848 they refused to obey orders. Soon afterwards regular troops panicked when a mob approached the government offices, someone fired a shot and eighty people were killed. It was probably an accident but it was enough to spark major rioting, with 80,000 manning the barricades. Paris was out of control and Louis Philippe had to abandon the city. Now the fact that the assembly had represented less than three per cent of the population left him hopelessly vulnerable. Not even the army came to his aid. Since his eldest son Ferdinand Duc d'Orléans had died in an accident Louis abdicated in favour of his nine-year-old grandson Louis Philippe, but it was too little too late.

Ex-King Louis Philippe who by this time was seventy-five sought refuge in England and lived for a while at Sheen House, Surrey. He died two years later and was buried in the family vault at Dreux.

This was the end of Bourbon France but for a while hope of restoration was not entirely lost. Young Louis-Philippe (1838-94) the grandson of the ex-King became the Comte de Paris and was the Orleanist candidate for the throne of France. As Captain P. d'Orléans he fought for the Union Army in the American Civil War including a spell with the Army of the Potomac under General George McClellan. As usual with this family he married his cousin, Marie Infanta of Spain (1848-1919) daughter of his uncle Montpensier and they had eight children. In 1873 when the National Assembly was considering a Bourbon restoration he generously waived his claims to the kingdom in favour of the legitimist candidate 'Henri V' Comte de Chambord, on the basis that when the childless Chambord died he would take over. But negotiations broke down because of Chambord's stubborn refusal to allow the use of the *tricolor* so the Third Republic took over instead and the last hope had been extinguished. When Chambord eventually died in 1883 the Comte de Paris was acclaimed Philippe VII of France by his few remaining followers but otherwise ignored. He lived in exile in Surrey and died at Stowe at the age of fifty-six.

The rival and legitimist candidate for the Bourbon throne, the former Henri V who had been king for a week at the age of ten, the Comte de Chambord, had in his early fifties refused a proposal from the pro-royalist assembly to take up the throne of France in 1873 unless the *tricolor* was replaced by the Bourbon flag. He married Marie Therese of Modena and they had no children, so apart from the Orleanist line the male heir was Juan Count of Montizon (1552-87), a Carlist Spaniard.

Henri died at Frohsdorf in Austria and was buried beside his grandfather in the Castanavizza Monastery in what is now Nova Gorica in Slovenia.

10

SPAIN: THE SPANISH BOURBONS 1815 TO THE PRESENT

FERNANDO VII EL DESEADO

'... he is very stupid.' Napoleon Buonaparte
'I detest despotism.' King Fernando VII

Fernando (1788-1833, king in 1808 and from 1814) had been so rebellious against his mother's favourite Godoy and so impatient to succeed his incompetent father Carlos IV that he was arrested by them in 1807 for justifiably suspected treason. As we have seen he was acquitted after his trial and emerged more of a hero than he deserved, largely because Godoy was so unpopular and his régime so corrupt. He was then briefly the king of Spain in 1808 when Carlos in a last despairing effort to save the dynasty abdicated in his favour, but he soon recanted his abdication. Napoleon summoned the divided royal family to meet him at Bayonne and cowed both father and son into appearing there, then replaced them both with his brother Joseph. For the next six years Fernando lived in comfortable exile at Valençay in France, noticeably making no effort to escape and no effort to help his countrymen when they rose up against the French invaders.

During the six years while Fernando was relaxing at Valençay many Spaniards were involved in a desperate guerrilla war to drive out their unpopular French King Joseph Bonaparte – Re Jose. The British victory at Vitoria in 1813 was the turning point and Fernando who had quite recently been sending grovelling letters to Napoleon found himself invited back to Madrid now that there was no longer any risk to his person. His father was still alive but his double abdication was now taken as read and besides the now elderly Carlos IV and his wife Maria Luisa were still relying on the hated Godoy even when all three were now itinerant exiles.

Fernando was now in his mid-twenties, already overweight, low browed, big nosed, pious and pompous. His education had been narrow with a heavy emphasis on religion but in the background he clearly nourished an Oedipal hatred of his mother's lover Godoy who was only eighteen years his senior and who had made the prince's father the laughing stock of the Spanish capital. At this point Fernando had been a widower for eight years as his first wife Maria Antonia of Naples, a Bourbon cousin as usual, had died unexpectedly in 1806 after only four years of marriage without giving him an heir. A year after his return to Madrid and nearly a decade after his first wife's death he married another first cousin, Isabel Braganza of Portugal but this marriage too was to be childless, short-lived and end so suddenly that there was suspicion of foul play. Later in 1819, when he took as his third wife yet another cousin, Maria Amalia of Portugal who also died after ten years of marriage there were questions asked retrospectively about Maria Antonia as well.

Meanwhile, however, Fernando was extremely popular, mainly because the Bourbons were no longer regarded as French. On his return to Madrid he protested his loyalty to the constitution of 1812 and announced his liberal attitudes. However, within months he was listening to the reactionary army officers and churchmen who surrounded him and had changed his mind. The constitution was forgotten and supporters of the previous régime were imprisoned, exiled or in some cases executed. The Inquisition was restored and the Jesuits allowed to return. Torture and arrest without trial were resumed, the army purged of liberal-minded officers and many sent to the African penal colonies.

Such a return to old-fashioned absolutism might just have worked if it had been efficient, but it was not. Spain had suffered greatly during the Peninsular Wars, industry was run-down and the flow of wealth from the Americas had ceased. Now the American colonies, which had grown restless during the war, resumed their calls for greater freedom. The long-term Spanish settlers resented the best jobs going to visiting Spanish grandees and resented the sending of gold back to the motherland. The surviving aboriginal inhabitants simply resented the huge level of exploitation. Mexico and Peru asked for their own Bourbon princes to be sent out but Fernando unwisely refused to listen, believing that despite his now much reduced army and navy he could still control his transatlantic empire.

For a couple of years that appeared almost realistic. In Venezuela the loyalists did drive out Bolivar in 1814 with the help of the brutal Llanero Indians. The Morelos rebellion in Mexico was put down in 1815, its leader executed and the Spanish general Morillo reconquered New Granada (Colombia) but after that things began to unravel. In 1816 Argentina declared independence followed soon afterwards by Paraguay and Uraguay as they realised the Spanish Navy was too weak to stop them. Then in 1817 came the rebellion of Chile under San Martin and two years later Bolivar won his victory at Boyaca River, helped by the Llanero Indians who had changed sides. Bolivar entered Bogota and was shortly appointed president of Greater Colombia.

So by 1820 Fernando had lost all the southern half of his South American Empire and his territories further north and in Central America were insecure. The humiliated army turned against him and there was a mutiny in Cadiz. A new junta was headed by his Bourbon uncle, the Cardinal of Toledo, and Fernando weakly once more agreed to abide by the constitution. He was only saved by three factors: the liberal parties were themselves deeply divided between the Moderados and the Exaltados, the army was at odds with itself as the royal guards opposed the ordinary régiments and the other kings of Europe did not want another revolution to succeed. So Louis XVIII of France sent an army of 100,000 men under the diminutive Louis Antoine, Duc d'Angoulême, his nephew and a Bourbon of course who a few years later became the last ever Dauphin and was to be King of France for twenty minutes in 1830. Angoulême made sure that Fernando recovered control but was later disgusted by the resultant reign of terror. Fernando for a second time reneged on his promise of constitutional government, executed over a hundred ringleaders of the rebellion, imprisoned more than 40,000 political opponents, exiled another 20,000 and purged the army of 100,000 disaffected soldiers.

The next ten years known as *la decada funesta* 1823-33 saw an ever-widening gap between the various political groupings, which gave the army an unhealthy ability to interfere. The economy failed to recover and the gap between rich and poor widened significantly. People accused of minor acts of rebellion were executed yet the despotism achieved no success abroad. Mexico had won its freedom in 1821 along with Peru and Venezuela to be soon followed by Ecuador and most of the rest of Central America. All that survived were Cuba, Puerto Rico and the Philippines.

In 1825 these disasters prompted Fernando's extremely ambitious and very right-wing younger brother Don Carlos (1788-1855) to attempt a coup. It was to be the first of many by this branch of the Spanish Bourbons whose arch-conservative stance and opposition to their own kindred were seriously to weaken the dynasty over the next century. They paralleled the similar rivalry of the Orléans branch with the main Bourbon dynasty in France. The particular advantage that Don Carlos had over his elder brother at this point was that his wife had produced three healthy sons, whereas Fernando's first three wives had produced only one girl between them and she had died almost at once. So the rebellious Don Carlos was heir to the throne and with his family posed a threat that was to be activated several times over the next fifty years.

To remedy this situation Fernando, now in his mid-forties, overweight and suffering from gout, in 1829 married his own niece, Maria Cristina of the Two Sicilies, a granddaughter of his mother Maria Luisa and either his father or her lover Godoy. Cristina bore a daughter, Isabella, in 1830 and later another daughter so Fernando, who was aging rapidly, faced an acute problem. Felipe V had introduced the Salic law of succession to Spain, so women rulers were not allowed. Don Carlos and his adherents bullied Fernando into upholding this law, but then as often before he went back on his promise, charged Carlos with treason and exiled him to Portugal, at the same time calling a meeting of the Cortez to change the law on female succession. Soon afterwards he died of a stroke leaving his throne to the only Bourbon female monarch, his daughter Isabella who was two years old.

ISABELLA II

'She had no steadying sense of responsibility whatsoever.' Martin Hume,
Spain: its Greatness and Decay

Since the first and last Bourbon female monarch was only two her mother Queen Cristina acted as regent. She was herself in 1833 still only twenty-seven but she was very much a Bourbon. Almost immediately her dead husband's brother Don Carlos from his Portuguese base at Estoril proclaimed himself as 'Carlos V' and so created a rift within the Bourbon dynasty that was to last four generations. The rift was reflected not just in the rivalry of the male heir challenging the, as he considered it, illegitimate female incumbent, but also in the different ideals of the two sides. Cristina lent towards a liberal approach whereas Carlos was an arch-reactionary, defending the tradition of absolute monarchy in association with the Catholic Church. In addition he soon created a geographical rift for he gained support in the Basque provinces and Navarre where he soon raised an army of 35,000 guerilleros under their leader Zumalacarregui. This began the first of the Carlist Wars, brutal civil conflicts which were to find an echo on the Civil War of 1936. Carlos himself was arrogant and prejudiced in almost every respect yet indecisive and a poor overall commander. Wellington described him as 'one of the silliest devils I have ever met', but he managed to establish an alternative capital at Onate and the war intensified so that at one point his army was close to Madrid.

Queen Cristina initially showed some acumen as regent and she is credited with the abolition of slavery in what remained of the Spanish Empire, but allowed her personal life to undermine her efforts. At the age of thirty the young widow fell in love with a corporal in her guard called Munoz and was too pious just to take him as a lover, instead secretly marrying him. What she could not for long keep secret was a succession of pregnancies, almost every year, which required absences in the country and the babies spirited out of sight to appropriate nannies. This was obvious enough to politicians close to her, so that they could threaten her with exposure unless she took their advice. The problem was that the war against Carlos cost money, it meant conscription and Spain was close to bankruptcy. The two wings of the liberal movement both failed to agree with each other and to provide competent government so they were beset by frequent populist risings by groups even further to the left.

In the end having fought themselves to a standstill after around 140,000 unnecessary deaths the two rival armies made peace with each other, largely ignoring the wishes of the two rival heads of the Bourbon dynasty. Carlos retired to France. Cristina meanwhile had been forced to revert to the 1812 constitution and seen her husband Munoz arrested. Her general Espartero had won the final battle, but that gave him an unhealthy ability to interfere in civilian politics, which was to be a feature of successful Spanish generals for the next hundred years. He became virtual dictator and Queen Cristina abdicated the regency. She moved to Paris and bought the Malmaison.

At this point Queen Isabella (1830-1904, *r.* 1833-68) was ten years old, a somewhat spoiled and lazy girl suffering from eczema who had seen little recently of her mother and was now to see even less. Her home life was far from normal and her training neglected.

Espartero once in power took little interest in his duties other than to suppress the Basques. After three years there was another military coup that brought in the more conservative General Narvaez, a paranoid womaniser and gambler who nevertheless was a reasonably competent if ruthless dictator. He brought back Cristina from exile and promoted her fertile but otherwise harmless ex-corporal husband, Munoz to a dukedom. His lasting achievement was the founding of the Guardia Civil but generally he provided a more stable decade with some economic recovery. Meanwhile Isabella had turned into an unruly teenager who ate and drank too much and despite the delayed onset of puberty was the most eligible bride in Europe. Unfortunately her choice was limited for the other powers would not let her have a French husband for fear of a Bourbon block. She rejected her cousin Carlos, son of the self-styled Carlos V, because he had a squint. In the end she was more or less forced to marry her first cousin Francisco de Asis (Francesco de Assisi) an army officer of uncertain sexual preferences – 'his sweet little voice... is it not a little disturbing?' commented Cristina, his future mother-in-law. At the same time Isabella's sister was to marry the French Duc de Montpensier, a much more virile candidate, but who was thereafter always tainted by the idea that he was part of a long-term Orléans-Bourbon plot to take over Spain for the French Bourbons. This was ironic since within two years the Bourbons were finally to lose the throne of France.

Thus occurred one of the most disastrous mismatches in history: the effete Francisco given the honorary title King of Spain and the sexually demanding Isabella II, now sixteen, who within months of her marriage felt obliged to take the first in a long line of lovers. To add to the problems of Isabella's fairly well publicised indiscretions Francisco's inability to hide his misogyny meant that there were always question marks over the legitimacy of their children which added to the increasing vulnerability of the dynasty.

The pleasure-loving Isabella was already putting on weight as she overindulged all her appetites. She was pious and full of good intentions but undisciplined and unpunctual, prone to party all night and stay in bed most of the day. After her first lover, the successful soldier Serrano, she picked an opera singer Mirall. First a miscarriage, then a son who died an hour after birth preceded the first healthy child, a daughter Isabella born in 1851 who for the next six years was to be the heir to the kingdom.

Meanwhile Queen Isabella's coming of age had provoked the Second Carlist War 1846-9, mainly again confined to the north and run by Don Carlos who was now based in Trieste while his son, the future self-styled 'Carlos VI' (1818-61) was acting the playboy in England. Isabella herself, undeterred by two failed murder attempts, was still popular, as the economy improved and affairs were relatively stable. Railways began to appear in 1848 and significantly the second line was from Madrid to the palace at Aranjuez with the last few yards of track made of silver.

Gradually, however, the seediness of her affairs, the profiteering she and her husband engaged in from contracts, and insider dealing led to serious erosion of her popularity which climaxed in the rebellion of 1854. Her new nickname was La Ladrona – the robber. She was forced to climb down and recall the more liberal Espartero, but this was soon followed by a succession of short-term military coups.

In 1857 came the longed-for son Alfonso whom Francisco rightly or wrongly but sensibly and not entirely credibly acknowledged as his own. Antonio Molto, Isabella's current lover was the main alternative candidate for paternity with a young American dentist also a contender. Meanwhile Spain enjoyed a decade of reasonable prosperity split between the alternating military leaders Narvaez and O'Donnell. Both tried to revive Spain's imperial image: in 1858 Spain intervened in Viet Nam but was outsmarted by the French who created three colonies in the area. More successful was O'Donnell's campaign in Morocco in 1860 after which Isabella walked barefoot in thanksgiving. The following year Spain reoccupied San Domingo, rashly contemplated a new intervention in Mexico, but wisely thought better of it. Now that both the French and Neapolitan Bourbons had lost their thrones Isabella was the only one still in power, albeit somewhat dominated by her generals.

The Carlists still continued to make trouble, still objecting to the female inheritance, but also attracting both right wing extremists and breakaway provinces like the Basques. The first Carlist 'Carlos V' had died in 1855 in his late sixties and his son the already balding 'Carlos VI' attempted a coup in 1860 but was captured and tamely abdicated his rights to his brother, the notional 'Juan III' (1822-87), who had kept out of trouble in England. However, once freed from imprisonment he reneged on his abdication, so there were two Carlist claimants until he died a year later in suspicious circumstances along with his wife and another brother, Fernando.

'Juan III' was too liberal-minded for most of the Carlists so in 1868 he was persuaded to abdicate his rights, such as they were, to his son the notional 'Carlos VII' (1848-1909) while he chose to live near Brighton with his mistress, calling himself Mr Montagu except for one final flurry in 1883 when he became the senior Bourbon and therefore pretender to the throne of France.

Not only was Isabella constantly challenged by the Carlists but also her brother-in-law, Montpensier, son of the last French Bourbon King, who tried a coup in 1866 and by her own husband who from time to time tried to get his own back.

In the late 1860's affairs began to go further downhill. Isabella's latest lover Carlos Marfori was fat, middle-aged and pretentious, so this caused more irritation than usual. A Spanish war against Peru and Chile was an expensive failure. The incompetence and corruption of the right-wing military governments were becoming more evident. A serious mutiny at the San Gil barracks was put down but then followed by another military coup, this time by Isabella's former lover the more liberal General Serrano who won a hard-fought battle at Alcolea in 1868. Facing deposition and reluctant to give up her lover Marfori, Isabella now aged forty headed for the French border and stayed for a while at the Château Pau, birthplace of the ancestor of all Bourbon monarchs, Henri IV, before buying herself a palace in Paris, now the Hotel Majestic.

For a while Serrano's new régime pushed forward with reform but was hampered by a long war to retain control of Cuba and the consequent need to maintain conscription. The Cortes was anti-Isabella, but not yet republican so there was a somewhat aimless search for a new king. Three male Bourbons all made attempts to win the role: 'Carlos VII' tried the usual Carlist invasion. Antoine of Montpensier (1824-90), the Orléans Bourbon married to Isabella's sister, fought a duel and killed the third claimant, his cousin and her other brother-in-law Enrique of Seville (1823-70). Then Isabella found the solution by at last abdicating in favour of her son Alfonso XII who was twelve.

Significantly Isabella's machinations had wide-ranging effects. It was on the question of the Spanish succession that Bismarck famously doctored the Ems telegram that enabled him to provoke Napoleon III into the war that resulted in the unification of Germany and indirectly, since Napoleon was thus too preoccupied to defend it, in the capture of Rome by the King of Italy, thus rounding off the task of Italian reunification. So the squabbles of the Spanish Bourbons contributed accidentally to the final consolidation of two great European nations which were to play a major role in Spain's civil war seventy years later.

Oblivious of these events the Spaniards meanwhile invited the Italian Amadeus of Savoy to be their king. Known as King Macaroni he made little effort to make himself popular. As riots erupted once more and the Carlists started their usual invasion he was forced to abdicate in 1873 after only two years and in the aftermath Spain's short-lived first republic was founded.

Isabella was to live on another three decades surviving her son Alfonso XII and dying in her mid-seventies. She spent some time after the restoration in the Alcazar at Seville but mainly lived in Paris as her son found her presence embarrassing. She had parted with her husband but latterly in exile began to see more of him until he died in 1902 having lived for some time with a large number of poodles all called after his wife's ex-lovers. Her reign had been characterised by forty changes of government, two attempts on her life, a civil war, two revolutions and around twenty military coups. She had let her personal life damage any credibility she might have acquired as a ruler and opened herself up to manipulation by those who could exploit her weakness. She had done nothing to rid Spain of the extreme divisions of class, ideology and wealth that created such deep fault lines in its society.

Altogether she had a dozen children, all of uncertain paternity, of whom only six lived to be adults.

ALFONSO XII

'When the people... suffer the ravages of this cruel epidemic it is only right I come to... offer my consolation.' Alfonso XII on the cholera epidemic of 1885

Alfonso (1857-85) was seventeen and a newly enrolled officer cadet at Sandhurst in England when news came in 1873 of the impending collapse of Spain's first republic. As usual the Carlists had exploited its difficulties to attempt a military conquest and with an army of 50,000 were based at Estella where the latest Don Carlos ('Carlos VII' 1848-1909) had himself anointed as King of the Basques. They won and lost a few battles but failed to make the vital breakthrough of capturing a major city such as Bilbao and their reputation was damaged by the atrocities of their troops. Meanwhile the loyalists or Alfonsists had been working away at a non-violent restoration while the various factions of the Cortes and the growing number of socialists and anarchists in the cities made democratic government almost impossible. In the end it was a military coup by General Pavia in 1874 that paved the way for the second Bourbon restoration.

From Sandhurst Alfonso issued a manifesto, Pavia made a *pronunciamento* and Alfonso headed first to Paris, then Madrid where he made the usual entry at the Atocha gate and received an enthusiastic welcome. Despite an unorthodox childhood he had grown into a remarkably well-balanced, good-natured young man, albeit with a fierce hatred of his mother's now long term lover, the unctuous Marfori. His schooling in Vienna and a term at Sandhurst made him rather more normal than previous kings, albeit more interested in guns and religion than politics. If his father really was Francisco de Asis then he was very much a Bourbon as all great-grandparents were descendants of Louis XIV. If on the other hand, as many suspected, his father was either Puig Molto the young Valencian engineer officer or even the American dentist McKeon, then he was still half a Bourbon and so far as the Alfonsists were concerned it was expedient that he be the legitimate head of state. He soon showed himself hardworking, smart, brave in battle, easy in company and blessed with an excellent memory for faces. The one problem was that he had a weak chest.

More than any previous Spanish Bourbon Alfonso accepted the reality of constitutional monarchy and for his first six years worked well with a conservative prime minister, Canovas del Castillo (1828-97). He enhanced his image by joining his own army in the fight against the Carlists and showing himself cool under fire. Soon 'Carlos VII' was driven put of Spain and went to England as an exile while Alfonso was hailed as *el rey Pacificador*. He kept his mother at arm's length, much to her disgust, for he realised that her poor reputation made her a liability. Though she spent some time in Seville she largely kept out of the way in Paris at the Palacio de Castilla, still in her mid-forties but increasingly obese.

Alfonso meanwhile for once in this dynasty did not have to submit to a compulsory arranged marriage, yet chose to marry just the way his predecessors had done, picking his Bourbon cousin, Mercedes de Montpensier whom he had met and fallen in love with in Paris. She was a granddaughter of the last French Bourbon king but like Alfonso also of Maria Cristina who was now in her seventies and living in France. Isabella, who hated the Montpensiers was furious, but the wedding went ahead in 1878 in the Church of the Atocha. Sadly the beautiful seventeen-year-old bride was dead of a fever six months later.

There is no doubt that Alfonso was devastated by his wife's death and perhaps never recovered his enthusiasm for life. He found some consolation from the re-conquest of Cuba and in an affair with an opera singer Elena Sanz who produced two sons for him. He survived two assassination attempts, one in 1878, the other after he had dutifully taken a second wife another cousin Maria Cristina of Austria (1858-1929). On each occasion he showed remarkable coolness and carried on as normal. The second marriage, however, was more than just a method of securing the dynasty for though his wife produced two daughters in quick succession she was shortsighted and over-formal, so he sought out another opera singer for company and consolation.

Meanwhile Alfonso's health deteriorated and his lifestyle did not help for he made extensive diplomatic tours round Europe, surviving a third murder attempt in Paris but doing useful work for Spain's relationships abroad. He made himself popular by standing up to the Germans in a row over the Caroline Islands – a German gunboat had claimed Yap Island for the fatherland. There were also worries at home for the power of the trades unions was increasing and strikes were frequent. Then came a severe earthquake in Andalusia in 1885 where despite his illness he toured the countryside and toasted sardines with the homeless on the beach at Malaga. Finally there was an outbreak of cholera in Aranjuez near the royal palace and he insisted on visiting the sick, travelling incognito by train to prevent his minders from stopping him.

Inevitably news of the King's poor health and the fact that so far he only had two baby daughters once more excited the perennial pretender 'Carlos VII' who from 1883 onwards after the death of the Count of Chambord added France to his dream kingdom. Even Alfonso's aging uncle Montpensier started renewing his plots. Maria Cristina was pregnant again but it might well be another daughter. The royal family, including even ex-queen Isabella, moved to El Pardo for the sake of the king's lungs but in vain. In November 1885 at the age of thirty he died. Six months later his wife produced a son.

In many respects Alfonso XII had been the most attractive of all the Bourbons.

ALFONSO XIII

'He will do.' Queen Maria Cristina, on her son coming of age

Alfonso XIII (1886-1941) was one of only two kings in European history to become a king in the womb. His pregnant mother Maria Cristina of Austria, herself not yet thirty was for the awkward six months after her husband's death the regent for their six-year-old daughter Mercedes who until the baby boy's birth was the heiress of Spain. As usual such a delicate situation was exploited by the other Bourbon claimants, the Carlist and Montpensier factions, but Maria Cristina proved a sensible regent who respected the constitution and did not damage her reputation by immediately taking a lover. Once the six months were over and she had produced a son her popularity was ensured.

The premature death of Alfonso XII meant that his wife was initially quite concerned over their son's health so his upbringing was notable for a concentration on the outdoors. The former queen Isabella had built a seaside lodge at Miramar (now a university annexe) in San Sebastian which thus became a fashionable resort and was the ideal place for the young king to grow up. Here he became good at sport, was a reasonable scholar but educated along somewhat conservative lines with a special love of all things military. Yet whereas his father had spent his formative years uncertain whether he would ever be restored, Alfonso was already king and took it all rather for granted.

Elsewhere it was a period of terrorist killings that included the murder of the prime minister Canovas in 1897. Executions as a form of reprisal simply prompted further violence. This atmosphere spilled over into the crisis which saw the final collapse of Spain's oceanic empire, for it was Canovas who had in 1894 sent General Valeriano Weyler (1839-1930) to suppress the latest nationalist rebellion in Cuba. Weyler is usually credited with the invention of the concentration camp shortly before the British used the same tactic in South Africa. His Cuban campaign resulted in some 200,000 deaths including many Spanish conscripts, so press barons like Pulitzer in the United States, which by this time had big investments in the Cuban economy, drew attention to the atrocities committed by Spanish troops. Thus Spain got the blame, perhaps rightly but more probably wrongly, for blowing up the United States warship *Maine* in Havana harbour and President Mackinley was forced by public opinion to back Cuban independence. This meant war, which neither he nor the Spanish government wanted and it soon revealed the ill-preparedness of both the Spanish army and navy. In a war that lasted 115 days the Spanish fleet was easily smashed in Manila Bay while a United States army, that included Teddy Roosevelt's Rough Riders, conquered Cuba and Puerto Rico. Spain had to accept a humiliating treaty that meant its withdrawal from those two territories and the Philippines. It was thus the weakness of Spain that caused the United States to enjoy its first taste of imperialism, with major consequences for the subsequent history of the world.

Alfonso was still only twelve when this revelation of Spain's military backwardness occurred. His mother Maria Cristina somewhat unfairly had as the regent to shoulder some of the blame and as usual in such situations there were rumblings from the Carlists, but 'Carlos VII' had somewhat lost interest as had his son 'Jaime III' (1870-1931) who served in the Russian Army before settling in the Château de Frohsdorf. Meanwhile the Spanish economy continued to drift, agriculture was backward, elections were rigged in favour of the conservatives, the army was still overmanned and the administration prone to incompetence and corruption. In addition the separatist tendencies of areas like Catalonia and the north still tended to amplify other political grievances.

Four years after the American war Alfonso came of age and took his oath of loyalty to the constitution not just as King of Spain but with a whole string of other meaningless titles that still included the Two Sicilies, the East and West Indies, Jerusalem and Gibraltar, none of which there was any real question of regaining. He was a personable young man, fit and affable with a good sense of humour, who could mix with his people even to the extent of sometimes wandering amongst them incognito. He rode and shot well, enjoyed the simple life of a soldier and was at this stage ready to work hard. However, his passion for the military led him to interfere with the government's efforts to prune the army down to a sensible size and a touch of old-fashioned royal high-handedness in his attitude, treating ministers as not much more than servants, was soon to make the politicians wary.

He chose his own bride the British princess Victoria Eugenie of Battenberg, or Ena (1887-1968), born at Balmoral Castle, a grandchild of Queen Victoria and niece of Edward VII who sadly brought with her the dreaded strain of haemophilia. One of the wedding bouquets tossed into her carriage contained a bomb that killed twenty-three people, yet Alfonso showed himself unperturbed, just as he had after an earlier assassination attempt. Their first son Alfonso (1907-38) turned out to be a sufferer rather like the heir to the Romanovs in St Petersburg, their second Jaime was a deaf mute, their third Juan (1913-93) was healthy as were two daughters whilst their fourth son Gonzalo (1914-34) was another haemophiliac. It was to be an added burden for a king already struggling to cope.

The problems of Spain continued during the pre-war period with riots in Barcelona, too many changes of government and resentment of the military call-up for war in Morocco. Another prime minister was murdered in 1912 and another attempt made against Alfonso, which he survived by adopting evasive tactics learned on the polo field. One very sensible decision he did endorse with his ministers was to remain neutral during the Great War. This enabled the Spanish economy to move forward when others were hampered by the war, but sadly the benefits of prosperity were confined to too few people, class antagonisms persisted. There were strikes, the threat of military coups and soon after the war in 1921 a third prime minister was assassinated. The one other good thing for Alfonso was that he gained a reputation for humanitarianism by the role he played in acting as a neutral negotiator for the rights of prisoners of war on both sides in the Great War.

As Alfonso entered his mid-thirties he began to behave like a middle-aged playboy. His marriage was wavering and his heir Alfonso who was frequently ill with his haemophilia developed into a spoiled, disgruntled teenager. The king became a reckless driver of fast cars, a heavy smoker and womaniser who spent too much time playing polo, posing with the fashionable sets at Miramar and Biarritz.

In 1921 Alfonso who despite his lust for military glory had kept on the sidelines during the Great War, was an enthusiastic proponent of the latest effort to subdue Morocco. Unfortunately a Spanish army was ambushed by the Riffs and in the ensuing scandal about army mismanagement Alfonso got some of the blame. In its aftermath came a military coup by General Primo de Rivera and Alfonso was too tired after a polo match to make any real effort to prevent him becoming virtual dictator at his side. It was a fashionable enough stance to take for the king of Italy had recently let Mussolini adopt a similar position. Like Mussolini Primo de Rivera set about a major programme of public works that solved the unemployment problem and like Mussolini waged war in Africa to try to create a glorious victory.

The partnership of Alfonso and de Rivera might have continued happily but for two things. One was the financial crash of 1929 which damaged commerce and showed up the dictator as having amassed a fortune, whilst the value of the peseta plummeted and ordinary Spaniards were impoverished. The image of Alfonso as a self-indulgent and permissive playboy had the same effect. The other was de Rivera's failure to keep control of his own army. He mishandled a mutiny by the artillery and executed some of the ringleaders. Alfonso effectively dismissed him and when the ex-dictator died soon afterwards in Paris he refused to attend the funeral, which made him look disloyal. There was another mutiny in the army and this time it was Alfonso who mishandled it by insisting on execution of the leaders. The next serious act of defiance was managed by Ramon Franco, an airforce pilot and brother of the future dictator, who bombed Madrid with republican leaflets. Alfonso and his ministers again overreacted by ordering the army generals take over the air force. As ever Alfonso gave brief support to one weak ministry after another but failed to build up any relationship with liberal politicians who might have saved his crown for him. In spring 1931 came local government elections intended as a prelude to national ones, which were meant to provide a rightist majority. Instead there was an unexpectedly large turnout and 90 per cent of town councils went republican. Crowds began to demand Alfonso's abdication. He did not abdicate but within two days of the election headed off to the frontier in the hope that things would cool down in his absence and that there would be no civil war. As Miguel Maura put it 'the monarchy was slain by its own hands, not ours.' By December Spain was a republic.

Ten years later in 1941 the exiled Alfonso in his mid-fifties began to suffer from a severe heart condition. His eldest son the haemophiliac playboy had died, bleeding to death after a car crash and the king had split up with his wife Queen Ena. Shortly before his own death in Rome Alfonso XIII at last abdicated and persuaded his deaf-mute second son to renounce his claims in favour of his third son Don Juan, another 'Juan III', but by this time the inheritance that he passed on was more a forlorn hope than a genuine expectation. Spain's second republic had been overthrown by General Franco in a bloody civil war and there was, for the foreseeable future, little likelihood that the Bourbons would be restored.

JUAN CARLOS

'The cult of the past should not be a brake on the evolution of a society.'
Juan Carlos before he became King of Spain

King Juan Carlos (1938-) was the only Bourbon monarch still to have a throne in the twenty-first century, all the more remarkable since his dynasty had already lost the throne of Spain three times and three times been restored. Born in Rome in 1938 as Juan Carlos Alfonso Victor Mari de Borbon y Borbon dos Sicilias he is the grandson of Alfonso XIII and was allowed into Spain for his education by General Franco in response to a request by his father, the exiled pretender to the throne. His education was thorough and in 1955 he joined the Spanish army for two years at Zaragoza. He was at this time involved in a tragic shooting accident at the family home in Estoril, Portugal, in which his younger brother Alfonso shot himself in his presence after being given a miniature gun by his father. Subsequently Juan Carlos spent time with first the Spanish Navy, then the airforce before reading politics and economics at university.

In 1941 when he was three his grandfather had died in Rome so that his father Juan (1913-93) took over as the notional 'Juan III' – there had been previously two king Juans of Aragon and a Carlist 'Juan III'. Born at La Granja as a Borbon y Battenberg Juan was the fifth child of Alfonso XIII, but of his two elder brothers one was an unstable haemophiliac later killed in a car crash and the other a deaf-mute, so before he died Alfonso not only abdicated his own rights but had organised Jaime the deaf mute to do the same in favour of Juan.

At the time of Alfonso abandoning his throne in 1931 Juan had been a cadet of eighteen and soon afterwards went to continue his training in England at Sandwitch College before serving in the British Navy till 1937 when his elder brothers had renounced their rights and he became the official heir. He twice asked to be allowed to join General Franco's army fighting the Civil War but was twice rejected by Franco so he did three university courses, meanwhile marrying a Neapolitan-Orléans Bourbon, Maria de Mercedes. They lived initially like his father in Rome, then at the Villa Roncailles in Lucerne, then Villa Giralda in Estoril, Portugal. Like his grandfather he had an excellent memory for faces, was dignified, charismatic, keen on hunting, golf and sailing and spoke four languages including Catalan, for he styled himself Count of Catalonia in the hope of winning popularity in that region.

It was after World War II when Juan was thirty-three that he probably stood the best chance of regaining his father's lost throne, for Franco's reputation had suffered badly from his association with Hitler and Mussolini. Franco temporised cleverly by encouraging the Cortes in 1946 to vote for the principle of hereditary monarchy to resume after his death, but arranging for there to be a popular vote on which candidate should be chosen. Thus Franco was able to play Juan off first against a new Carlist candidate Hugo Carlos, then against his own elder brother Jaime who had recanted his renunciation, then finally against his own son Juan Carlos. Thus Juan was kept for two decades in frustrating suspense. The basic problem was that he had positioned himself surprisingly as a more liberal and less centralist alternative to the Falangist dictatorship and Franco regarded him therefore as too left wing, so likely to undo the good work he regarded himself as having done in restoring the stability of Spain. Franco also undermined Juan's case by himself moving slightly leftwards and reducing controls on the Spanish economy so that there began a period of steady economic improvement.

Meanwhile Juan met Franco in 1948 when Juan Carlos was ten to ask that his son should have a Spanish education. This was agreed to include a period of service in all three Spanish armed services and attendance at a Spanish university, despite the fact that Juan was concerned that Franco's Opus Dei advisers would browbeat the young man into a rightist mindset.

In 1956 came the family tragedy in which Juan's younger son accidentally shot himself. Juan distracted himself with yacht racing and a re-enactment of Columbus's first crossing of the Atlantic. Whilst never reconciling himself to the idea that the wily Franco would aim to skip a generation he must have been increasingly concerned that Franco was only sixteen years older than himself, that time was running out, so that Juan Carlos as a candidate younger and brought-up under his influence might be a more attractive prospect. Besides Juan Carlos, though six feet three inches tall, gave the impression of solidity rather than initiative and this suited Franco who above all wanted continuity.

Finally in 1969 when Franco was approaching eighty and Juan was past sixty Juan Carlos reached the new minimum age of thirty, set by the Cortes for the next king. He had also recently married Sofia of Greece and produced two daughters. So Franco made his decision and declared Juan Carlos his official heir. The Carlist leader Hugo Carlos was expelled from Spain.

Juan, who had waited such a long time for restoration, was furious both with Franco for sidelining him and with Juan Carlos for his disloyalty in agreeing to it. Yet both talked of the greater good and after a few months Juan accepted the situation. For the next six years Juan Carlos played the dutiful understudy, avoiding any criticism of the Franco régime. He attended official engagements without causing any controversy and lived in the Zarzuela Palace in Madrid while Franco was at el Pardo or the Orientale. He also had a holiday home at Palacio Marivent in Majorca and in 1972 sailed for Spain in the Olympic Games.

Then when Franco died in 1975 Juan Carlos at the age of thirty-nine was restored to the throne of his ancestors. He quietly set about removing most of the features of dictatorship favoured by Franco so that Spain managed a fairly peaceful transition to democracy. There were two attempted coups, but both were easily suppressed, the worst problem being the violent separatist movement amongst the Basques who had received so much encouragement over the years from the rival Bourbon branch the Carlists.

In 1978 thirteen years after the birth of their second daughter Juan Carlos and Sofia had a son, the Prince of Artemis. In 1993 at the age of eighty, his father, the frustrated Juan, died in Estoril.

ITALY: THE NEAPOLITAN AND PARMA BOURBONS 1815-60

FERDINANDO I

Having regained the Neapolitan half of his kingdom from Marshal Murat in 1815 after the Battle of Tolentino won for him by the Austrians, King Ferdinando IV of Naples and III of Sicily, who had already been on at least one of his two thrones now for fifty-five years and was in his mid-sixties, was still more interested in hunting than in politics. From 1808 the British had made him delegate even the rule of Sicily to his son Francesco and he was later obliged to do the same in 1820 when his ultra conservative stance made him even more unacceptable to the Neapolitan populace.

In a brief flash of enthusiasm after his return he set about dismantling the Sicilian constitution which he had so reluctantly granted and to try to create a sense of nationhood he united his two thrones of Naples and Sicily into a single entity to be known as the Two Sicilies. So he reinvented himself as Ferdinando I. At about the same time he aimed to rejuvenate himself by a morganatic marriage to a Lucia Migliacio who was twenty years his junior.

However, the influence of the Carbonari had infiltrated his army and there was a military coup under General Guglielmo Pepe which forced Ferdinando to accept the 1812 constitution. This so alarmed the Austrians, who hated the idea of their own province in Italy being contaminated with republican ideas, that they sent an army to help Ferdinando beat General Pepe. Ferdinando who had twice sworn an oath to defend the constitution now repudiated his oath for the second time. The rebels in Sicily were brutally suppressed as were the Carbonari in Naples. Undeterred by his unpopularity and total loss of credibility amongst his royal peer group Ferdinando continued his lavish lifestyle, for example laying on an extravagant fête for a visit by his granddaughter Marie Louise, the widow of Napoleon. At the age of seventy-four he was still passionate about hunting and after one such outing and catching a slight cold he died in his bed of a stroke.

FRANCESCO I OF THE TWO SICILIES AND JERUSALEM

'All his virtues were domestic' Harold Acton, *The Last Bourbons of Naples*

Francesco (1777-1830) was born in Naples the son of Ferdinando I and his Austrian wife. So genetically he was about half Germanic-Austrian, quarter Italian and quarter French-Hispanic Bourbon. Initially he was more popular than his father as he appeared to have more liberal ideas. In 1812 he had his first taste of power when the British who were protecting the rump kingdom of Sicily (all that the Bourbons had left after their expulsion from Naples), asked him to act as regent in place of his intractable father. However, in 1815, after the fall of Napoleon when his father was restored he reverted to the status of heir in waiting. When there was a threatened revolution in 1820 he came back as regent for his reactionary father but by the time of his father's death in 1825 he was beginning to become a reactionary himself and on becoming king at the age of forty-eight he failed to fulfil his earlier promise. In 1828 the former liberal blessed the savage repression of the Cilento rebellion.

Meanwhile Francesco had married twice: the first time to Maria Clementina of Austria who died young, then to his first cousin Maria Isabella who at thirteen was half his age. They had twelve children. She survived him and nine years after his death when she was fifty she married a Count Balzio who was sixteen years her junior.

Francesco in his disillusioned middle age left the work of government to his favourites and his police force, hid away from the public because of his fear of assassination and spent a lot of time with his mistresses. Overweight and dressed in ill-fitting military uniforms he made no serious effort to improve his kingdom. He was only fifty-three when he died after a reign of barely five years.

FERDINANDO II RE BOMBA

'It is a negation of God erected into a system of government.' William Gladstone after visiting Naples in 1850

Ferdinando Carlo (1810-59) was born in Palermo during one of the periods when his father and grandfather had been ejected from Naples by Napoleon. The son of Francesco I and his Spanish second wife he was very much a Bourbon/Borbone and inherited the throne in 1830 unexpectedly early when he was only twenty. Genetically he was the usual mixture of Neapolitan, Parmesan and Spanish Bourbons. To begin with, like his father as a young man, he had liberal ideas, was popular with the *lazzaroni* and promised his people to work for 'the greatest happiness of the greatest number.'

As good as his word, he cut taxes and reduced expenditure. He had the first Italian railway built, albeit that ran from Naples to his palace at Portici. He installed a telegraph from Sicily to Naples and his navy boasted the first Italian steamship. Then he began to find his benevolence unrewarded. His plans for reforms in Sicily were blocked by corruption and conservative vested interests. In 1836 his first wife Maria Christina of Savoy produced a son for him, Francesco, but she died only two weeks later, soon to be hailed as a saint. In 1837 the Sicilians rebelled again for a new constitution. He repressed them with considerable violence. In 1847 there was another period of rebellion in Reggio Calabria and Messina which was put down by his army. The next year saw further risings in Palermo and Salerno which got out of control, a pattern that was evident throughout Europe. He backed down and granted a constitution based on the charter of 1830, but within months his confidence revived, for his opponents were divided between the aims of the middle class liberals and land-hungry peasants; so he back-tracked again and dissolved the parliament. He could not be trusted or as Acton puts it 'What would the boisterous young man do next?' Meanwhile he acquired a second wife, Maria Theresa of Austria, and they had thirteen children.

Despite his later reputation for cruelty he was not adulterous or extravagant in his personal tastes, often to be seen playing with his own infant children. He preferred the simple life of his villas at Quisinia above Castellamare or Gaeta to the formality of Caserta. His favourite foods were macaroni and pizza, which perhaps accounted for his weight problem. Famously he would have to stand up quite often in the theatre to hitch up his trousers, resulting in the entire audience also rising as they thought he was about to leave, which he often did during the performance of operas like Verdi's *Trovatore* which he perhaps regarded as more duty than pleasure. He preferred the popular new Neapolitan songs like *Santa Lucia* which was first sung in 1849 and heralded a whole new wave of tenor favourites. As the British ambassador William Temple observed 'Unfortunately His Majesty has a great distaste for business.'

The next year came a further rebellion in Sicily led by Ruggeru Settimu who announced the King's deposition. All Sicily fell into rebel hands with Messina being the last town to surrender and the rebels offered the crown of Sicily to the Duke of Genoa who tactfully refused. The numerous squadre of brigands took the rebel side until bribed by Ferdinando to change. Ferdinando now sent in an army of 20,000. His navy carried on shelling Messina for eight hours after the rebels had surrendered, killing large numbers, after which he was given his nickname 'Re Bomba'. The numbers of casualties on both sides were high and both were guilty of atrocities.

It is perhaps no coincidence that about this time it is believed by most authorities that the Mafia first appeared in Sicily, although it may have existed previously under another name and without some of the iconic rituals which it borrowed from other secret societies such as the White Hand. It was a reflection on long years of sustaining an archaic feudal system in which landlords delegated the management of their estates to the ruthless *gabelloti*, so that the peasants and tradesmen were forced to look for protectors against exploitation.

A combination of lazy government and lazy landlords with deep-seated political unrest made the island, particularly the vast lemon orchards round Palermo, an excellent breeding ground for the Mafiosi. Even back in 1800 Ferdinando had used the criminal element to help his attempt to reconquer Naples and in 1860 Garibaldi was to do the same, so criminal thuggery was condoned and harnessed to politics. This atmosphere also led to substantial emigration of Sicilians to the United States, some of them taking with them the Mafioso concept. The Maffie are mentioned amongst the supporters of Garibaldi in 1860 and the term became more widely known after the success of the play *Mafiosi della Vicaria* in Palermo in 1863.

In his Neapolitan kingdom as in Sicily Ferdinando suppressed the liberals. With the help of his Swiss mercenaries and the *lazzaroni* he staged a May coup that enabled him to dispense with the parliament. Under pressure to help Sardinia in its war of Italian liberation against Austria, he at one moment reluctantly sent troops and the next had them recalled.

The period after 1849 was one of severe repression with 2,000 political prisoners behind bars: it was in 1850 that Gladstone made his famous visit and spread the news of Ferdinando's unsavoury régime round Europe in a scathing attack. The king made no effort to win friends for the British had substantial business interests in Sicily, particularly the vital sulphur mines which supplied British factories, but he interfered and in 1856 both Britain and France recalled their ambassadors. That same year Ferdinando was nearly assassinated by a disaffected soldier and it is believed that the bayonet wound sustained in the attack was at least partly responsible for his early death three years later at the age of forty-eight.

Meanwhile the erratic history of the Bourbon duchy of Parma had continued with the restoration of Carlo Luis, one time King of Etruria, who had waited patiently for the death of Napoleon's widow, his cousin Marie Louise in 1847. Meanwhile he had had to content himself with the tiny Duchy of Lucca. However, his restoration at Parma did not last long for, like other cities, in 1848 it underwent a revolution. He abdicated in favour of his son but was imprisoned, eventually getting away to end his days in comfort in Nice. The son Carlo III (1823-54) was nicknamed Danduccio, an elegant cavalry officer with a pointed moustache who was murdered in the streets of Parma five years after taking over. He was in turn succeeded by his six-year-old son Roberto (1848-1907) who was deposed five years later when Parma was incorporated into a united Italy. Despite this he managed to keep most of his wealth for he still had a private train with eleven coaches, a castle at Schwarzau near Vienna another at Chambord in France and the Villa Pianore. He married Maria Pia of the Naples Bourbons and significantly out of their twelve children, six were later declared to be mentally defective.

FRANCESCO II RE BOMBINO

'A young man of lofty but limited principles' Harold Acton, *The Last Bourbons*

Francesco II (1836-94) was too little too late. Like his father and grandfather before him he was a liberal in his youth and might have still been one in middle age, but he was not given the chance. He was the son of King Ferdinando Re Bomba and his saintly first wife Maria of Savoy who died soon after his birth, so he had an awkward upbringing with a dozen step-siblings who nicknamed him Lasagna, perhaps as Acton suggests because of his pasty complexion, perhaps because of his eating preferences. Once he became king in 1856 he unfairly inherited the diminunitive version of his father's nickname to be called Re Bombino. Sadly after his mother Maria Christina's death when he was two weeks old he was in the usual way disliked by his ambitious stepmother. He received a fair education with a strong Catholic bias but sadly given the future turn of events he was given no military training.

He became king unexpectedly at the age of twenty-three after his father's premature death. In his brief period on the throne he was the most conscientious of the Bourbon kings in Naples since Carlo IV. He organised every conceivable kind of reform and improvement in an incredibly short time, but on a paternalistic basis with no concessions to democracy, for he was very much under the influence of the reactionary camarilla. At the same time having taken over a kingdom that was deeply in debt he simply made the financial situation worse. He ignored the sound advice of his prime minister Filangieri to form an alliance with the Piedmont dynasty to carve up Italy between them, for he had religious scruples about attacking the independence of the papal enclave in Rome. When he once more refused to provide a constitution Filangieri resigned.

Francesco's most disastrous move was his handling of a mutiny by his Swiss Guards who were the backbone of his army and as mercenaries less prone to listen to liberal ideas. He let General Nunziante shoot the ringleaders and soon afterwards he disbanded the one régiment that might have saved his throne. The rest of his army and navy were already beginning to disintegrate. Though they managed with great violence to suppress yet another rebellion in Sicily the resentment just went briefly underground.

In this situation Garibaldi (1807-82) who was on the look-out for a weak spot in the Neapolitan kingdom (and who had just been deeply shocked by the infidelity of his new wife) decided to risk everything in a new invasion of Sicily. He landed in two ships at Marsala with his Thousand Red Shirts – *I Mille* – and defeated a Bourbon force of three times his numbers at Calata in April 1860. Within six weeks he had captured Messina and Palermo, where the populations rose up to welcome him. By September he was entering Naples as King Francesco II fled in the opposite direction with his wife. He had by this time at last granted a constitution but he was far too late.

The Bourbon army managed one more stand at Volturno but Garibaldi's prestige was now so great that the regulars lost confidence and were defeated. Francesco and his wife retired with a few remaining troops to the massive fortress of Gaeta. There in an unexpected display of courage they held out against a siege by the Piedmont army for three months, with Maria Sofia aged barely twenty gaining the reputation of being a 'warrior queen' by her steadfast devotion to the wounded, giving her own food to the troops and defying the Piedmont artillery. Despite an outbreak of typhoid in the fortress there was a surprisingly high level of loyalty to the royal couple. But at last they had to surrender and moved quietly to Rome. Meanwhile the triumphant Garibaldi was persuaded for the good of Italian unity to step aside, so Naples and Sicily were absorbed into the new united Italy ruled by another dynasty, the age-old rivals of the Bourbons, the House of Piedmont led by Vittorio Emmanuele II of Savoy, who became the new nation's first king.

Francesco lost nearly all his property so that he and his wife Maria Sofia of Bavaria became fairly impoverished exiles. Their luck was no better when their only child died soon after his birth in 1869. Francesco died in 1894 in the Schloss Arco in the Tirol, still only fifty-eight and his wife lasted till 1925.

One of the strange reminders of this almost forgotten dynasty was Prince Luis of Orléans Braganza whose great great grandmother Teresa, sister of Ferdinando II of the Two Sicilies, had married the scholarly Emperor Pedro II of Brazil (1825-91). Their saintly daughter Isabella married the Bourbon grandson of King Louis Philippe, Gaston d'Orléans, Comte d'Eu (1842-1922) and their grandson Prince Luis (1938-2009) became pretender to the crowns of Brazil, France and the Two Sicilies, should anyone care to pay any attention. He lived in Sao Paulo, was known unofficially as Dom Luis and died when Air France flight 447 disappeared over the Atlantic in 2009.

AN ARMCHAIR TOUR OF THE BOURBON MONUMENTS OF THE WORLD

PROPERTIES OF THE BOURBONS BEFORE THEY BECAME ROYAL

THE BOURBONNAIS

Set to the northern end of the volcanic mountain ranges of the Massif Central it was a largely fertile area in the valley of the River Allier dotted with lakes and large stretches of forest. The Forêt de Tronçais measuring 10,600 hectares became the private hunting ground of the Sires and Ducs de Bourbon until it was confiscated by King François I in 1523. The area is still relatively isolated and preserves its folk music traditions of the musette (bagpipe) and hurdy gurdy (stringed instrument).

CHÂTEL DE NEUVRE Little trace is now evident of the original family that later became the Bourbon dynasty, but its first known member Adhemar was holder of a castle here in 910 on behalf of the Count of Auvergne and its prominent position overlooking the valley of the winding River Allier which flows northwards from here some fifty miles to join the Loire. The twelfth- century church of St Laurent, with portions from an earlier church here survives.

Adhemar attended the founding ceremony of the famous new monastery at CLUNY fifty miles to the east and five years later founded one of its first daughter houses on his own land at SOUVIGNY ten miles to the north. The splendid priory church in this delightful golden-stoned village survives with the fine tombs of two of the later Bourbon dukes. It houses also the tombs of two of the early abbots of Cluny who were both declared saints and died here in retirement, Mayeul and Odilon, helping to make this an important pilgrimage stopping point on the route to Santiago de Compostella. There are also the remains of a small early Bourbon mansion, now embedded in more recent housing.

Adhemar also held the castle of BOSTZ at BESSON just to the north of Châtel de Neuvre, and it has recently been restored by a Bourbon descendant, Charles-Henri de Lobkovich. It also has a surviving twelfth-century church.

Before his death Adhemar's eldest son Aimon married the heiress of the nearby castle at BOURBON now BOURBON L'ARCHAMBAULT, named after the old Celtic god of hot springs, (*Aquae Borvonis*). Just below the castle rock which dominates the valley of the Burge there is an eighteenth-century spa built over hot springs earlier much frequented by the Romans. The castle first mentioned around 751 dominated also the old Roman road from Bourges to Clermont. Aimon was succeeded by nine generations of Archambauds/ Archibalds, Sires de Bourbon, one of the first of whom rebuilt the castle around 947. In 1288 it was further rebuilt with fifteen massive towers and much improved accommodation ready for the marriage of Beatrice de Bourbon to a royal prince. The castle was twice captured by English or Gascon mercenaries during the Hundred Years War and Duke Louis II added twenty meters to the height of the towers so that he could better use artillery. He also added the new tower known as *Qui qu'en grogne*. Sadly all but three of the great towers were later destroyed, as was the castle's magnificent Sainte Chapelle, but the remaining ruins are still very impressive. Below the castle there is also a fortified mill and the twelfth-century church of St George.

MOULINS

As its name suggests this was a medieval mill town on the River Allier and legend based its foundation on the story of one of Adhemar's successors getting lost on a hunting trip there and falling in love with a miller's daughter who rescued him. As a reward he built a small castle here for his new mistress and in due course it became the main seat of the Bourbons. The old fortress was converted into a renaissance château by Duke Pierre in the 1490s. The tower keep, *Donjon de la Malcoiffée* survived a fire in 1755 and was used as a prison till 1945. The Pavillon de Anne de Beaujeau (Pierre's royal wife) is all that survives of the Vieux Château and now houses an art gallery. The Cathedrale de Nôtre Dame was extended in 1474 by Duke Pierre II who is shown with his wife Anne on a fine fifteenth-century triptych by the 'Master of Moulins' while the stained-glass windows help project the image of the early Bourbon dukes. The Jacquemont Belfry built 1232-1451 is forty-five meters high and symbolised the town's free status under Bourbon patronage. Situated on the highest navigable point on the Allier for sea-going ships it became a significant port.

LE MONTET

Fifteen miles south-east of Moulins, this was acquired by the Bourbons around 1050 by Archambaud III. A Benedictine priory was founded here by Mahaut de Bourbon, the mother of Archambaud VII, around about 1190 and the Bourbons also had a castle here. The twelfth-century church of Saints Gervais and Protais survives.

HÉRISSON

The magnificent château was built twenty-five miles west of Moulins by Archambaud II to guard the ford over the Aumance and, according to legend its design was inspired by a curled-up hedgehog. It became a major fortress for the Bourbons during the Hundred Years War and features in the various rebellions of Charles Duc de Bourbon and his machinations with his villainous brother-in-law Rodrigo de Villandrando who leased Bourbon's lesser castles south of Bourbonnais at Châteldon in the Puy de Dôme and Montgilbert at Ferriere near Vichy where there is a fine Bourbon chapel. Château Hérisson was dismantled on the orders of Mazarin, but significant ruins remain along with parts of the old town walls. Near Hérisson was the castle of LA ROCHE OTHON built by Duke Louis II.

BILLY

This huge fortress overlooking the Allier was built in the twelfth century and taken over by the Bourbons soon afterwards.

RONNET

This ruined keep thirty metres high along with Château de l'Ours, a round tower once nearly as high, on its motte overlooking the Allier were built by Guy de Dampierre, Sire de Bourbon, around 1210 to defend Montluçon from attack from the south.

CHÂTEAU DE LA BRUYERE-L'AUBEPIN

Was built by Archambaud VIII, captured by the Gascon ex-mercenaries fighting for the English in 1369 and retaken by Duke Louis II. It was destroyed during the religious wars. Nearby, north of the Tronçais Forest is AINAY LE CHÂTEAU where parts of a twelfth-century Bourbon château survive.

MONTLUÇON

This fine medieval town on the River Cher is the economic heart of the region and was acquired by the Bourbons round about 1050 when Archambaud III was Sire de Bourbon. His grandson William built the castle, which was revamped in 1370 and became the favourite residence of Duc Louis II with a huge rectangular tower set in a rectangular enclosure. Louis also gave the town some fine churches such as the Église de Nôtre Dame, which survives. The Bourbon Château now houses a museum of musical instruments. Archambaud VII de Bourbon married Beatrice de Montluçon around 1200. Sections of the medieval town walls also survive.

MURAT

Ruins survive of this six-towered château midway between Montluçon and Le Montet by Thizon. It was considered the third most important fortress of the early Bourbons after Bourbon l'Archambault and Chantelle. Beatrice died here. It was first built around 1050 by Archambaud de Montet and extended by Duke Louis II. It was destroyed by Louis XI in 1465 to teach the Bourbons a lesson, confiscated and destroyed again by King François I in 1523 due to the suspected treachery of Charles Duc de Bourbon, the Constable.

HURIEL

Dominating the valley of the Cher seven miles west of Montluçon still has its twelfth-century Bourbon keep, the Donjon de la Toque acquired by Archambaud VIII and first built around 1090, so probably the oldest surviving Bourbon castle, now partly a museum.

CHANTELLE

This favourite castle of the early Bourbons, particularly Pierre and Anne of Beaujeu, was built on a promontory high above the River Bouble near the site of the Abbey of St Vincent which incorporated some of its ruins. Here was founded the Order of the Golden Sword. It was destroyed on the orders of François I after the fall of the Constable in 1523 and replaced by a Benedictine Abbey. Some of the old town wall survives and there is a legend that Charles the last Duke of Bourbon, during his hasty escape from here, left behind treasure, which has never been recovered.

BUSSET

The Bourbons of Busset, descended from a bastard son of Duke Jean II, were one of the minor branches of the family that lasted more than fourteen generations. Situated between Vichy and Châteldon this exotic château overlooking the Allier owes some of its extravagance to the fact that its Bourbon owner Louis married Louisa, the sister of Cesare and Lucrezia Borgia.

AIGUEPERSE

Only the Sainte Chapelle survives of the great Bourbon château at Aigueperse which was the home of the Montpensier Bourbons. The hill of Montpensier rises to some 1400 ft above the village and was surmounted by an older fortress where Louis VIII died in 1226 and which was destroyed on the orders of Richelieu. It is in the Limagne area of the volcanic Puis de Dome, Auvergne. The newer castle was held by English mercenaries until it was captured from them by Louis II Duc de Bourbon in a sudden attack using primitive bombards. It came to the Bourbons when its heiress Marie de Berri married Jean Duc de Bourbon (-1434) as her third husband and their son Louis became its count.

His son Gilbert (1448-96) was the general in the Italian wars and grandson Charles was born here, rose to be Constable of France but under provocation from François I deserted France to fight for the emperor and died capturing Rome in 1527. The property became a duchy in 1539 and went initially to the younger son of the Duc de Vendôme, then by marriage to the Orléans branch of the Bourbons – famously it was the female warrior and nearly life long spinster Anne de Montpensier or La Grand Mademoiselle who helped Condé and the Frondeurs in 1652. However, by this time the old castle had been demolished on the orders of Richelieu and only the ditch is still visible.

Montpensier went finally to Antoine, son of Philip Egalité who married the notorious Queen Isabella's sister and on the strength of it tried for the Spanish throne himself.

The medieval village of Verneuil in the Limagne has the ruins of a fourteenth-century castle. The now ruined Bourbon castle of Montgilbert, perched on a rock above the Vareille, a tributary of the Allier at Ferrieres sur Sichon was held by the villainous Villandrando in 1434. The thirteenth-century castle at Montaigu was built for King Philippe Augustus. The twelfth-century castle at Gannat was regarded as the gateway to Aquitania, was dismantled in 1566, then reused as a prison, now a museum. A fine eleventh-century church survives in the nearby village of Jenzat with its Bourbon keep. There was also a Bourbon castle, later rebuilt as a fine renaissance château, which survives at Jaligny sur Besbre. It came to the Bourbons by marriage in 1081 and was captured by the English or their Gascon mercenaries in 1367. The impressive castle Châteldon, perched on a rock south of Vichy, was taken by force by one of the Archambauds or during the period of Mahaut in 1200 in their drive to extend Bourbon power southwards. Later like Vichy the town became well-known for its water.

THIERS
Was the Montpensier Bourbon town that specialised in sword and cutlery manufacture but was taken from them in 1527 after the fall of the Constable. Many fiftennth-century houses survive.

CLERMONT
The Bourbons acquired Clermont in Beauvais, Picardy, when Louis IX's younger son Robert married Beatrice, the heiress of Bourbon in 1272. Remains of their huge keep survive. Later the Bourbon Marie de Clermont married Robert of Tarento the self-styled emperor of Constantinople. Nearby was Château La Fère, originally built by a Capet prince in 1206. It is not far from later Bourbon properties such as Chantilly and Compiègne.

DAMPIERRE SUR BOUT ONNE
This château came into Bourbon hands in 1196 when Guy de Dampierre married Mathilde/Mahaut de Bourbon. The magnificent current château was built in 1675 for the Duc de Chevreuse and has its sumptuous Louis XIV dining room.

NEVERS
Archambaud IX de Bourbon became Comte de Nevers on the Loire by marrying its heiress Yolande in about 1230. He died in Cyprus and the property was given away as part of his granddaughter's dowry in 1265. The fine ducal castle is of later date.

Other properties associated with the early Bourbons include Germigny l'Exempt where the now almost vanished castle was the site of the infamous Aimon of Bourbon's climb-down when faced with royal troops.

Charolles north of Mâcon, the seat of the counts of Charollais was briefly Bourbon and there are still ruins of the castle. In 1684 it was given to the Great Condé by the King of Spain in lieu of cash for his mercenary service.

LA MARCHE

The 'border county' on the Creuse came to Louis the later first Duke of Bourbon in 1327, passed on to his younger son the Constable Jacques in 1356, lost by the Bourbons from 1435-77, then restored till the fall of the Constable in 1523. Its castle was at Ahun – Château de Chantmille.

FOREZ

North-east of Thiers on the Loire came to the Bourbons in 1371 by marriage and included the fortress at Roanne of which the eleventh-century donjon survives.

VENDÔME

This old town, almost encircled by the River Loir (as opposed to the Loire), was once a major stopping place for pilgrims on their way to Santiago de Compostela. The old, now ruined Château of the counts of Vendôme and La Marche was built in the thirteenth century on a rocky outcrop high above the river and was acquired for the Bourbons by Jacques de Bourbon round about 1360. His third son later styled himself King of Naples. Louis de Bourbon Comte de Vendôme led the left wing at Agincourt and was one of the supporters of Joan of Arc. It was this branch of the Bourbon family, who became Ducs de Vendôme in 1515, that later produced Henri IV. The younger sons of the first duke were given La Roche sur Yon and were made Ducs de Montpensier by marrying the Constable's sister in 1539. The ruins of the old Bourbon castle La Roche sur Yon lie south of Nantes and have been incorporated in a more modern château.

When Henri IV became king he no longer needed the title of Vendôme and in due course gave it to his bastard son César whose descendant was one of Louis XIV's most brilliant but least moral generals.

LAVARDIN

This magnificent château near Vendôme survives with its half-ruined eighty-five feet high tower and ramparts on a rock above the River Loir and the pretty village with its Romanesque church and half-timbered houses. It was sold to the Vendôme family in 1130 and rebuilt twice, once by Jean Count of La Marche in the 1380s then by his successor Louis I de Bourbon, Count of Vendôme the supporter of Joan of Arc in the 1430s, before being dismantled on Henri IV's orders during the wars of 1590.

CASTRES

In Languedoc on the River Agout came to Jacques Bourbon Count of La Marche in 1374 along with Vendôme. At the time it was in a poor state due to plague and war damage. In 1585 it was a Protestant stronghold used as a base by the future Henri IV and in 1629 it was one of the protestant enclaves captured by Louis XIII who had the fortifications dismantled.

CHAMPIGNY SUR VEUDE

Built by Louis de Bourbon, who gained it by marriage to the heiress of the Montpensier Bourbons in 1472, and his son Louis II, the château was a major base of the Vendôme Bourbons, but it was destroyed by Richelieu. The chapel similar to the Sainte Chapelle in Paris survives with fine stained glass memorials to the early Montpensier Bourbons.

LA FÈRE

This property in Picardy near Reims also came to the Bourbons of Vendôme along with Clermont and again through the Montmorency connection. Ruins of the early castle built by the Dreux family survive alongside the sixteenth-century replacement, which has been converted to a hotel, its vast cellars holding substantial stores of wine. The first Prince of Condé was involved in a battle here.

CHÂTELLERAULT

On the River Vienne near Poitiers was given to Anne of France or Beaujeu in 1505 after her marriage to Pierre Duc de Bourbon and was handed over to the Constable Charles of Montpensier whose younger brother was made the first Duke of Châtellerault in 1514, only to be killed in battle a year later. The Constable then took over the dukedom and had the river dredged so make it more canal-like up to the château. After his disgrace in 1525 it was confiscated by the crown and later in 1548 transferred somewhat meaninglessly to the Scotsman, James Earl of Arran for his help organising the marriage of Mary Queen of Scots to the Dauphin François. Arran's successors the Dukes of Hamilton thus built their own Châtellerault near Hamilton in 1739.

Henri IV built the bridge over the Vienne at Châtellerault which until the new bridge over the Rhone at Avignon was built was the longest in France.

BEAUJEU

The original main town of the Beaujolais area came to the Bourbon line at the time of the 1272 wedding and was well to the east of Bourbonnais on the edge of the separate Duchy of Burgundy, so Duke Louis II had to repel Burgundian invaders in 1410. It is particularly associated with Duke Pierre II and his formidable wife the princess Anne of Beaujeu who used it as her special name. A wooden house of their period is now used for wine tastings. Villefranche still has the magnificent façade of its Nôtre Dame de Maria donated by Duke Pierre II and his wife Anne.

Nearby at Nièvre was the Bourbon Château Chinon which was demolished in 1565 and of which little remains. Even further to the east beyond the Saone was the remote glacier-scoured Bourbon estate of Dombes acquired by the Bourbons in 1400 with its main centre at Trevoux. At the time of Duke Charles III, the Constable, it was technically outside French territory and under the control of the Holy Roman Emperor, hence his famous defection and its confiscation by François I. This remarkable waterlogged plateau has a thousand lakes, is fertile but was formerly unhealthy due to mosquitoes. It was returned to the Montpensier Bourbons in 1561 and then passed over by Anne Marie, the fighting Duchess to one of Louis XIV's bastards as the price of her faithless lover Lauzun's release from prison.

Pau

This fine château in the south-west, inland from Biarritz was the birthplace of Henri IV as his mother the Joanna d'Albret heiress of Navarre was keen that he should be born in the area and dashed away from her husband Antoine of Vendôme to her father's home at Pau, which was the capital of his county of Béarne. Marie Antoinette enjoyed coming here to tend the garden. It was also lived in later by the scandal-ridden Bourbon Queen of Spain Isabella II after she had been forced to abandon her throne and was refurbished by Napoleon III.

The other base of the Béarne family was NERAC a delightful but now badly ruined castle in Lot-et-Garonne south-east of Bordeaux.

Condé

This title may have emanated from either of two Condés. Condé en Brie which has two châteaux, Grand and Petit, was first acquired for the Bourbons when Jacques de Bourbon, brother of Pierre the second duke, married its heiress round about 1350. Jacques, despite being known as 'the flower of chivalry', was on the losing side at both Crécy and Poitiers and was killed at Brignais. The first Bourbon Prince of Condé was Louis I (1530-69).

The other candidate for the title is Condé sur l'Escaut whose credibility is enhanced by the fact that it is close to D'Enghien, which is now over the Belgian border. It had a castle from 1410 and the area was seized from the Habsburgs in 1676 by Louis XIV after which Vauban built a moated fortress.

The main later base of the family was Chantilly acquired when Henri Prince of Condé married Charlotte of Montmorency having snatched her from the clutches of Henri IV.

Conti

The junior branch of the Bourbon Princes of Condé took their title from this modest property near Amiens but grew nearly as wealthy as their peers. It came with Eleanor of Conti (*d.*1564) who was the wife of Louis Prince of Condé. The first Prince of Conti was Armand de Bourbon, younger brother of the Great Condé who was given the title on his birth in 1629. Despite being destined for the church he became military leader of the Fronde and was defeated by his own brother at Charaton. He later had a quite distinguished military career under Louis XIV and died partly due to an earlier venereal affection at his Château de la Grange des Pres on the River Peyne near Pezenas in Languedoc, a property rebuilt in 1575 after being acquired by the Condé Bourbons from the Montmorencys in 1537 along with Château Montmorency. There was then a break in the line of Princes of Conti until François Louis Le Grand Conti.

The Château Conti on the L'Isle Adam on the River Oise was rebuilt round an earlier fortress during the reign of Louis XIII.

PROPERTIES OF THE BOURBONS AFTER THEY BECAME ROYAL

FRANCE

Paris

The earliest surviving landmark in Paris associated with the Bourbons is the Pont Neuf, the oldest bridge in Paris, which was begun in two halves in 1578 but completed at the expense of Henri IV, its twelve rounded arches decorated with humorous grotesques. The nearby Place Dauphine was also built for Henri IV as a triangular block of houses, some still the original, and dedicated to the Dauphin, the future Louis XIII. The St Merri Church also dates from the reign of Henri IV as does the Tour St Jacques originally the starting point for the pilgrims going to Santiago de Compostella. Henri IV also founded the Hôpital St-Louis after the plague of 1606. It subsequently became a skin hospital. The Places des Vosges-Place Royale was conceived by Henri IV in 1605 as the first large symmetrical square in Paris and as part of his plan to transform the Marais.

It was Henri IV's promiscucous first wife Marguerite de Valois who first made the Faubourg St-Germain fashionable by building a now vanished mansion on the river. What survives is the Palais Bourbon built in 1728 for the Duchesse de Bourbon, illegitimate daughter of Louis XIV and Madame de Montespan. Louis XVI sold it to the Bourbon Prince of Condé who got it back after the revolution, but after the death of the last Condé in 1827 it was used by the National Assembly. The nearby Fontaine des Quatres Saisons dates from Louis XV and was paid for by the father of Turgot, minister under Louis XVI.

The Tuileries Gardens were begun by Henri IV's mother-in-law Catherine de Medici who wanted a new château near the Louvre and established an Italian style garden here, but never finished the château because of a prophesy that she would die there. Henri IV added the Pavillon de Flore and Louis XIV the Pavillon de Marsan and French Garden but Louis XV was the first to use it as a palace, in which later Louis XVI and his wife were kept prisoners after the revolution. Henri IV also completed the Bord de l'Eau Gallery, which Richelieu used as his mint and Louis XIV as workshops for artists.

The Louvre itself was substantially rebuilt by Louis XIII as a much bigger palace than it had been before, and with a new Horloge Pavillon. Louis XIV made substantial additions, rebuilt the Apollo Wing and added the Colonnade but in 1682 after this huge expenditure the court left the Louvre for Versailles. The entire set of buildings was then badly neglected and close to collapse until 1770 when it was restored under Louis XVI. In 1792 the Tuileries were sacked by the mob and parts were later used by the republican régimes. Napoleon began restoration work again and added his triumphal arch. In 1827 Louis XVIII was the only French king to die here. There was further damage during the riots when first Charles X and then Louis Philippe were dethroned and the main Palais de Tuileries was finally burned down by the Commune in 1871. The idea of using the Louvre as a museum had begun with Louis XIV who had over 2,000 paintings though it was François I who acquired the Mona Lisa. The three post-Restoration Bourbons all added to the museum – Louis XVIII bought the Venus de Milo in 1820 – and its use as a royal residence declined.

The Place de la Concorde at the Tuileries end of the Champs Élysées was created as an octagonal moated feature to commemorate the survival of Louis XV in 1755. It was the scene of the firework display for Louis XVI's wedding in 1770 when 133 people were crushed in the panic, and also of the guillotining of the king in January 1793. The obelisk was acquired from Luxor by Charles X in 1829. The Place de la Nation was created to celebrate Louis XIV's wedding.

The Champs Élysées itself began as an avenue, the Cours-la-Reine designed for Henri IV's widow, Marie de Medici in 1616. It was replanted, straightened-out and renamed Champs Élysées in 1709 under Louis XIV. He had commissioned the Marly Horses and when his mansion at Marly was destroyed in 1795 they were brought here. The Étoile was added under Louis XV and now has Napoleon's Arc de Triomphe as its centrepiece, a monument ironically completed by Charles X to celebrate the conquest of Algeria.

The Bassompierre Mansion on Chaillot Hill was built for Catherine de Medici and later used for a convent by Henrietta Stuart, wife of the Duc d'Orléans but demolished by Napoleon. The Place du Trocadero was named after the fort near Cadiz where the French Army was sent by Louis XVIII to help his Spanish Bourbon cousins in 1827. The nearby Champs de Mars now dominated by the Eiffel Tower was developed as a military parade ground in 1765 under Louis XV. At the far end is the École Militaire built by Louis XV's favourite banker with help from Madame de Pompadour. Napoleon was a cadet here.

Hôtel des Invalides a vast complex built for Louis XIV in 1670 as a retirement home for 7,000 injured soldiers. He typically collected money to pay for it from soldiers still serving in his army. It had the Church of St Louis des Invalides and the Napoleon Chapel. Louis XIV's other humanitarian foundation was the Hôpital Salpêtrière, established in 1656 as a hospital for the poor of Paris with room for 10,000 and a St Louis chapel. It was on the site of Louis XIII's gunpowder works – hence the name. The idea was to clean up the streets of Paris, which at that time had 55,000 beggars.

Amongst the great Bourbon churches are the Dôme Church, Sorbonne, St-Louis-en-Ile the Église St-Roch, the classical St Gervais completed in 1657, the St-Sulpice and Val-de-Grace built for Louis XIV, the Church of St-Paul-St-Louis founded under Louis XIII as was the basilica of Nôtre-Dame-des-Victoires. The Madeleine was begun under Louis XV but had an erratic history of stop and start till completed as a church under Louis XVIII. Louis XV also founded the Panthéon after his miraculous recovery from illness in 1744 though it was not completed till 1789 and its huge size and massive Dôme meant that there was always a struggle to find the necessary money. The serious restoration of Nôtre Dame Cathedral was begun by Louis Philippe after the scandal about its dilapidation caused by Hugo's *Hunchback*. The Chancel recalls the dedication of France to the Virgin Mary by Louis XIII when he at last had a son after twenty-three years of marriage. It was under Louis XIII that the Ile St-Louis was joined to the Ile Nôtre Dame. One church that caused trouble for Louis XV was the St Medard which became the focus for a masochistic group practising self-mortification in memory of a Jansenist deacon who tortured himself to death. The King clamped down on the sect and closed the cemetery.

The Gobelins tapestry factory dated back to 1440 but came to prominence under Louis XIV producing thousands of tapestries promoting his glory and later that of Louis XV.

The Conciergerie built by King Philip the Fair was part of the old Royal Palace and the Palais de Justice. It was used during the Terror to house important prisoners such as Marie Antoinette and Philippe Egalité. The Place Vendôme was created under Louis XIV on the site of the Duc de Vendôme's mansion in 1685.

The Palais Royal near the Louvre was built by Richelieu and he left it in his will to Louis XIII. Louis XIV and his mother Anne of Austria lived here until the Fronde. Later he lent it to the exiled Queen Henrietta of England followed by her daughter Henrietta who married his brother the Duc d'Orléans. The palace was thereafter mainly held by the Bourbon dukes of Orléans and was the scene of their orgies and sometimes plots against their royal rivals. It was extended when Louis Philippe from that family became king in 1830. Comédie Française was founded in 1680 by Louis XIV. The Place de l'Odéon was the site of the Condé Bourbons' main Paris residence until 1782.

The Palais du Luxembourg was built in the Italian style by Marie de Medici, widow of Henri IV, who disliked the Louvre. It was here that she hatched her plot to have Richelieu dismissed in 1630. When it failed her son Louis XIII turned against her and she was exiled to Cologne for the rest of her life. The Hotel de Ville was entirely rebuilt in 1874 but replaced a series of earlier buildings including the one completed by Henri IV whose façade it copied and where Louis XVI first kissed the *tricolor*.

Les grands Boulevards (the word means a rampart terrace) mark the line where after 1660 Louis XIV demolished the defensive ramparts of Paris which had been completed by his father Louis XIII and which by his time were no longer needed for defence. Triumphal arches replaced the old fortified gates, for example the Porte St-Denis commemorated the capture of forty towns on the Rhine by Louis XIV in 1672 and the Porte St-Martin the victory over the Spanish, German and Dutch troops in 1674. Similarly the Place des Victoires with its statue of Louis XIV celebrated the military successes of 1685.

The Paris Observatory was built by Louis XIV's great minister Colbert in 1672 on what became the longitudinal centre of the world till 1822, the Paris Meridian. The royal hunting grounds which had been levelled by Colbert, the Bois de Boulogne were opened to the public by Louis XIV and include the Bagatelle, the mansion built for a bet in sixty-four days by the future Charles X when he was still the Comte d'Artois and a friend of Marie Antoinette.

The Château Vincennes was a medieval fortress modernised by Mazarin during the minority of Louis XIV who spent his honeymoon here. The old keep or donjon was used as a prison and Bourbon prisoners included the Great Condé, the Prince of Conti and later the Duc d'Enghien who was famously executed here by Napoleon. A royal porcelain factory was also built here. Under Napoleon and Louis Philippe there was a major arsenal and barracks for the defence of Paris and the Germans destroyed much of it in 1944.

The Parc Monçeau was established in 1778 by the Duc d'Orléans with a variety of follies and other features. The Jardin des Plantes dates back to the court doctors of Louis XIII who set up a new medicinal garden in 1626.

The Élysée Palace, now the official base of the president, was at one time the home of Louis XV's mistress Madame de Pompadour. The Carreau du Temple recalls the long demolished Templar Tower used as a prison where Louis XVI and his wife were kept prisoners before their execution and where their son young Louis XVII died at the age of ten. Similarly only paving stones marking its walls survive from the Bastille demolished in 1789. Part of the old Arsenal nearby was converted into a law court by Louis XIII and into a public library under Louis XV.

OUTSIDE PARIS

VERSAILLES

In 1634 Louis XIII built himself a hunting lodge on the site of a farm where he enjoyed hunting round this, then marshy, wooded area. Though it was too wet for growing plants yet too dry to supply water for fountains Louis XIV undertook the massive task of re-engineering the landscape to allow for a massive palace, huge gardens and extravagant water features. By 1664 he was able to hold receptions there and by 1682 it became the seat of government. The palace could accommodate a thousand aristocrats and their 4,000 servants whereas the ancillary buildings round about could take another thousand lesser aristocrats, 5,000 more servants and 9,000 soldiers. By thus creating a venue for his top layer of subjects the King aimed to prevent them flouting his authority or nursing unhealthy ambitions away from court. Features include the Hall of Mirrors, Grand Apartment, Royal Opera, Mars Salon, the suites of the Queen, Mme de Maintenon, Mme du Barry and Mme de Pompadour. The gardens include the famous Parterre, Grand Canal and fountains. In the years that followed Versailles was imitated by virtually every royal family in Europe, especially the Bourbons in Spain and Italy.

Louis XIV used the original Le Grand Trianon for his affair with Montespan but then rebuilt it in pink marble for Maintenon. It then fell on hard times till reused by Madame de Pompadour with Louis XV in the 1740s. She added the New Ménagerie and the Pavillon Français. It was restored by Napoleon. Le Petit Trianon is part of a complex of buildings organised by Louis XV that once included a menagerie and a botanical garden. Louis XVI gave the château to his wife Marie Antoinette. She put on plays in her Queen's Theatre and the gardens had a Temple of Love on an island and other features much copied by Catherine of Russia and others. Round the Grand Lac were built a dozen thatched peasant cottages, the Hameau, for Marie Antoinette's make-believe rustic idylls.

ST DENIS

The great Gothic Basilica was begun by Abbot Suger in 1136 and contains the tombs of all the Bourbon kings up to Louis XVIII. It was here that Henri IV made his final dramatic reconversion to Catholicism in 1593. Many of the royal tombs were desecrated during the revolution but more than seventy survived.

RUEIL MALMAISON

The seventeenth-century château Malmaison was famously bought by Napoleon's first wife Josephine Beauharnais and later by the exiled Queen Isabella of Spain.

St-Germain-en-Laye
The new château was begun by Henri II and completed by Henri IV who liked to make the fountains squirt unexpectedly at his guests. Louis XIV was born here and Louis XV died here. It was also occupied by the exiled James II of Great Britain. Charles X demolished it. The Old Château still survives. Louis XIV turned the turret into living accommodation and an observatory.

Sèvres
The royal porcelain factory was transferred here from Vincennes in 1756. It used a process leaked from Dresden and kaolin discovered in Limousin.

Compiègne
Notorious in earlier days as the place where the Burgundians captured Joan of Arc the original Compiègne château was a hunting lodge acquired by the kings of France in 1374, enjoyed for its good game and closeness to the military exercise areas by Louis XIV and rebuilt as a classical palace by Louis XV who was even more obsessed with hunting. Thereafter it became a favourite summer retreat for royalty and now houses three museums.

St Cloud
The seventeenth-century château here is associated with the Orléans Bourbons and was destroyed by the Prussians in 1870 but the gardens, fountains and Grand Cascade survive in the Parc St-Cloud.

Meudon
This Orléans château was burned down during the revolution.

Saint Fargeu
The five-sided, five-towered château Saint Fargeu, between the Loire and the Yonne, belonged to the soldierly Grande Mademoiselle, Anne-Marie of Orléans, who came to Condé's rescue during the Fronde and refurbished it 1653-7.

Dreux
The royal chapel here housed the tombs of the Orléans Bourbons including King Louis Philippe. It had earlier been the site of Condé's defeat by the Catholics in 1562.

Fontainebleau
There was a royal hunting-lodge here as early as 1130 and then it was developed first as a fortress and then as a renaissance château under François I. It came to the Bourbons in 1589. The horseshoe shaped staircase *Escalier du Fer-a-Cheval* was added in 1634 during the minority of Louis XIV.

RAMBOUILLET

The castle here, red bricked with five stone towers, was founded as a royal hunting lodge and country retreat twenty-seven miles south-west of Paris. The old fortified château was reused as a residence by Louis XIV in 1683 and later rebuilt for Napoleon's son the Prince of Rome. Charles X was here when he heard that his deposition was imminent. It was later used as a country home for the presidents of France.

CHAMBORD

This began as another royal hunting lodge but was rebuilt in the 1530s, perhaps to a design supplied by Leonardo de Vinci for François I. The double helix staircase bears his hallmark. Set on the River Closson, a tributary of the Loire it is the largest of the Loire châteaux and was completed by Louis XIV with 440 rooms in 1685. From 1725 to 1733 it was used by the exiled King of Poland who was Louis XV's father-in-law.

BRUNOY

This château on the Ile de France fifteen miles from Paris was built by Philip VI in 1346 and renovated under Louis XV.

CHANTILLY

The estate twenty miles north of Paris near Senlis was acquired by the Bourbon Princes of Condé in 1643. This happened after Henri II of Condé married the daughter of Anne de Montmorency Constable of France whose son had been executed during the Fronde. His son the Grand Condé built a superb renaissance château here in the 1660s with magnificent park and fountains designed by le Nôtre that included a grand canal. Here Condé entertained famous literary figures like Molière and la Fontaine. This was all but destroyed during the revolution but in 1709 Henri of Condé had built the Grand Château. It was rebuilt in the 1820's and then refurbished when gifted by the last of the Condés (Louis's son and heir the Duc d'Enghien had been shot on the orders of Napoleon) to Louis Philippe's son the Duc d'Aumale who turned it into a museum and left it to the nation.

The Grandes Écuries were built by Louis Henri Prince of Condé who had acted as chief minister during the minority of Louis XV and who later believed that he would be reincarnated as a horse. He also set up a porcelain factory and a centre for scientific research. A few years after the death of the last Condé the first official horse racing began here in 1834. Louis de Condé (d. 1818) had also built the Jeau de Paume and Château d'Enghien, developed Chinese Gardens and a fake peasant village or hameau like the one Marie Antoinette had at Petit Trianon.

Other later Condé properties included Saint Leu where the last Prince of Condé died – he was found hanging from a window. Suicide was regarded as unlikely and murder was suspected because of the legacy to his mistress, the former Miss Dawes, but there is also the theory of accidental death while seeking sexual stimulus. Château Taverny in de Boissy, Montmorency in the Val d'Oise nine miles from Paris came to the Bourbon Condés after their marriage to the heiress. In 1689 it was renamed Enghien in memory of their lost lands in what is now Belgium. Rousseau wrote his *Emile* here. The Condés preferred Chantilly and the nearby magnificent Château D'Ecouen, built in 1538, which the last Condé designated as an orphanage but which is now a museum of the Renaissance. Mortefontaine was a seventeenth-century property in Oise which had belonged to Joseph Bonaparte.

Château Ouen has a monument to Condé's son the Duc d'Enghien who was shot as a traitor by Napoleon.

NEUF BRISACH

Overlooking the Rhine opposite Freiburg is a fine surviving example from 1698 of the fortification skills of Vauban under Louis XIV as he consolidated the new eastern frontier of France in Alsace. It has the typical octagonal citadel.

VALENÇAY

This château of Valençay is west of Bourges and was built in 1540. It was acquired in 1719 by the Scots banker John Law during the Orléans regency when he was helping to fund the development of Louisiana. Later Napoleon made his minister Talleyrand buy it to house the dethroned Bourbon King of Spain, Fernando VII in 1808.

BELGIUM

ENGHIEN

Enghien, now Edingen, in Hainaut (thirty kilometers from Brussels) was held, theoretically, by the Bourbons of Vendôme from 1487 when François acquired Mary of Luxembourg as a bride. She also brought Condé en Brie. Its castle built in 1410 became part of the Condé inheritance till 1569 when it was lost due to a legal mistake. In 1689 the name was transferred to Montmorency outside Paris when the junior Condés began using the title of Ducs d'Enghien. The château is modern but has fine restored gardens.

SPAIN

As the Bourbons have provided kings or queens of Spain with a few breaks ever since 1700 there is a significant architectural legacy from their presence.

MADRID

The El Pardo began life as a royal hunting lodge in 1406 on a hill outside
Madrid but was destroyed by fire in 1604. Felipe V the first Bourbon King of
Spain used it for diplomatic occasions and it was the scene of the unpopular
Convention of Pardo with the British in 1739 which presaged the war
of Jenkins's Ear. It was re-built by Carlos III in the 1760s, using Francesco
Sabatini as architect. It was used by General Franco after the Civil War and
since his death has been used for visiting heads of state. Part of the same
complex is the more modest Palacio Zarzuela also a former hunting lodge
which Carlos IV rebuilt to house his huge collections of clocks, tapestries and
porcelain. It is now used by King Juan Carlos and his family.

The Palacio de Oriente, or Real, is in the western area of Madrid and east
of the Manzanares River. It was built on the site of the old Moorish fortress,
or Alcazar, on the orders of the first Bourbon King of Spain Felipe V in 1734
after a fire had nearly destroyed its predecessor. His architect was Giovanni
Sachetti, an Italian chosen by Felipe's wife Isabel Farnese. It was occupied
by their son Carlos III and was the largest palace in Europe after the Louvre
with 135,000 sq. metre space. It contains numerous works by Velasquez,
Caravaggio, Goya etc. The Parque del Retiro occupies most of the area
covered by the former Retiro Royal Palace and includes the statue of Alfonso
XII. Some of the buildings survive as museums etc.

The Prado was built by the fourth Bourbon King of Spain Carlos III,
known sometimes as 'Madrid's best mayor'. It was originally intended as a
building for botanical research and the Jardines Botanicos founded by his
half-brother Fernando VI were moved alongside. Carlos laid out the Plaza
Canovas del Castillo with its fountain and statue of Neptune, the Paseo del
Prado and several other avenues and fountains throughout the city. Carlos III
also built the Alcala Gate and organised numerous improvements of the city
infrastructure. Real Academia dates from this period.

The Archaeological Museum was founded by Isabella II in 1867.

The Ritz hotel was built by Alfonso XIII to entertain his guests. The Teatro
Real was built as an opera house by Queen Isabella II in 1850.

The Basilica of Our Lady of Atocha had a special significance for the
Bourbon monarchy but has had a chequered history. Originally built on the
site of an earlier church by Philip/Felipe II in gratitude for the Virgin's help in
the Reconquista it was developed by the Bourbons after 1700 and regularly
used for royal weddings. It was beside the great Atocha gate into the city, the
place for ceremonial entrances, but Napoleon's troops used it as a barracks in
1808 and it began to deteriorate. Isabella II tried to revive the cult but failed to
stop the decline and most of it was demolished in 1885, leaving only the bell
tower and part of a cloister. It was rebuilt on the orders of Alfonso XIII in 1924
but destroyed again in the Civil War, then rebuilt in 1951. It has now resumed
its role as the venue for Bourbon royal weddings. The cathedral of Madrid

Nuestra Senora de la Almudena is also a modern building, only finished in 1993. Churches dating from the Carlos III period include San Francisco el Grande, San Jeronimo el Real where King Juan Carlos was crowned, Ermita de Santa Antonia de la Florida which was decorated by Goya for Carlos IV and where the painter was buried in 1828. From that period also comes the Real Fabrica de Tapices. Las Salsas Reales was a foundation of Fernando VI.

ARANJUEZ

The Palacio Real is some thirty miles south of Madrid and was built by the Habsburg Felipe II with massive gardens and water features that required the rivers Tagus and Jarama to be diverted with a man-made island. It was substantially re-built by Carlos III and Carlos IV, and it was the scene of the mutiny of Fernando VII against his father Carlos IV.

SAN ILDEFONSO

This huge palace complex La Granja de San Ildefonso just south of Segovia was built by Felipe V in imitation of his grandfather's similar rural retreat at Versailles. The site was chosen for the same reason – its excellent hunting – and he had bought it from local monks in 1519. It was further extended in 1728 after Felipe's brief attempt at abdication in 1724 and when he reluctantly came back to the throne after his eldest son's death he began to move the government out here. The town of San Ildefonso had to be expanded with a barracks, accommodation for civil servants, the Holy Trinity Church and a royal glass works. Felipe liked it so much he was buried here, though in one of his typically depressed periods he had complained 'it cost me 3 million and has amused me for 3 minutes.' It has a garden of 1500 acres, an artificial lake, Baths of Diana and twenty-six sculpted fountains some with jets rising forty meters into the air. His successor the even more depressive Fernando VI gave the palace to his stepmother Isabel Farnese, and then Carlos III took it over and used it as his summer palace.

Nearby is the Palacio Real de Riofrio, also built at the instigation of Isabel Farnese in 1722 and thereafter rarely used except as a hunting pavilion.

SANTIAGO DE COMPOSTELLA

The flowering of Bourbon Baroque or Churrigueresque architecture is seen in the new façade of Santiago de Compostella from 1738-49, the square at Salamanca and Valladolid University.

SEVILLE

Isabel and Felipe V also lived for a while in the magnificent Alcazar of Seville, a Moorish palace added to by the Emperor Charles V. This was because Felipe was always so close to mental breakdown that it suited Isabel to keep him out of the public gaze. This palace was also associated much earlier with

King Pedro the Cruel who treated his Bourbon wife so badly. The San Telmo Palace here was used by Isabella II's sister and her ambitious husband the Orléans Bourbon Montpensier. The Plaza Espana, with its tiled tableaux of the Spanish Empire, was a 1929 effort in the last years of Alfonso XIII to sustain the imperial image.

SAN SEBASTIAN
Miramar Palace, chosen by Isabella II as a healthy place to bring up her delicate son the future Alfonso XII, became a popular summer palace for Spanish royals and is now part of the university.

PALMA
Marivent is now the summer residence favoured by King Juan Carlos.

THE CANARY ISLANDS
The Canaries were conquered by Castile in 1479, and by the time of the Bourbons were in decline but they introduced cochineal as a cash crop to revive the economy. They were fortified by Alfonso XIII against American attack in 1898 and gained economically from the introduction of bananas soon afterwards.

ITALY

The Bourbons held the kingdom of Naples or the Two Sicilies plus the duchy of Parma with short breaks from 1733 -1860 and as in Spain left a substantial architectural legacy.

NAPLES
The Castel Nuovo predated Bourbon Naples but was lived in by Carlo IV when he first arrived in Naples in 1734. It was refurbished in 1823. The old Palazzo Reale now houses a theatre and museum.

The Palazzo Capodimonte was begun as a new summer palace for Carlo IV in 1738 with the objective of showing off the magnificent Farnese art collection which he had brought with him. The Porcelain Factory was added in 1743 on the instigation of his German wife and in imitation of the one in her native Meissen.

Teatro San Carlo Opera House was also organised by Carlo and designed by the same architects, Antonio Medraso and Angelo Carsale. It opened in 1737. At the time it was the largest opera house in the world and could hold 3,000.The décor was in the blue and gold Bourbon colours. In 1816 it had to be rebuilt after a fire but Ferdinando I achieved the work in a remarkable ten months. Verdi wrote his *Alzira* for it in 1841 and it was refurbished again by Ferdinando II in 1854. Surprisingly Ferdinando allowed a performance of *Nabucco* in 1848 and also surprisingly Verdi wrote a royalist anthem for Ferdinando: *La Patria*.

Also in Naples Carlo IV built the huge Albergo Reale dei Poveri in 1751, a massive 300 metre long five-storey building to house the destitute of Naples.

The medieval church of Santa Chiara had its Cloister of Claristes rebuilt in 1742 under Carlo and is the burial place of the would-be early Bourbon Empress of Constantinople Mari de Clermont. Capella Sansevero is another example of Bourbon baroque.

CASERTA

The magnificent palace here, twenty miles north-east of Naples, was built between 1752-74 by King Carlo IV of Naples, the first Bourbon king there, in imitation of his great-grandfather's palace at Versailles. It has a vestibule lined with statues leading to courtyards and a superb 'staircase of honour' with sixteen marble steps. To help with the vast labour force required Carlo used his galley slaves.

A few miles away was the favourite hunting lodge of Ferdinando IV at San Leucio. As an excuse for his philandering or to escape the memory of his son's death Ferdinando began to develop a utopian concept of a new industrial city with good housing and working conditions, rather like David Dale's New Lanark which came a few years later. Named Ferdinandopolis, it was abandoned in 1800 due to the spread of revolution but the silk works still survive in Piazza de la Seta.

PORTICI

The fourth of Carlo IV's new palaces was Portici built, dangerously, at the base of Mount Vesuvius and five miles south of Naples. It is now part of the university agriculture department. Nearby Pompeii and Herculaneum were rediscovered during the reign of Carlo IV and excavations undertaken.

South of Capua was an additional magnificent hunting lodge with a façade 300 metres long at Carditello in a marshy area where there were plenty of pheasants, wild boar and deer. It also suited the buffalo, which were milked to provide the basis for mozzarella cheese, a royal favourite.

POZZUOLI

Lake Fusaro near Pozzuoli west of Naples was prized by Ferdinando IV for its supply of fresh oysters and mussels as well as more good hunting, so he bought it in 1773 and built his Casino Reale on an island. Many years later when he had reinvented himself as Ferdinando I of the Two Sicilies and acquired a new young wife, Lucia Duchess of Florida (morganatic so she was not the queen), he built her the Villa Reale. This stands on Vomero Hill in what is known as the broccoli area of Naples. There she had a menagerie including eighteen kangaroos and a tiger.

GAETA

This town fifty miles north of Naples was significantly where the Naples Bourbons both began and ended their period in power. It was the scene in 1734 of the siege where Carlo IV watched by Bonnie Prince Charlie finally overcame the Austrians and captured the fortress. Ferdinando II enjoyed Gaeta and also another modest palace at Quisinia above Castellamare. Nearly fourteen decades later Gaeta was where Francesco made his last stand against a united Italy and finally surrendered after a four-month siege in which his wife Maria famously played a gallant role. The massive castle still towers above the cliffs and town. Offshore is the remote island prison of San Stefano from 1795. The other notorious Bourbon prison was on Nisida.

LUCCA

This city was given to the Bourbon Dukes of Parma from 1815-47 as an independent dukedom whilst their cousin Marie Louise, second wife of Napoleon, was allowed to keep Parma till her death. Maria di Borbone, the duchess, transformed the town walls into a tree-lined walkway. The Palazzo Ducale, Villa Reale and numerous other palaces survive.

PARMA

Its ducal palace was built in 1561 but enlarged after the Bourbons took over under Don Felipe in 1748 with their usual extravagant French ideas. Also the Palatine Library, picture gallery, botanical gardens and Royal Printing Works had Bourbon makeovers.

PALERMO

Palacio Colli was the residence used by Ferdinando during the French revolutionary period. There are also remains of the grim Bourbon prison of Ucciardone of 1807. The Chinese Villa was built by Ferdinando IV/I in 1799 during his exile here, and thirty miles south of Palermo is the Ficuzza Palace, his favourite hunting lodge. Caltagirone has another fine Bourbon prison.

AUSTRIA

STYRIA

Krohsdorf, otherwise known as Krotten Hof or Krottendorf, was a Bourbon hideaway from 1844 owned by the Angoulêmes. Château Fruhsdorf in Lanzenkirchen was acquired by one of Napoleon's sisters in 1817, later by Carlo III of Parma, by the Angoulême Bourbons in 1844 and finally by Jaime Borbon Duke of Madrid in 1880. The last semi-serious Bourbon claimant to the French throne, the Comte de Chambord, died here in 1883. Schloss Arco near St Martin in upper Austria was the final home of Francesco II, the last king of the Two Sicilies who died here in 1885. It became known later as the evacuation home during World War II for the Lippizaner stallions of the Spanish Riding School. Kirchberg on the River Jagst was one of the refuges for the exiled French Bourbons, whilst Schwarzau am Stenefeild was a Habsburg castle used for the marriage of the last emperor of Austria-Hungary to Zita, seventeenth child of the last Bourbon of Parma.

GERMANY

DRESDEN
Uchendorff and Weisstropp were two castles near Dresden acquired by Carlo II of Parma, the former Bourbon King of Etruria.

SLOVENIA

NOVA GORICA
This town, formerly in the Italian part of Austria and famous for its roses, was where Charles X, the last of the main French Bourbon line, came to die and where he was buried in the monastery of Castanivizza on Kostanjevica Hill. His only surviving son the Duc d'Angoulême was also buried here.

GREAT BRITAIN

EDINBURGH
Edinburgh's Holyrood Palace was twice the place of refuge of the penultimate French King Charles X. The first time was during the Napoleonic wars, when he was still just the Comte d'Artois, and the second was after his deposition by Louis Philippe in 1830.

Only the stable block survives of Sheen House in Surrey, similarly the place of refuge for ex-king Louis Philippe after 1848. He died at Claremont near Esher. Other Bourbon exiles were also scattered in Surrey.

Bermondsey was the birthplace in 1910 of the chocolate sandwich biscuit initially called Creole and later Bourbon.

NORTH AMERICA

Generally North America was the scene from the sixth century onwards of a three-sided competition between three European powers, France, Spain and Britain to see which could gain the most lucrative colonies and the losers in all areas were the native Americans.

Britain largely dominated the north-east coast, and France tried to create a river-based empire stretching from Canada to the Gulf of Mexico, while Spain expanded slowly northwards from its central American heartland to take the south and west coasts. The mid-eighteenth century saw all three states involved in warfare with each other and a change of ownership of large areas, with the French Bourbons being the main losers, the Spanish Bourbons both gaining and losing and the British overall winners. While the primary original objectives of the Spaniards were to find gold and convert the heathen, the French were more interested in fur though they did some converting, whilst the British were more interested in long-term settlement and cash crops.

CANADA

It was François I in pre-Bourbon times who first took the bold step of defying the Pope to send French settlers to Canada. Jacques Cartier from St Malo was really looking for gold along the St Lawrence in 1534. Then came the epic journeys of Samuel de Champlain who was sent out in 1603 on the orders of Henri IV and founded two key trading posts vital for the fast growing fur trade. The interest of the French was greatly stimulated by de Champlain's book Des Sauvages and Henri commissioned further exploration. It was he who pioneered the policy of using the Algonquin tribe to fend off the Iroquois. As a result of his letter to Louis XIII in 1610 Charles de Bourbon, Comte de Soissons, was appointed Lieutenant General of New France but he died soon afterwards and was succeeded by another Bourbon, Henri II Prince of Condé.

Nova Scotia
Port Royal, now named Annapolis, was the first of Champlain's settlements. It was set up with great difficulty in 1605 after an abortive attempt on Saint Croix Island, and a replica of the original fort has been created. Grand Pré is another well-preserved remnant of the French occupation of Acadia. The French were ethnically cleansed from here by the British in 1755 but many managed to return five years later.

Newfoundland
This island retains some reminders of the French attempt to dominate it under Louis XIV. In 1692 they built the Castle Hill fort at Placentia, then known as Plaisance. The islands of St Pierre & Miquelon have survived numerous attacks to remain a part of the French empire, valuable as a base for North Atlantic fishing.

LOUISBOURG

The largest fortress in New France was built on Cape Breton Island as a major military base during the regency of Orléans in 1715, after Louis XIV had been forced to abandon Newfoundland to the British but still wanted to maintain French interests in the Grand Banks fishery. It was captured in 1745, regained in 1749 and finally captured again by the British under Wolfe in 1758. The fortifications were destroyed but have been restored.

MONTRÉAL

Champlain first landed at the Pointe-a-Callière in 1611 and this was the area, now excavated, where settlers under Maisonneuve developed the first real settlement, the Ville Marie in 1642. The town was built on an island, part of a group downstream from the junction of the Ottawa and St Lawrence Rivers so it was an ideal base from which to expand the fur trade, for the *coureurs du bois* and the *voyageurs*. Amongst surviving early buildings are Chapelle Nôtre Dame de Bonsecours, first built in wood as a sailors' church in 1657; the Vieux Seminaire de Saint Sulpice, from 1685; and the Château Ramezay, a long, low, stone-built mansion put up in 1705 for Governor de Ramezay and later used as the headquarters of the Compagnie des Indes.

QUÉBEC

The city still retains a fine Bourbon heritage and was founded by de Champlain in 1608. The site of his habitation is now occupied by the Place Royale which was laid out as the town centre in 1688. The town became the capital of New France. The Hôtel-Dieu Hôpital was built in 1640 by Augustinian nuns, the Seminaire de Québec in 1663 as a training school for priests by the city's first bishop and the Église Nôtre Dame des Victoires in 1690 to celebrate the retiral of a British fleet which had been threatening the city. The Couvent des Ursulines has been rebuilt over the centuries but dates back to an original foundation in 1639 as a school for both French and native American girls.

The massive Citadel built originally on a smaller scale by the French had to be largely rebuilt by the British who had captured it in 1759. The Parc des Champs de Bataille marks the area where General Wolfe died in the moment of defeating the French General Montcalm who also died of his wounds. In Artillery Park are numerous other remnants of the original fortifications of Québec, barracks and powder magazine.

The Ile d'Orléans seven miles from Québec has the original settlement founded by Jacques Cartier at Sainte Petronille. Other monuments from the Bourbon period include the Sainte Famille church built in 1749 and the Basilique Sainte Anne de Beaupré on the other side of the river, rebuilt on a seventeenth-century site.

KINGSTON
This was established as Fort Frontenac in in 1673 but refounded as Kingston in 1784.

MIDLAND
Sainte-Marie among the Hurons, the Jesuit mission station founded in 1649 on the Wye River, has been reconstructed. Its purpose was to convert the Huron people on the peninsula between Lake Huron and Lake Ontario. Ten years later the Iroquois attacked it, massacred most of the Hurons and tortured the Jesuits. Similar was the Mission du Hurons de la Pointe de Montréal du Detroit, founded in 1761.

UNITED STATES

Louis XIV was responsible for a major drive southwards with the pioneering journey of De La Salle from Canada to the Gulf of Mexico in 1668. He claimed the territory he called Louisiana for France though it included much more than the modern state of that name.

MICHIGAN

DETROIT
This was founded as a French fort in 1701 by Antoine de la Mothe Cadillac for Louis XIV as part of the drive to link French Canada with the Gulf of Mexico. It stood strategically on the narrows Pontchartrain and was captured by the British in 1760. Fort Michilimackinac founded on its island in 1695 was the first French settlement in the area.

NEW YORK STATE

TICONDEROGA
This originally French fort by Lake Champlain was the scene of a battle between the French and Iroquois in 1618 and later a bloody siege by the British.

OGDENSBURG
Fort La Presentation, a mission founded by Abbé Picquet near the town, dates from 1750 and has been reconstructed. Fort Ste Marie de Gannenbatha near Syracuse dates from 1656.

PENNSYLVANIA

PITTSBURGH
The Bourbon Fort Duquesne, renamed Pittsburgh by the British after they captured it in 1759, was founded by the French, in 1753, at the river junction of Allegheny and Monongahela. Traces were found in Point State Park. Nearby were forts of De La Riviere aux Boeufs and De La Presque-Isle du Lac.

VERMONT

Had its Fort St Anne from 1666, foundations of which have been preserved.

WISCONSIN

Fort St Nicholas was founded in 1680 on the Mississippi near Praire du Chien, but nothing survives. The site of Fort St François is marked.

MISSOURI

ST LOUIS
Surrounded by Native American mounds the orginal city was founded by Father Jacques Marquette and Louis Jolliet, a fur trader from Canada, in 1673 during the expansion in America encouraged by Louis XIV. The first wooden St Louis Cathedral was built in 1725 and rebuilt in stone in 1789. A trading post developed in 1763, and eventually the town was laid out like New Orléans on a grid by the levée. It had moved to the west side of the Mississippi, which at this time became the border of British territory and was the capital of Upper Louisiana. Then in 1763 it was handed over to Spain with the rest of Louisiana, was Spanish till 1800, then very briefly back under France until sold to the USA in 1803. The Soulard Market, or Vieux Carré, dates mainly to the Spanish period. Casa Alvarez, built in 1790, survives from the period when this area was included in the transfer of French Louisiana to Spain in 1763 and belonged to the clerk of the Royal Treasury.

SAINTE GENEVIEVE
This has one of the finest groups of French colonial buildings dating back to the mission founded in 1703.

ILLINOIS

CHICAGO

This area was developed by Jolliet and Marquette in 1673 and became part of French Louisiana in 1713 but was transferred to the British in 1713 after the Treaty of Utrecht. Fort Checagu was founded by the French on Lake Michigan in 1683 and was the antecedent of Chicago.

In 1680 La Salle set up Fort Crevecoeur which was overrun by native Americans two years later and replaced by Fort Louis du Rocher near Utica.

There was also Fort Pimitoui, otherwise known as Illinois. Fort de Chartres dates from 1720, and Cahokia Courthouse dates from 1739.

KASKASKIA

Kaskaskia on the Mississippi was founded as a French fur station in 1703 and has its Immaculate Conception Church.

KENTUCKY

Bourbon County was established in 1765, an area that soon produced a surplus of corn hence the fact that at Fort Harrod, a convenient port on the Ohio River, the locals began producing whiskey which was given the name Bourbon.

MINNESOTA

DULUTH

Duluth was a French settlement founded in 1679 by Daniel du Luth in an area surveyed by the French in 1630. Other French forts included Fort St Charles from 1732 and Fort L'Hullier founded by Le Sueur on the Blue Earth River in 1700.

MISSISSIPPI

BILOXI

This was the capital of French Louisiana till 1723 when New Orléans took over. The first settlement had been at Fort Maurepas, now Ocean Springs, after d'Iberville's voyage down the Mississippi. Fort Rosalie at Natchez dates from 1716. The Old Spanish Fort on Krebs Lake was a French fort founded in 1718 by La Pointe but taken over by Spain in 1783.

INDIANA

Fort de Vincennes, originally founded in 1680, was named after the governor who was murdered by Indians. Only the cemetery survives.

SOUTH CAROLINA

Has the site on Parris Island of a French Huguenot fort dating from 1562 and of a Spanish Fort San Felipe.

ARKANSAS

The first French settlement of Henri le Tonti by Lake Dumond dates from 1686. John Law, bank pioneer during the Orléans regency, tried to set up a colony here but the location is uncertain.

TENNESSEE

Nothing remains of Fort Assumption founded by Le Moyne in 1739.

LOUISIANA

New Orléans

La Nouvelle Orléans was founded in 1718 on a commercially brilliant but geographically flawed site by the French Mississippi Company at the instigation of Philippe Duc d'Orléans who was acting as regent for his nephew Louis XV and a year later the first cargo of black slaves arrived from Africa. Two decades earlier Des Moines had camped on the Pointe du Mardi Gras at the mouth of the river and given its new name to Lake Pontchartrain. Six years before that in 1668 de La Sale had claimed the territory of Louisiana for France. New Orléans took over from Biloxi as the capital of the colony in 1723, and the wooden Cathedral of St Louis was built in 1725 and rebuilt in stone in 1789. By 1725 the first black slaves had escaped and set up camps as maroons in the bayou. The Charity Hospital was founded by a sailor Jean Louis in 1735 and ten years later the Place de Negroes was laid out for the early versions of the Mardi Gras. 1764 saw the arrival of French Canadian refugees from Acadia and they became known as Cajuns, while the descendants of mixed Afro-French relationships were known as Creoles.

BATON ROUGE

Pierre le Moyne d'Iberville established the first settlement here in 1699 and named it after a red marker-pole fixed in the ground by the Native Americans. It had to be handed over to the British by the treaty of 1763 but after sixteen years it was conquered from them by the Spaniards, led by Bernardo de Galvez who also took Pensacola. Thus Baton Rouge was a Spanish city from 1779-1810. Surviving from that period are the Magnolia Mound Plantation House of 1791 and Tessier Lafayette buildings from 1800. There is also the Old Arsenal Powder Magazine. Point Coupée was founded in 1756.

COLORADO

Named as the red area. The Spaniards built Fort Talpa in 1819 as they tried to defend their Mexican frontier and the same year Sangre de Cristo Fort at Oak Creek.

ARIZONA

It was the Spaniards who had first introduced horses to this part of America and later the concept of *vaqueros* or cowboys. The Pimeria Alta Franciscan missions date from just before the Bourbons took over Spain in 1700.

TEXAS

The French attempted to set up a Fort Saint Louis near Vittoria in 1684 but its founder de la Salle was murdered and the colony abandoned in 1688. Texas was ceded to Spain along with the rest of Louisiana in 1763 and remained Spanish till independent Mexico took over in 1821. The early immigrants including the Hispanic Tejanos rebelled against Mexico in 1836.

EL PASO

El Paso, founded on the Rio Grande in 1659, became the capital of the original New Mexico.

SAN ANTONIO

San Antonio was founded by the Spanish Bourbons in 1716 with Villa Fernando as first administrative centre of Texas and Alamo as a fortified mission. Nuestra Senora de la Ascencion de Opodepe dates from 1704.

LOREDO

The mission here was founded by Guadalajara and the San Augustin Church dates from Bourbon times in 1755.

San Luis de las Amarillas was founded in 1757 on the River Saba as part of the Spanish drive to convert the Apaches as was Santa Cruz de San Saba which was soon afterwards destroyed by the Comanches. Tubac Presidio, founded near Santa Cruz in 1752, was the base for the expedition to find the new 700 mile route from Sonora to California encouraged by Carlos III.

NEW MEXICO

Nueva Mexico, developed by Spain after 1515. There was a Pueblo revolt 1680-92 after which the Spanish general de Vargas had to reconquer the area. It became part of the United States after the Mexican wars of 1848. Albuquerque was founded by Felipe V (the first Bourbon King of Spain) in 1706 when he supplied land for new settlers. The church of Felipe de Neri survives as do a number of old adobe houses from the period.

GEORGIA

A number of Spanish missions, such as Santa Gallina on St Catherine's Island, were overrun by the South Carolinans under General James Moore in 1702, before 1732 when the British finally established a new colony under George II and run by Oglethorpe.

FLORIDA

Spain lost Florida to the British from 1763-83 but was given French Louisiana instead. Spain regained Florida and finally sold it to the United States in 1819.

Earlier the French Huguenots established Fort Caroline in 1764 near where Jacksonville now stands but it was captured by the Spaniards and replaced by their St Augustin. There was a Spanish stone fort of San Marcos de Apalache.

At Escambe the Spanish mission San Cosmo y San Damian de Escambe set up in the seventeenth century in the Florida Panhandle near where Talahassee now stands was destroyed by Creek Indians, paid for by the aggressive régime in South Carolina in 1704. The same fate applied to Santa Catalina on Amelia Island.

PENSACOLA

Pensacola was founded by the Spaniards in pre-Bourbon times in 1557 but reoccupied and strengthened in 1698 when the French started to make encroachments towards Florida. The British captured it in 1719, took over control in 1763 and built Fort Barrancas but the Spanish recaptured it in 1781. The United States took it over as a potential naval base in 1820.

ALABAMA

MOBILE

First colonised by Spain in 1559 but then more seriously developed by the French Pierre de la Moyne Sieur d'Iberville in 1698 as part of Louis XIV's drive to control the mouth of the Mississippi. In 1702, during a period of savage war against the native tribes which involved large numbers of French troops, they developed Dauphin Island as a deep water harbour and potential capital of the region and then built Fort Louis at Twenty-seven mile Bluff. Fort Condé de la Mobile was built in 1704. From 1710 the Boeuf Graf society of Mobile held an annual parade. In 1763, the town was taken by the British and then by the Spaniards in 1780.

CALIFORNIA

It was Carlos III of Spain who first began the serious colonisation of California in 1769 because he was alarmed by recent Russian encroachments there – the Russian trappers were keen on sea otter. He appointed Gaspar de Portola as first governor and sent him along with Father Junipero to set up a chain of twenty-one missions: El Camino Reale.

SAN DIEGO

San Diego was founded in pre-Bourbon times in 1602 but relatively neglected until Gaspar de Portola was sent by Carlos III to tighten things up. He founded the Presidio de San Diego as the base for colonising the rest of California, now Presidio Park and the Alcala Mission which was rebuilt in 1774 but closed in 1821 when the colony became part of independent Mexico. Aqueducts were built to supply the town in 1795.

SAN FRANCISCO

San Francisco was explored by Portola in 1769 and a fort erected at the Gate in 1776. Then came the mission San Francisco de Asis on Dolores Street founded originally by a Lieutenant Moraga and Father Palou but rebuilt in adobe as it stands today in 1791. The Hospital of San Rafael was added in 1817.

LOS ANGELES

San Gabriel Archangel was the fourth of the Junipero missions set up with the help of the local Native Americans the Garbileno. In 1781 a group of farmers expanded from the settlement to found El Pueblo de Nuestra Senora la Reina de Los Angeles. The Avila Adobe, still surviving, was built in 1818 to house the mayor of the settlement, a rancher called Don Francisco Avila. The San Antonio Mission in Monterey dates from 1770.

In 1825 after Mexico won its independence from Spain California became part of the new Republic of Mexico. Gold was discovered in the San Fernando Valley in 1842 and after the Mexican War of 1848 California became part of the United States.

PUERTO RICO

This island was used as a major military base by Spain during the eighteenth century and remained in Spanish control along with Cuba long after most other colonies had sought their freedom. The San Juan National Historic Park includes the Spanish forts of San Geronimo, San Cristobal and San Juan de la Cruz, powder houses and parts of the city walls mostly dating from the 1760s and the reign of Carlos III.

CENTRAL AMERICA

This entire area was dominated by Spain from the days of Cortez and only minor inroads were later made by other nations. For example the British illegal log-cutters of Campeachy Bay gained a foothold in what was later Belize. For Spain the isthmus was a source of bullion, of potential converts to Catholicism and a transit area for goods coming across the Pacific and from Peru.

MEXICO

In 1764 after the disasters of the Seven Years War Carlos III sent out José Galvez to sort out the Central American colonies. He expelled the Jesuits but the drive for lay efficiency was unpopular with the Creoles. In 1800 Bourbon Mexico was the wealthiest area in all the Americas and Mexico City the largest town. Nueva Espagna had a garrison army of 27,000 troops and 10,000 clergy to look after a population of six million.

Generally the Bourbon period in Mexico saw the building of a large number of fine baroque churches in the highly decorative style of the Churriguera family. Tepotzotlan has San Francisco Xavier church, a superb baroque building built in 1755. Similarly at Churrigueresque there is the church of Nuestra Senora Dolores built in 1570 and the site of Father Hidalgo's attempted revolution in 1810. The Dolores Hidalgo in Guanajuato was founded in 1710 by the Viceroy of Mexico, Marques de Montecarlos, as a haçienda for cattle. Ocotlan the silver town has its Sanctuary baroque cathedral from 1745 and Taxco its church San Sebastian y Santa Prisca from 1751-8.

MEXICO CITY
Mexico City is the site of the Sagrario Metropolitano which was built in Bourbon times.

ACAPULCO
This was the key port of arrival for the annual Manila galleon and the transfer of its valuable spice cargo across the isthmus to Portobello.

HONDURAS

This area, named by Columbus for its deep water, came under the Captain General of Guatemala and was valued for its mineral resources. Comayaqua and Tegucigalpa were the two main Spanish cities. Like many Spanish cities in Central America Comayaqua had to be rebuilt after an earthquake. In 1821 it was freed from Spain but came under the authority of Mexico and then the United Provinces of Central America till its collapse in 1838.

PANAMA

This was a vital area for the co-ordination of Spanish trade and Portobello with its outlying Fort Chagre and Fort Lorenzo was the key port for slaves arriving and bullion departing, hence the number of times it was attacked by the British. Some of the Bourbon battlements still survive. The Scots made their ill-fated attempt to build a base at Darien just at the start of the Bourbon period.

NICARAGUA

Its capital Granada dates back to 1524 but had to be rebuilt in Bourbon times, including the fortress La Polvora. The cathedral in Leon built in 1747 was the largest in Central America.

GUATEMALA

Guatemala was a Spanish colony from 1518 and had a captain general reporting to the Viceroy of New Spain. It specialised in the production of sugar, cocoa and cochineal red dye for sending back to Spain. An earthquake destroyed much of the capital Antigua Guatemala in 1773 by which time it was the third largest city in the Americas and it was rebuilt in the Emritqa Valley. Surviving from Bourbon times are the Casa de la Moneta of 1735, the Cathedral rebuilt in 1743 and 1784, the former University from 1763 and the Capuchin Convent facing the volcanoes from 1736. In 1821 Guatemala became part of independent Mexico, then till 1838 the UPCA.

COSTA RICA

Was named for wealth that never quite materialised until 1808 when coffee was introduced and found to be more valuable than elusive gold. With seven active volcanoes it was neglected until the coffee boom. The Spanish foundations included Heredia, San Jose and Alajuela.

EL SALVADOR

Became free of Spanish rule in 1821 when a bell was rung from the la Merced church, but remained initially under Mexico till 1824.

THE WEST INDIES

In the early days after Columbus Spain regarded itself as having a monopoly of the West Indies but the English, Dutch and French Bourbons began to make inroads, often as pirates or illicit traders. The first big dents in Spain's hegemony were when the French took half of Hispaniola in 1659, and the British acquired Jamaica in 1655.

CUBA

Cuba was a long-term Spanish colony taken over by the Bourbons in 1700 when it had a population of around 30,000 and was divided into the provinces of Havana and Santiago. The Bourbons tightened up its economy and granted a tobacco monopoly which helped growth, but there was a planters' revolt which was put down with eleven executions. In 1740 the local merchants created the Real Campania de Commercio de la Habana to control all Cuban business. The British captured the island in 1762-3 and returned it to Carlos III who strengthened its defences with forts such as the huge San Carlos de la Cabana. He founded a new town of Pinar del Rio.

HAVANA

Havana has Palacio de los Capitanes Generales, Santa Clara Convent and Castillo de la Real Fuerza. The former Jesuit centre became Havana Cathedral in 1789. Cuba prospered during the American War of Independence and the Creoles won concessions from the Bourbons in 1814. The slave trade increased rapidly till 1841 as plantations expanded. The major revolt of 1898 resulted in the appointment of General Weyler as governor and his use of *reconcentrados* or concentration camps to subdue the population – some 200,000 died. Then the blowing up of the USS *Maine* in Havana harbour brought the United States into the war and they helped Cuba win its freedom in 1899 after close to 200 years of Bourbon rule.

In the 1730s Cuba was a base for the aggressive guarda costas who on the orders of Felipe V waylaid so many British ships in the run-up to the War of Jenkins Ear.

HAITI

The western half of the island of Hispaniola, now known as Haiti, was more suitable for sugar production and the eastern half, now known as the Dominican Republic, was better for cattle and meat production.

The French Bourbon colony on the island of Hispaniola, San Domingo, was established in 1659 under Louis XIV but there had been a base for French pirates on Tortuga since 1625. The French West Indies Company took over management in 1664 and rapidly developed production of tobacco, indigo, cotton, cocoa and later sugar. When the indigenous Taino had been wiped out they had to bring in slaves who numbered 800,000 at the colony's peak and had to be replaced at the rate of 20,000 per year. In 1764 came an influx of French refugees expelled from Acadia by the British, but in St Dominigue they were treated as just one rung above the slaves or escaped slaves, the Maroons. In 1681 Louis XIV introduced the Code Noir which put some minor restraints on the maltreatment of slaves. Their food needs were partly met by fish supplied from the Grand Banks fisheries which the French operated from Louisbourg. St Dominique became one of the richest colonies in the French empire, supplying 40 per cent of European sugar and 60 per cent of coffee. The mix of Catholicism and African religions resulted in the development of the hybrid cult of Voodoo. In 1791 the slaves rebelled and by 1804 the colony had become the first black republic.

Santo Domingo was retained by Spain after the cession of Western Hispaniola to France in 1659 and supplied meat for the sugar plantations of the East.

GUADELOUPE

This volcanic island was taken over by the French in 1635 under the aegis of the Compagnie des Iles d l'Amerique. The local Caribs were virtually wiped out and it became a formal colony in 1674 under Louis XIV with its main centre at Point a Pitre. It is now a department of France.

MARTINIQUE

Another volcanic island under French rule it still has reminders of the Bourbon period in the Clement House Plantation, Fort-de-France and Plantation de Leynitz.

TRINIDAD

Was visited by Columbus in 1498 and became Spanish territory till passed to the British in 1797. Spain found settlers reluctant to come here so they opened up the island to any catholic European. There were missions at San Fernando and Savonetta. Port of Spain was made the capital by the Bourbons in 1757 and their grid layout including the Plaza del Marina still survives.

CURAÇAO

The Dutch took over this island and became the middlemen for the transfer of slaves from the West African coast, mainly Angola, to the Spanish colonies. There were a number of tragic incidents with Spanish slavers operating after the official ban on the traffic such as the mutiny on the *Amistead* in 1839.

SAINT LUCIA

This island regularly changed hands between the French and British. The Vieux Fort survives with the Lighthouse Moule à Chique.

SOUTH AMERICA

Spain and Portugal split South America between them in the famous Treaty of Tordesillas in 1494 and Spain took the lion's share. Particularly in the Habsburg period the main emphasis was on searching for bullion and converting the heathens to Christianity, so the administration was left to the initiative of the church and temporary viceroys. The Bourbons were anxious to tighten control so they could extract maximum revenue, so they reduced the role of the church, particularly the Jesuits, refocused on high value crops like tobacco, sugar and coffee, and had to increase the slave labour force.

GUIANA

The French had tried a colony in Sinnimary in 1604 and again in Cayenne in 1643 for the pepper trade, but it was Louis XV who encouraged a major settlement with the promise of gold and management by the Compagnie des Indes Occidentales although most of the settlers died. Some fled to the islands including the notorious Ile du Diable which was used as a penal colony in post-Bourbon times from 1852. When slavery was abolished in 1848 the plantations were no longer viable.

VENEZUELA

Was colonised by Spain from 1522 but largely neglected until the Bourbons indulged their taste for chocolate by encouraging cocoa production. This required an extra influx of slaves and under Felipe V Venezuela was incorporated into Nueva Granada with its capital at Bogota.

CARACAS
This was the birthplace of Simon Bolivar who trained as a lawyer in Madrid. After the declaration of independence in 1811 he was driven out but re-entered the city in 1814 and proclaimed himself dictator. He was driven out again but after a long campaign waged from his base in the West Indies he drove out the Spanish troops in 1824. In 1821 he had been declared president of the new nation of Colombia which comprised Venezuela, Colombia and New Granada. Venezuela detached itself from the new republic in 1829 after which Bolivar resigned.

BOLIVIA

Bolivia was originally the upper part of the Spanish viceroyalty of Peru. In 1824 Bolivar drove the Spaniards out of Peru and the southern half was renamed in his honour as Bolivia. However, he and his army were driven out, as the population disliked his new constitution.

LA PAZ

La Paz was founded in 1548 by the Spaniards at a height of 3,600 meters above sea level. The area round Santa Cruz has a number of fine Jesuit mission stations dating from the Bourbon period and Sucre, formerly La Plata, at 2,700 metres above sea level was the scene of South America's first 'cry for freedom' from Bourbon rule in 1809 and has a number of fine eighteenth-century buildings. Potosi centre of the silver mining area has a fine baroque church from the Bourbon period.

COLOMBIA

BOGOTA

In Bourbon times Bogota, then known as Santa Fé, was the regional capital of the reorganised colony of Nueva Granada which included what are now Colombia, Ecuador and Venezuela. Bogota has a Bourbon cathedral built 1807-23 just before independence. It has La Candelaria and Primada Cathedral.

CARTAGENA

Cartagena was a key base on the north-east coast which was unsuccessfully attacked by the British in 1741 with its great fortress of San Felipe de Barajas.

In 1821 Bolivar helped found the new republic of Colombia which briefly included Venezuela and New Granada.

ECUADOR

Was added to the new republic of Colombia by Bolivar in 1822. Quito has a baroque church of the Bourbon period and the old city is a World Heritage Site. Esmeraldas has a number of very high-altitude Bourbon-era haciendas, some converted into hotels.

PERU

Peru was a Spanish colony from its conquest by Pizarro in 1535 till independence in 1821, so it was under Bourbon rule for 121 years. Arequipa la Ciudad Blanca developed as a key Spanish staging post on the route from the Bolivian silver mines. A Jesuit church, La Campania, survives and the bishop's residence has been converted.

LIMA

Ciudad de los Reyes was founded by Pizarro in 1535 and became capital of the viceroy of Peru. It was largely destroyed by an earthquake in 1746 and rebuilt under the Spanish Bourbons. The town revived briefly under the Bourbons when silver production rose but went into economic decline when the Bourbons transferred control of the Potosi siver mines from Peru to the new viceroys of La Plata in 1776. Generally the centralising policies and heavy taxation of Carlos III upset the Criollo who supported the rebellion of Tupac Amaru in 1780. Cuzco and Lima both produced an elite Creole population which thrived on illicit trade across the Pacific

URUGUAY

MONTEVIDEO

Montevideo was founded by Spaniards in 1726 and was the most important new city of the Bourbon era in South America although the area had been taken over by Spain 1516 and the Portuguese driven out in 1524. It became the capital of independent Uruguay in 1828. It retains its Palacio Pittamiglio and Catedral Metropolitan.

Further expansion of Uraguay, at the expense of Portuguese Brazil, had been undertaken by the Bourbons in 1778.

PARAGUAY

ASCUNCION

Paraguay was part of the Great Province of Indes created in 1537 with Asuncion as its capital. In 1603 came the first Synod for the conversion of slaves. Asuncion still has the Casa de la Independencia, a Bourbon-era townhouse from 1772 where the revolutionaries met in 1811 to plot independence. The old part of the city Manzana de la Rivera also survives.

Paraguay was the centre of the unique Jesuit experiment for protecting the Native Americans from slavery by converting them to Christianity. Amongst the fine Jesuit Reducciones surviving are San Cosme y Damian, Jesus de Tavarangue and Santissima Trinidad de Parana (1705). There was trouble when some territory had to be ceded to the aggressive, slave-hungry Portuguese in 1756 and the Jesuits were expelled in 1767 on the orders of Carlos III.

In 1731 under Bourbon rule there was a rebellion led by Jose de Antequera that included criollos and mestizos. Then came independence in 1811.

CHILE

Chile was taken over by Spain in 1541 and was under Bourbon control from 1700 to 1817 as part of the viceroyalty of Peru.

SANTIAGO
Of the two main towns both Santiago and Valparaiso, founded 1516, developed fairly slowly until independence. Surprisingly a local junta rebelled against the rule of Napoleon's brother Joseph in 1810 and declared themselves for the deposed Fernando. Once Fernando was restored to Madrid he showed his gratitude by attempting to take back Chile by force till in due course the royalist forces were defeated in battle by the Chilean general Bernardo O'Higgins, helped by the Argentinian Jose de San Martin.

ARGENTINA

BUENOS AIRES
The River Plate estuary was first colonised by Spain in 1515, and Buenos Aires was founded as a part of Peru in 1580. In the early days the population lived mainly by smuggling because Lima had the monopoly. It was Carlos III who encouraged the city's development by allowing it to trade freely and in 1776 established the Viceroyalty of Rio de la Plata. In particular Buenos Aires became the outlet for silver from the mines in Potosi. During the Napoleonic wars Buenos Aires had its first junta and after 1814 Jose de San Martin created Argentina as an independent state. Catedral Metropolitana has an eighteenth-century nave and dome.

Amongst fifteen partially ruined Jesuit missions that survive are San Ignacio Mini and Nuestra Senora de Loreto.

ASIA

INDIA

PUDICHEN
The original French base in India was founded at Pondicherry (now Pudichen) on the Coromandel Coast in 1643 and was the headquarters of the Compagnie des Indes founded by Colbert for Louis XIV. It was originally divided between a *ville blanche* and a *ville noire*, separating Europeans from the native inhabitants. From here its most famous governor, Joseph François Dupleix, planned the French expansion in India in 1741. This led to the capture of Madras from the British using sepoy mercenaries and an attempt to rally client native rulers

against the British, which eventually provoked the retaliation organised by Robert Clive. Reminders of this period survive in the mansion Ananda Ranga Pillai, dated from 1738, the home of Dupleix's assistant, in L'Eglise Nôtre Dame, and the statues of Dupleix himself and of Joan of Arc. The Raj Nivas palace of 1742 also shows elements of French style. Pondicherry was taken by the British in 1763 but was returned to France in 1814 for another 140 years until it became part of independent India in 1954.

CHANDANAGGAR

The second largest Bourbon enclave in India was at Chandernagore (now Chandanaggar) sixteen miles above Calcutta which was its British rival. Founded by the French under Louis XIV in 1673 on the Hughli River it had its Fort d'Orléans and when Dupleix was governor here he built 2,000 brick houses, many built well above ground to keep out snakes. It was captured by the British in 1757 and again in 1794 but was back in French hands from 1816 till 1950 when it became part of the new India. Surviving buildings from the Bourbon period include an Église du Sacré Coeur, the residency and a seventeenth-century gate.

The third French base was Mahé named after a French Captain Mahé de la Bourdonnais who landed here in 1721. Lying on the south-west coast of India it was fortified by the French in 1724, with a further Fort St George at Cherukallu. Surviving monuments include an Église Ste Therese, a Marianne statue from 1789 and a residency from 1855. It remained in French hands till handed over to India in 1954.

There were also French factories at Kasimbazaar and Balasore.

BHOPAL

Jeanne Philippe de Bourbon (see p.45), who according to legend had fled France after killing a relative in a duel, came to Bengal around 1560. He found employment in the court of the Mogul emperor Akbar, allegedly in charge of the imperial guard at Delhi. His descendants thus became nawabs and hereditary governors at one time of the imperial seraglio, acquiring estates at Narwar near Gwalior. In 1775 they moved to Bhopal where they became senior advisers of the Nawab of Bhopal until 1930. Known as the Bourbons of Bhopal or Fratcis their most recent representative was the lawyer Balthazar Napoleon Bourbon. Their private chapel became the Catholic cathedral of Bhopal. Several magnificent mosques survive from their period of service here.

TAIWAN

Spain founded a colony and Fort of Santo Domingo in 1629 at what is now Tamsui but it was taken over first by the Dutch and then during the Opium Wars by the British.

PHILIPPINE ISLANDS

Las Islas Filipinas were turned into a Spanish colony from 1570 when Fort Santiago was built. It was the base for the spice trade and the famous Manila galleon which sailed each year for Acapulco. It was captured by Commodore Anson during his round-the-world voyage when the British were at war with Felipe V. The islands were governed from Mexico until 1821 when Mexico won its independence and thereafter direct from Madrid. Spain lost the islands under Alfonso XIII in 1898 after the war with the United States.

MANILA
Manila had a walled city Ciudad Intramuros and the Bourbons built a succession of cathedrals, their last, from 1870, was destroyed by bombs in 1945.

Other Bourbon baroque churches include Santa Anna, Nuestra Senora de los Remedios Las Pinas on Luzon Island. On Mindanao there was Fort Pilar and on Batan the Church of San Jose.

MICRONESIA

The Nuevas Filipinas, an archipelago north-east of New Guinea were renamed the Carolinas after Carlos III but only properly claimed by Spain in 1875 which caused a minor crisis till one of them was sold to Germany in 1899. The island of Guam de Mariana was used as a penal colony for Bourbon political prisoners.

There were early Spanish forts at Tohula and Rum by Tidore in the Moluccas and Castella, and Santa Lucia and Kalanata on Ternate Pulau. In Borneo at Sabah there was Semporna.

MARQUESAS ISLANDS

This vast archipelago in the Pacific was discovered by Spain in 1595 but not colonised until the very last of the French Bourbon kings Louis Philippe tried to earn his spurs as an imperialist and created French Polynesia in 1842. Tahiti was conquered in 1843 and is still a department of France.

AFRICA

The French and Spanish Bourbons had two things in common with regard to their objectives in Africa. The first during the seventeenth and eighteenth centuries was their need for slaves in the American plantations. The second in the nineteenth century was their need for easy military victories to create some cheap glory and credibility for their weakening régimes.

MOROCCO

Spain acquired parts of Morocco as early as 1497 when Melilla became part of Spain. The area was a place of refuge for the sephardic Jews of Moroccan descent who were expelled from Spain in 1492. Ceuta became part of Spain in 1580. In 1847 Spain captured the Islas Chafarinas including the Isla Isabel II. In 1912 as part of the scramble for Africa Alfonso XIII presided over Spain turning Morocco into a Protectorate that lasted till 1956. This led to a series of crises with Germany which were amongst the contributing factors to the start of the First World War. Morocco was also the base from which Franco launched his attack on the Spanish Republic in 1936. The Rio d'Oro and Spanish Sahara, now the Mahgrib, was snatched by Spain in 1884 in the hope of finding the gold which had earned it its name but none was found. The area was later split between Morocco and Mauretania.

ALGERIA

The penultimate Bourbon King of France Charles X decided on a last-minute attempt to win popularity by achieving a glorious conquest at the expense of the Arabs. The excuse for the war was that the Dey of Algiers had slapped the face of the French envoy with his fan. Thus in 1830 France conquered what they called Algeria, though most of the work came after the fall of Charles X.

SENEGAL

The island of Gorée just off Dakar at the Cape Vert peninsula was taken over by the French Bourbons in 1677 as its main collection depot for the African slaves needed to work their plantations in Louisiana and the Antilles. It still has its Maison d'Esclaves from 1780 and is a World Heritage Site. Also contributing to the trade were the female managers of St Louis, the Senegalese capital which had a population of Franco-African Creoles or Metis. Slavery was abolished by France in 1794 but the colony remained French till 1960.

EQUATORIAL GUINEA

Spain had for centuries relied on British, French and Dutch slavers to do much of the dirty work in supplying slaves to the American empire but towards the end of the eighteenth century began to look for its own sources. In 1778 Count Argelejos based in Montevideo led an expedition for Carlos III to annexe for Spain the islands of Fuarto, Bioko and Annobon at the mouth of the Fernando Po which was used as a slave depot well after the abolition of the trade in the British Empire. Port Clarence (Malabo) and Santa Isabel were founded in 1843. Cocoa and Coffee were introduced to Spanish Equatorial Guinea, which was made largely independent in 1968.

INDIAN OCEAN

The French Bourbons occupied a number of island bases on the route between the Cape of Good Hope and India. These included Reunion (1642), east of Madgascar, formerly an East India Company base called Ile de Bourbon with its Creole style capital, St Denis Cathedral and other buildings surviving from Bourbon times. Also Kerquelen and Iles Crozet (1772), Amsterdam (1843), St Paul Juan de Nova and Tromelin (1776). Mauritius was occupied by the French in 1722 and has its Vieux Grand Port of St Louis with the well-preserved La Loge from this period.

ANTARCTICA

In 1840 King Louis Philippe of France claimed the territory of Adelie.

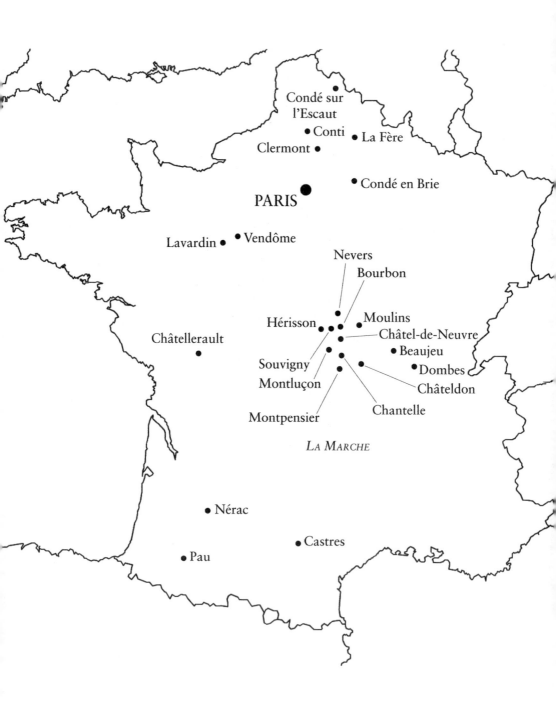

Condé sur
l'Escaut

• Conti
• La Fère

Clermont •

• Condé en Brie

PARIS ●

Lavardin • • Vendôme

Nevers

Bourbon

Hérisson •
Moulins
Châtel-de-Neuvre

• Beaujeu

Châtellerault

Souvigny
• Dombes

Montluçon
Châteldon

Montpensier
Chantelle

LA MARCHE

• Nérac

• Castres

• Pau

BIBLIOGRAPHY

Acton, Harold, *The Bourbons of Naples*, London, 1963.

Acton, Harold, *The Last Bourbons of Naples*, London, 1961.

Antonetti, Guy, *Louis Philippe*, Paris, 1994.

Autrand, François, *Charles VI*, Paris, 1986.

Barker, Juliet, *Agincourt*, London, 2005.

Beach, V.W., *Charles X*, Boulder, 1971.

Bergamini, John, *The Spanish Bourbons*, New York, 1974.

Bridge, John S.C., *A History of France from the Death of Louis XI*, Oxford, 1921.

Cannon, Gwen, ed., (Michelin) *Auvergne Rhone Valley*, Greenville, 2007.

Chateau, Jacques, *Les Bourbons avant Henri IV*, Charroux, 2005.

Cobban, Alfred, *A History of Modern France*, 3 Vols, London, 1965.

De Sauvigny, G. de Berier, *The Bourbon Restoration*, trans. L.Cass, Pennsylvania, 1966.

Denizeau, Gerard, *Larousse des Châteaux*, Paris, 2005.

De Vries, Kelly, *Joan of Arc*, Stroud, 1999.

Erlanger, Philippe, *Louis XIV*, transl., Cox, London, 1970.

Fraser, Antonia, *Marie Antoinette*, London, 2001.

Greengrass, Mark, *France in the Age of Henri IV*, London, 1995.

Grizelle, Rex, *Auvergne and the Massif Central*, London, 1989.

Hardman, John, *Louis XVI*, Yale, 1993.

Hargreaves-Mawdsley, W.N., *Spain under the Bourbons*, London, 1973.

Howard, T.E.B., *The Citizen King*, London, 1961.

Jones, Colin, *France*, Cambridge, 1994.

Knecht, Robert, *The Valois Kings of France*, London, 2004.

Mansel, Philip, *Paris between the Empires*, London, 2001

Mansel, Philip, *Louis XVIII*, London, 1981.

Mitford, Nancy, *The Sun King*, London, 1966.

Montague, Violet, *Sophie Dawes, Queen of Chantilly*, London, 1912.

Petrie, Charles, *Alfonso XIII and his Age*, London, 1963.

Petrie, Charles, *Charles X*, London, 1971.

Polnay, Peter, *A Queen of Spain, Isabella II*, London, 1962.

Ross, Christopher, *Spain 1812-1996*, London, 2000.

Salch, Charles-Laurent, *Dictionaire des Châteaux du Moyen-age*, Strasbourg, 1979.

Shennan, J.H., *The Bourbons*, London, 2007.

Woolf, Stuart, *History of Italy 1700-1860*, London, 1979.